The Saturday Book

NINTH YEAR

SATURDAY night at Vauxhall Gardens, 1784, after Rowlandson

EDITED BY

LEONARD RUSSELL

THE

Saturday Book

BEING THE NINTH ANNUAL ISSUE

OF THIS CELEBRATED

REPOSITORY OF CURIOSITIES

AND LOOKING-GLASS OF

PAST AND PRESENT

THE BOOK DESIGNED BY
LAURENCE SCARFE

THE PUBLISHERS ARE

HUTCHINSON

MADE AND PRINTED
AT THE MAYFLOWER PRESS
(OF PLYMOUTH) AT WATFORD
BY WILLIAM BRENDON AND SON LIMITED
FOUR COLOUR PLATES
ENGRAVED AND PRINTED BY
THE GROUT ENGRAVING COMPANY LIMITED
PUBLISHED OCTOBER 1949

The Front Parlour

THERE WE WERE, SITTING despondently at our desk trying to think up something new for THE SATURDAY BOOK, when two letters from readers flooded in. One suggested, politely enough, that our Mr Fred Bason was too good to be true and must be an invention; the other curtly requested the publication in these pages of a few personal details about the editor.

This, we said, flying suddenly into a paddy, is a fine thing. Those contumacious readers of ours are beginning to suffer from delusions and fancy that we are something dreamed up by Marcel Proust or even the author of *The Dove in the Eagle's Nest*. Not content with denying the very existence of that vital spark, Mr Bason, they ask us to prove our own identity in our own pages. There had been nothing like it, we felt, since Swift had decreed Partridge the almanac-maker to be a dead duck.

Thus, you see, it became necessary to demonstrate in this volume that we existed in our own right and were not the figment of somebody's imagination; and from this it was but a short step to the idea of proof

Edwin Smith and Olive Cook
(p. 49)

Desmond MacCarthy (p. 35)

Fred Bason (p. 90)

by photograph. Trust the people, we said. Let the people decide whether this editor really exists or not. And the same went for Mr Bason. And for Mr Laurence Scarfe, Miss Olive Cook, and Mr Edwin Smith, heroes of the annual fight to get THE SATURDAY BOOK out in good order—let them all be photographed.

So now you know why, in this front parlour of the book, pictures of our undistinguished selves appear cheek by jowl with those of such distinguished persons as Mr Desmond MacCarthy, Miss Dilys Powell, and Miss Virginia Graham. It was necessary to show that no one had invented us; we just happened to be born this way.

14 Albion Street, W.2. L. R.

The Contents

Mural

Sabbatical

Fred Bason's landlady (p. 90)

Petra (p. 191)

Dilys Powell (p. 216)

Virginia Graham (p. 264)

Siamese studies (p. 241)

Laurence Scarfe

Pictures on the Wall

Giving Prized Paintings of some
Eminent Contemporaries, chosen by
them from their own collections
for exhibition in these pages

Oh, give me a nail and a hammer
A picture to hang on the wall.
MUSIC HALL SONG

From the collection of
DAME EDITH EVANS
by FELIKS TOPOLSKI

Henr: Chicheley 1414.

From the collection of the
**ARCHBISHOP OF
CANTERBURY**
*Henry Chicheley, Archbishop of
Canterbury, 1414*

J.TISSOT.
"Going to the City."

From the collection of
VISCOUNT KEMSLEY
Going to the City
by TISSOT

From the collection of
MISS REBECCA WEST
Portrait of a Young Man
by LE GROS

From the collection of
SIR KENNETH CLARK
Baigneuse Blonde
by RENOIR

From the collection of
SIR EDWARD MARSH

Portrait of a Lady
by ZOFFANY
Mr Christopher Hassall
by ENID MOUNTFORT

From the collection of Mr.
MICHAEL REDGRAVE
Miss Rachel Kempson
by ANTHONY DEVAS

From the collection of Mr
J. ARTHUR RANK
Scotney Monty and Scotney Dinah pointing
by WARD BINKS

From the
SATURDAY BOOK COLLECTION
Suspense
by the late celebrated C. Burton Barber

In which Mr. Schwartz, by way of a thumbnail autobiography, contrasts the full, rich life of our present social democracy with the bleak materialism of the England of his youth. He is followed in this section by other 'Sunday Times' contributors who gladden our Sabbaths.

Drabness Is All

by GEORGE SCHWARTZ

THIS will be a drab version of a drab life. For I am a product of that drab Britain which, as Mr Herbert Morrison has explained, earlier generations had left us through being too obsessed with money and things, and too little concerned with people and the needs of their minds and spirits.

Perhaps I can sum up the drabness by saying that owing to the grim choice by Providence of the time for planting and marooning me in these islands I have never seen anyone kicked to death or lynched in any other way, nor have I ever seen the corpse of a woman strung up by the heels. The traditional obsession with money and things ruled out these diversions for my contemporaries.

To start with, I can recall running in a race for the infants' class in the local celebrations of Queen Victoria's Diamond Jubilee. The course was round a tree and back to the starting point. I came in first and was disqualified for the entirely irrelevant reason that I had not run round the tree. Such was the treatment of children in an age which gave precedence to material over mental and spiritual needs. The drab psychology of the times failed to foster in me a proper sense of this injustice, which carefully nurtured could have rankled within my bosom until the day, circa 1945, when it could have been profitably avenged upon society at large. Unfanned it died down, and it is only with an effort and the assistance of modern textbooks that I can recall the memory of these old unhappy far-off things.

Similarly it is only in retrospect that I can appreciate how the drabness of the age constrained my Sunday School teacher to withhold the assurance that *The Swiss Family Robinson* was true from beginning to end. Most of the virtue must have gone out of me at that revelation, and in an age of Santa Claus economics I now have to battle without a belief in fairies.

My parents did little for me apart from feeding, clothing, and sheltering me, and providing for my education as a preliminary to turning me

17

c

loose at the age of 20.   There were only four of us children and we lived in a drab amity that must have concealed nameless repressions, nameless at that time.   Probably because they had been thwarted themselves and possibly as the only recourse in the prevailing drabness, my parents took an undisguised interest and pleasure in what was then regarded as the progress of their children.   We were brought up drably, *anglice* respectably, on a working-class income, and when Father lit up his threepenny cigar on Sunday you would have thought he was getting a kick out of it all.

If he, and grandfather before him, had put their backs into it I might have had the cinema, radio, and the motor-bike in my youth.   But the wheels of capitalist Britain had long been running down and my bleak portion was the magic-lantern, push-bike, and the occasional sight of a balloon ascent.   Sunday School treat in summer, Sunday School tea at Christmas.   Call it a childhood.

Behold me then packed off with my lunch to the County Ground at Hove to watch Ranji and C. B. Fry, a couple of drab performers if ever there were any.   Behold me then in the choir on the cantori side operating on the precept that the mouth had to be opened to the width of two fingers.   Behold me stuffed with the drab literature of the Authorized Version and the equally drab liturgy of the Prayer Book, to say nothing of the forlorn strains of Hymns Ancient and Modern.

> *He shall come down like showers*
> *Upon the fruitful earth*
> *And joy and hope like flowers*
> *Spring in His path to birth . . .*

Heaven help me, I still think that verges on the poetical.

As a drab setting for this adolescent life there was the English Channel in the foreground and the South Downs for a backcloth, and, as I always say, once you have seen one of the South Downs you have seen all of them.

The progress of the world depends upon the people who think up a more powerful atomic bomb while shaving.   My drab intellectual furnishing can be gauged from the performance I put up in the bathroom.   It consists of dipping the razor in the hot water and mouthing vacuities.

> Heat me these irons hot, and look thou stand
> Within the arras. (*Down the right cheek,*
> *Under the jaw*). When I strike my foot
> Upon the bosom of the ground, rush forth
> And bind the boy which you shall find with me
> Fast to the chair (*Right upper lip, left upper lip,*
> *Round the jawbone*). Be heedful. Hence and watch.

Second Shaver. I hope your warrant will bear out the deed
(*Up the left cheek, lower lip and chin*).
First Shaver. UNCLEANLY SCRUPLES! fear not you: look to't.

In 1909 one Ferrer, a Spanish theoretical anarchist, was shot in peace-time for the offence of political agitation. My generation hysterically resented this challenge to its drab complacency and smashed the windows of the Spanish Embassy in nearly every capital of the world. It then returned to its materialistic trough and its obsession with money and things. Thus the initiation of the age of the common man by the process of bumping off the political opposition was held up for a decade.

Two years in a training college in the West-country and, as I always say, once you have seen one of the Cotswolds you have seen all of them. I now realize that the Welsh had been enfeebled by decades of mal-nutrition, that their performance on the Rugger field was a manifestation of despair and that their three-quarter line never really got moving until 1945. It didn't seem so at the time when we were being pushed around by Newport second XV.

Up to London to work in 1912 under the grand delusion that a boat out on the Serpentine was floating on top of the world. It was floating next to a powder magazine. Perhaps it was to hear people say 'What are economics?' that I took up the study of that subject, for decades of sloth-ful ease disguised as continuing prosperity had almost thrown it into the discard. The currency was managed without anyone proclaiming the fact, consequently the terms inflation and deflation had no meaning except in the context of bicycle and motor tyres. The few professors in the faculty maintained the drab tradition of intellectual integrity, and it is amazing how they kept ahead of the times. My Professor of Economics forecasted in 1895 the probable advent of a declining population in this country and then got on with his other work. The Professor of Statistics was broaching the doctrine of public works in times of depression when informed thought was taking an indefinitely prolonged rest from the bimetallic controversy. He it was who cramped my style and disqualified me for fame in a planned world by saying to me mildly one day, 'Please tell Mr So-and-so that the Almighty himself cannot guarantee the third significant figure.' The world today is an oyster for the man who will vouch for the estimate that the grain consumption of the United Kingdom in 1952 will be 7,674,000 metric tons, and that the tertiary production requirements of the Yugo-Slavia of 1960 will embrace 2,345 dry-cleaning establishments. These experts pass like night from land to land. Washington, London, Paris and Geneva are their footstools and the five continents their washpot, while the non-worshipper of Baal decays in his non-priority wilderness.

The degree course entailed dashing off from work five nights a week for three hours attendance at lectures. The 26 tram was regularly boarded at Lambeth by a bevy of boisterous charwomen on the way to Government offices. If these lineal descendants of the wife of Bath represented the oppressed proletariat they successfully concealed it by an exchange of obstetrical badinage conducted with a gusto that reddened the ears of a young cub of 21.

The rush to the Colours in 1914 of the under-nourished denizens of the capitalist hell came up against some exacting recruiting officers, who couldn't have known the facts of life. In some places the adjutant would stalk in and pack off anyone under 5 ft. 9 in. with a summary, 'Trot off home, sonny.' Anyone with glasses might be dismissed with a cruel 'We're looking for men.' Those who got through the mesh were a gallant comely crowd and when they moved off in column of fours the drab town halls outside of which they paraded took on a glow which has not yet faded for some of the survivors.

That war provided my first contact with the men of the North. If I had known the extent of their degradation by the Industrial Revolution I would never have supported their kindly, good-humoured tolerance of the soft Southerner. 'Hey oop, blöody schoolmäaster,' a stocky Geordie would say after watching our amateur exhibition of truck-unloading. He would then make a pass with a short wooden roller and a crowbar, whereupon sawn tree trunks would obediently rise on their hind legs and dive docilely over the side of the truck. Kill off nearly a million of that type and you get your post-war world without any reference to the particular economic system that prevailed beforehand.

Ten days convalescent leave in early 1918 gave me my first chance to have one on the State, for I stretched a free railway voucher to Leeds, even though it meant sleeping in the Y.M.C.A. hut. Briggate was a shining boulevard, and a £500 travel allowance wouldn't buy me the same exhilaration today.

Subsequently twenty-one years of academic life served as an apprenticeship to journalism for, as I always say, once you have been in one Common Room in this country you have been in all of them. There are academic standards and it is a waste of time going round looking for a departure from them. Sort of drab uniformity, if you know what I mean. It was something to sit alongside Keynes, and others who wouldn't thank me for the advertisement, puzzling over the economic problems of the inter-war period. Too little concerned with people and the needs of their minds and spirits? What can you expect in the line running down from Hume and Adam Smith?

Having preached the necessity for the mobility of labour I was under some constraint to practise it, and the approaching end of a war seemed to provide the necessary fluidity in the labour market. For once I kept under the shower after turning it on to the cold, and after recovering my breath smote myself on the chest 'No weakness, Danton' and set out for The Street. A journey by tube and then a wait for the bus. It came along eventually and the number was 18B, incidentally and significantly the worst service in London. *Pas trop de zèle, Danton.*

I had been lured into journalism by the films, and before the end of a month I knew there was something wrong with the script. I got it soon after when I observed the Editor walking slowly along the corridor. The Bishop to the life. The Deputy-Editor fell into his place as the dean of the chapter, and there were canons to the right and left of me. No wonder they have chapels in this industry. I was in a cathedral and all I had done was to enlarge the circle of friends to none of whom would I give a reference for the job of running a concentration camp. I suppose there are about thirty of these friends whose list of agenda and non-agenda constitutes what could be called a drab code, and I don't think at this stage of life I shall bother with any other.

For the new set-ups in process of creation strike me as still drabber. It may have been a drab assumption of the old order that murder is murder, loot is loot, and rape is rape whatever the time and place, but there is a drab ignominy about the formula which asks who killed your mother before deciding whether it was a crime to blazon to all eternity or a necessary purge to clear the way for the establishment of the new order. The lucubrations of the apostles of this new order induce in me a vast fatigue over their whole range from sour priggishness to bloody-mindedness. I concede them the first three items on the nine o'clock news for the daily record of their departures from the old drab standards. 'Get it over,' I growl. 'What's the latest fake trial? Who's been expropriated this time? To what bestiality are we now to remain indifferent, or even to subscribe?' Let them go on persuading themselves that the history of Britain is summed up in the Dissolution of the Monasteries, the Enclosure Acts, the Peterloo Massacre, the Tolpuddle Martyrs, and the Great Depression. Let them paint a picture of a hell upon earth. Let them wrap the whole story round the thesis that Sam Weller was a despicable hireling. I will go on contending that the British people have been the favoured children of Providence over the past 300 years, and I am drably superstitious lest the selfsame Providence should turn round and rend us for the bleating ingratitude that informs current ideology.

Behold, they make all things new! In 1912 the submerged cockney newsvendor served me with a deferential *'News* it is, me young cock sparrer.' Since then humanity has struck its tents and has been on the march. Today the emancipated serf greets me with a new-found independence. *'News* it is, me old cock sparrer.' That, for me, sums up the Revolution of Our Times.

*An obituary upon the charm of London in the 'twenties;
together with a croak over its current glumness*

Good-bye to London

by *RAYMOND MORTIMER*

'BUT then you never saw Karsavina!' 'None of them can hold a candle to Lenglen!' 'Melba was in a different street!'—what could be more maddening than such remarks? Every new generation is submitted to them. My elders tried to crush my youthful enthusiasms with talk of Patti and Irving. So, when I catch myself pulling a long face over London as it is today, I feel obliged to consider how far London used in fact to be more enjoyable, and how far I found it so only because I was younger and more ready to enjoy it.

To show the superiority of Melba, I have only to play records of the same *aria* sung by her and by any songstress now vociferous. About Karsavina, on the other hand, I can prove nothing, dead certain though I am that she was an artist of a different order to any *ballerina* whom I can see today. I may find it, I fear, similarly hard to substantiate my sense that London was once incomparably more delightful than it is now.

The years between the Wars can be divided into two periods,
1919–1929 and 1929–1939. The second of these decades was a period
of ever increasing anxieties—a slump, hideous unemployment, Hitler's
evolution from a local nastiness to a universal menace. Though London
continued to offer many delights beneath these black clouds, it is to the
earlier period that my thoughts most frequently return. The 'twenties,
I assure you, were enchanting. War seemed a horror banished for ever:
in any case there was no Power that threatened or insulted us. The
world, after an appalling ordeal that had brought mourning to most
families, seemed to have recovered its normal health. The faith in progress, which the War had never entirely prostrated, seemed more buoyant
than before. Hopefulness saturated the air. There was money to spend,
and not only among the very rich. Never had pleasure been more widely
available, more fervently pursued. One can reasonably apply to the
period Wordsworth's description of an earlier flowering of human hope:

> *Bliss was it in that dawn to be alive,*
> *But to be young was very heaven!*

Of course some people were indignantly censorious. If you can't
enjoy something, you can always enjoy disapproving of those who do.
This has always been a great consolation to the elderly. Indeed I used
once to look forward to shaking my grey head over the frivolity of the
young. Instead, I am shocked by their seriousness.

One has now, I know, to take a great deal of trouble in order to have
even a fairly good time, and most of the young don't seem to take it.
In the 'twenties there was much chin-wagging over 'the Bright Young
People.' For my part I associate youth with brightness, and I altogether
prefer those disgracefully bright young people, many of whom were my
friends, to the Dull Young People whom I sometimes encounter, with
their earnest chatter about socialized public houses or moral rearmament.
Today I might not be anxious to attend a midnight party at a swimming-
bath, into which the guests dived in the intervals of dancing. But it
was a more seductive London in which such pleasing follies were devised
and enjoyed.

IN THE 'TWENTIES FANCY DRESS was given the deep thought that it
has habitually excited in the most civilized societies. Perhaps indeed a
society can be thought civilized in proportion to the energy it expends
upon what is unpractical or materially unnecessary; the decoration of

rooms, for instance, and sport and the refinements of cooking. In tenth century Japan a gentleman was judged by his gift for improvising poems, his handwriting, his dancing, and his taste in scent. In France, during what is still glorified as *le grand siècle,* Lewis the Fourteenth, in the intervals of extending the powers of the throne and the frontiers of his kingdom, gave as much consideration to his fancy dresses as to the latest novelties from the pens of Racine and Molière. Very few of us have the talent to project our daydreams in verse or painting or acting. Many can do so by dressing up. Shall I make out with psychological jargon that this is therapeutic through a temporary objectivization of the *persona*? It well may be, but I'll be content to say that it is great fun. And, though I now have little wish to dress up, I should like to see other people doing so.

Parties and all that were only the more conspicuous or orchidaceous of the pleasures that flowered so bountifully in the London of the 'twenties. The Muses linked hands with the elegances; supreme art became positively fashionable. There were evenings when you could choose between *Rosenkavalier* unsurpassably given by Lotte Lehmann, Elisabeth Schumann, Delia Reinhardt, and Richard Mayr, and the Diaghileff Ballet with Karsavina, Lopokova, Massine, and Idzikovsky dancing to new music by Stravinsky and Falla, or in new settings by Derain and Picasso. You had time to dine before the show, and restaurants welcomed you after it. Pleasanter still, you would meet friends, some of them from abroad, in the entr'actes, and could improvise a party, after the performance, in your home, since you could count on finding there something to eat and lots to drink. Today, unless we have just been remembered by some angelic friend in America, we are all Mother Hubbards.

Food! It is a measure of our degradation not that this subject is now always cropping up but that we are concerned with the materials for cooking instead of with cooking as an art. Food in London has now reached a dizzying degree of nastiness. In some of the large hotels, that are called 'exclusive' because they are avoided by all who don't care to pay through the nose for bad service and worse cooking, I have been treated to meals from which a stevedore in Marseilles would recoil with disgust and amazement.

The best food in England has always been found in private houses, and to these now you can seldom be invited because of the paucity alike of rations and of cooks. I do not pretend that good cooking, except in the simplest style, was ever easy to find in London. But the simplest style does very well when the material is prime. Today it appears that calves are born without tails, livers or sweetbreads, and lambs without saddles. The grouse, for all I know, has joined the dodo as an extinct species; and, judging by London restaurants and clubs, one must suppose that no hen now lays an undried egg.

THE PICTURES IN LONDON were another source of ever new delight. By 'pictures,' I fear I must explain, I do not mean photographs projected in rapid succession upon a screen; these are seen more easily and more cheaply in the country. The pictures I care for are the hand-painted sort which used to be brought in large numbers from abroad, where they have always been good at this type of thing.

Our cultivated rulers now prevent the import of pictures from France. The Foreign Secretary, we know, guffaws at the mention of French books, as if he were a bookie relishing a limerick. Can it be that the Chancellor of the Exchequer and his Treasury officials suffer from a similar delusion about French pictures? Their veto cannot be due to a shortage of francs, since this does not exist. Are they seeking to protect our morals? I can assure them that the pictures I want to see could not shock anybody, however prudish, except perhaps the venerable President of the Royal Academy.

London picture-dealers used to compete with one another in finding and bringing here the most remarkable pictures, new and old. How pleasant it was to wander from Leicester Square to Albany courtyard, and then up Bond Street, touring the shows! A French picture—dare I add?—could be all the more enjoyable when you found a friend in a French hat looking at it. Today Bond Street has been invaded by purveyors who seem to have moved from the Edgware Road; and the frocks and hats in London are as dingy as the bombed or unpainted houses that form their background. If I run across anyone I know with the right sort of nonsense on her head, 'You're just back from Paris!' I exclaim, and in this I am seldom wrong.

Shopping used to be most exhilarating. Whenever I was depressed by a letter from my banker about an overdraft, I would cheer myself up by dashing out to choose some ties and to order some shirts. Today shopping gives one the blues. Purchase-tax is intended to prevent you from buying anything not utterly necessary; it is difficult to find anything of good quality and design; and if you do find it, it is sure to be marked 'For export only.'

Sometimes, on top of all this, rudeness supervenes. Manners certainly are not what they were, but I don't agree with those who call them atrocious. Londoners, if less polite than Florentines, are not nearly so rude as Parisians and New Yorkers. (To discover just how insulting people can be, I recommend a visit to one of the large stores on Fifth

Avenue.) If you worked in a London shop, might you not become a trifle uncivil yourself? Never to have the gratification of finding for a customer just what he wants; always to be clipping tiny squares of paper; always to be saying 'Oh, yes, it will wear wonderfully' about goods you know to be shoddy—what wonder if salesmen, thus frustrated in the higher reaches of their art, sometimes vent their vexation on the customer? Mrs Harris, I must add, who keeps the village post-office and shop that I go to in the country, never seems put out.

Paris and Rome may not be what they were, but they remain stimulating and vivid. Indeed, if you go from London to Rome, you have the ironical impression that you have come from a defeated to a victorious country. (The impression, I must own, is superficial, though the industriousness of the Italians has worked wonders.) The causes of London's degeneration are not, I suspect, merely economic. Our rulers seem prejudiced against all pleasures that they do not think elevating. But they would not dare impose needless austerities if there were not in the public a puritanical strain that accepts drabness with docility and even a degree of perverse satisfaction. Consider the new street-lighting, which makes people look as if they had been exhumed. It might have been devised by some Purity League, bent upon discouraging casual encounters. In what other country would the population consent to be thus disfigured?

London has become the most unpracticable as well as the glummest of great cities. In the district between Bond Street and Shaftesbury Avenue it is quicker to walk than to take a taxi, even when you can find one. The streets, narrow enough already, are blocked by stationary vehicles. If in the middle of the West End the streets were kept rigorously clear all day of parked cars and vans discharging beer, pastries or packing-cases, those who have to come to this district would be saved at least half an hour every day. Tough on car-owners? Yes, but the present jam is even tougher on those of us who are not car-owners; and, fanatically as I believe in the rights of minorities, I cannot see why the 5 per cent who use their cars in Dover Street and Vigo Street and Brewer Street should inflict so much waste of time on the 95 per cent who use buses and taxis.

IT IS THE PLEASURES OF FRIENDSHIP that now drag me to London. Of the people I like best probably more than a half live in the country. Yes, but in different parts of the country. They are scattered from Kent to Wiltshire, from Cambridgeshire to Dorset. What have I not learnt, during two rural hibernations, about the impediments to cross-country journeys! The artful arrangers of railway and omnibus time-tables seem to have conspired to make travellers wait for two hours whenever they have to change. Paradoxically, one of London's chief merits is that it is so easy to get away from. In the old days a friend would sometimes meet me in the street and say, 'I am motoring to the Riviera the day after tomorrow,' or 'I am flying to Munich,' and add, 'Why don't you come with me?' And I could not always see why I shouldn't. (Earning one's bread and butter with a pen is not the rosy, indolent job some people suppose; the easier a thing is to read, the more difficult it is to write. Yet the privilege of not being tied to an office is enormous.) On a country walk evidently one is unlikely to be tempted by such sudden invitations to break all engagements and rush to sunny shores or snowfields. But in any case the delight of unpremeditated travel has been taken from us. Having got to Kitzbühel or Cannes, what would you live on, when your ration of foreign currency has long since been used? London has ceased to shine even as a jumping off ground.

So good-bye to London; and, hey-nonny, let me surrender myself to bucolic joys. Several years ago I remarked that there were only two classes left in England, cow-owners and non-cow-owners. The farmer belongs to the upper class, and all Londoners to the lower, except the few who have discovered the whereabouts of that wonderful-sounding Black Market. (I suppose it must be possible to buy cream in London, but having no notion where, I have never been tempted.) Apart from the satisfaction of joining the upper class, I find that the country offers an important and seldom mentioned advantage: you are never obliged to go out of doors. No trudging through deluges, fogs and blizzards, because you have accepted an invitation, or because there is no food in the house. In good weather there are strolls and gardens, with birds to watch, flowers and cows to smell; in bad, there is a wood-fire and a book or the wireless. The choice of music available is far wider in the country than in my part of London, where I cannot get the Third Programme; and I would far rather listen to an orchestra by broadcast than in any of the resorts that so inadequately replace the Queen's Hall.

Some day London, I hope, will be herself again. If I am still alive, I shall be very, very old, but I shall come back to die where I was born. I shall hobble to superb performances of operas and ballets. I shall drink Veuve Clicquot from satin slippers. Fireworks will coruscate above streets gay with masqueraders. And the young and fair will whisper: 'It's worth while talking to that old codger: he actually saw Karsavina, and Lenglen, and Melba.' I shall pretend to have seen Patti also and Irving; and even—as dotage creeps on—Grisi and Malibran, Mrs. Siddons and Farinelli and Camargo.

Concerning first nights, and the mistaken idea that regular first nighters are allowed free tickets, and the ways of dramatic critics, and the convention which forbids their applauding the performance, and much more besides.

The Dramatic Critic: His Job

by HAROLD HOBSON

T is about half past nine on a summer evening—to be exact, June 30, 1948; and the curtain is falling on the first performance, at the Aldwych Theatre, of William Douglas Home's comedy, *Ambassador Extraordinary*. It has been a not unamusing evening. Mr Raymond Lovell, as heavily built as Mr Bevin, but more courtly, has given a superb rendering of a British Foreign Secretary faced with the dilemma of sacrificing either his country to a load of atom bombs from Mars, or his daughter to the Martian ambassador. With a host of hesitations, qualifications, and reservations that barely conceal the fact that from the very beginning he has had no doubt whatever as to the answer he will give, Mr Lovell has placed the public weal before private honour.

The curtain falls, and rises again in response to some applause from the stalls. Mr Lovell steps forward to acknowledge the reception, but as he opens his mouth a noise like the baying of wolves comes from the gallery. There are shouts of 'Rubbish,' and there is a great hissing. At this point a figure in a dinner jacket strolls on to the stage. We understand that it is the author. 'I like heckling,' he says casually. 'Please go on. We have the night before us.' The booing continues. A photographer rushes forward and takes a picture. Mr Home gives him a little bow and says 'Thank you, sir.' In the intervals of the abuse (for even the gallery must pause for breath) Mr Home, speaking as easily and lightly as if at a tea party, thanks the cast for their excellent performance. For his last words he turns to the hooters. 'I hope some people have enjoyed the play,' he remarks. 'As for the others, it doesn't much matter whether they like plays or not. Because, if they don't learn the lesson of compromise taught here tonight, in six months' time that gallery won't be there.'

He spoke this rather melodramatic threat in the coolest possible way, and then strolled off the stage as nonchalantly as he had strolled on. It was a magnificent exhibition of self-possession and calmness, and far and away the most dramatic event of the evening.

The Aldwych holds eleven hundred people, and that night it was full. Of these all but about a hundred and sixty had paid for their seats. It is often thought that a first night audience for a new play is made up of friends of the management and company who are invited in free. This is not so. At West End first nights not more than two hundred seats are given away, and their distribution is carefully watched. The Press gets 44 pairs of stalls, and 18 pairs in the dress circle. Herbert Smith, the managing director of Keith Prowse, gets one pair in the stalls. The general managers of the theatrical agencies have 12 pairs in the dress circle. The author has two stalls free, the director two, and the dress designer two. The theatre owner has four seats in the stalls, and another four in the dress circle. The holders of all seats but these must pay.

The first choice for paid seats goes to members of the cast, who can buy them for their friends, and there are about twenty regular first nighters who are also given the refusal of seats for sale. Among these the most constant are Mrs Nathan (Henry Kendall's aunt) and Sir Louis and Lady Stirling. The last two invariably occupy the centre seats of the front row of the stalls for everything except Shakespeare (though Laurence Olivier has been known to lure them even to the Old Vic). Sprinkled about the first half-dozen rows of stalls there are generally to be found film stars, writers, and politicians, but the composition of these varies. Sir John Anderson, Sir Stafford Cripps, Terence Rattigan, Noel Coward (when he is in England), Sir Bronson Albery, Henry Sherek, Stewart Granger, Godfrey Tearle are frequently to be seen at first nights.

MOST OF THE AUDIENCE of 1,100 saw the scene at the end of *Ambassador Extraordinary* that I have described. In fact, everybody saw it except some of the dramatic critics. For those dramatic critics who write for the daily papers have to flee from the theatre the moment the curtain descends, or they would be late with their copy. As soon as the last line is spoken you will see A. V. Cookman of *The Times* and W. A. Darlington of the *Daily Telegraph* rise from their seats at the end of the second and third row of stalls, and glide silently down the aisle to the exit, followed by their colleagues on the daily Press. It is only once-a-week dramatic critics, like Ivor Brown and John Trewin of the *Observer,* Eric Keown of *Punch,* and myself of *The Sunday Times* who have leisure to wait for such episodes as that which brought *Ambassador Extraordinary* to its extraordinary conclusion.

Extraordinary it was, for the usual thing, even when the play is obviously not a success, is to disguise its failure with the trappings of applause. Generally speaking, not more than three plays a year are hooted at curtain-fall. The sort of journalist who rejoices in brawls, tumults, and demonstrations had better not choose dramatic criticism for his profession.

Now I come to think of it, I am not sure that many of my colleagues (or myself, for that matter) can be said to have chosen dramatic criticism at all. It is unlikely that one will become a dramatic critic unless one has some liking for and understanding of the theatre. On the other hand, the number of first-class dramatic critics (which is small, anyway) who were born with the determination to spend every other evening within smelling distance of a theatre bar is infinitesimal. Dramatic criticism is rarely a vocation. One of my most brilliant colleagues is known to have graduated to it from the Civil Service. It is said that at his first appearance in his office, after coming down from Oxford, he was sent to Northampton to make a report on the latrines of that interesting town. He passed three weeks in this occupation, and then handed in his survey. 'Is there much of this kind of work in the Civil Service?' he inquired. 'There's practically nothing else' was the reply. He promptly resigned, and became a dramatic critic.

My own introduction to dramatic criticism may be considered to be the accident of an accident. Had I not chanced at Oxford to be a member of the same college—Oriel—as Erwin Canham, now Editor of *The Christian Science Monitor,* I should never have become a journalist; and had I never become a journalist I should never have become a dramatic critic. One day early in our acquaintance I lent Canham my copy of Maitland's *Domesday Book and Beyond,* and in a casual return he suggested that I should write something for the *Monitor,* a junior member of whose staff in Boston he had been before he came to Oxford as a Rhodes Scholar. I wrote a thousand word essay on the desirable qualifications of an intelligent voter, of which I recall the main theme as advice to read Walter Bagehot's *English Constitution.* The article was reduced by 750 words in Boston and printed as an editorial. After that I wrote other editorials, and came to London in 1931 as a leader writer.

The London dramatic critic of the paper at that time was the celebrated J. T. Grein, a rotund little man who at seventy possessed the physical and mental energy of a youth of seventeen. He had no liking for musical comedy, and when Jack Buchanan appeared in *Stand Up and Sing,* he did not trouble to review it. The then London editor, Roscoe Drummond, suggested half in jest that if I wrote a notice of this show that the *Monitor* printed, the paper would refund me the price of my seat. This was my introduction to dramatic criticism.

The greatest professional opportunity of my life came to me in the same apparently accidental manner. It was whilst I was acting as Leonard Russell's assistant on the literary staff of *The Sunday Times* that the greatest of modern dramatic critics, James Agate, began to lose his health. The editor of *The Sunday Times,* Mr W. W. Hadley, very generously offered me the chance to deputize for him, which I did with a review of the Regent's Park *Midsummer Night's Dream* in 1945. After that, whenever James was away from the theatre, I took his place.

Of course, it is not really as casual as this makes it appear. No one can make even a passable dramatic critic who has not for as long as he can remember had burning inside him a love for the theatre. I was fascinated by the theatre long before I had ever been in one. For various reasons I was in childhood more or less confined to my home; but every Sunday evening, about the time I was eight years old, an insurance agent called Gibson used to visit my parents' house in Sheffield.

This young man, a very lively fellow, must have had a great liking for the theatre. He was always talking about it. He used to slouch his shoulders, pull his mackintosh up to his neck, push his trilby hat over his eyes, and recite, 'It is a far, far better thing that I do than I have ever done. It is a far, far better rest that I go to than I have ever known.' He was vastly excited, too, about a play in which I understood him to say that the hero tore his eyes out with knitting needles.

These things made an impression on me that has never been effaced. They made the theatre seem in my eyes a place of magic and enchantment. When, years later, I repeated this young man's experience, and saw Sir John Martin-Harvey in *The Only Way* and *Oedipus Rex,* the impression was strengthened and confirmed.

MARTIN-HARVEY WAS THE IDOL of my youth. I found myself quite unable to regard dispassionately any actor whom I chose to classify as a rival of his. For this reason I was never able to do justice to the splendid talents of Fred Terry and Julia Neilson, and even to Henry Ainley, who used to write me very pleasant letters when I was a boy, I gave only a reluctant admiration. I admired Ainley, in fact, chiefly as a cinema player, and for me the ideal screen versions of *The Prisoner of Zenda* and *Rupert of Hentzau* will always be those in which he appeared with Gerald Ames.

Before I went to Oxford, then, my theatre-going was dominated by Martin-Harvey. The only other actor who came near to having as powerful an effect on me was the young Henry Baynton, whose *Hamlet,* in the superb dawn of a career that faded very early into the common day, astounded me by the extraordinary beauty of its speech.

It was Oxford, both the Playhouse and the New Theatre, that, to my appreciation of the romantic and the poetic, added the realistic, the modern, and the philosophic. During the day I read history in that university, and at night gazed at greasepaint. At the old New Theatre, in 1924, I was exhilarated by the extraordinary vitality of Maidie Andrews in *Archie,* and enormously excited by Dennis Neilson-Terry in a not very good thriller, *No Other Tiger.* At the Playhouse, I think my most memorable experience was Galsworthy's *The Skin Game,* which first showed me that modern industrial and social problems can make a play every bit as gripping and as moving as a piece of romantic heroism.

I came down from Oxford with the theatre firmly fixed in my mind as the place where, if I was not going to earn my living, I was at least going to spend my leisure. But three years had still to pass before I received my first payment for professional criticism.

THE FINANCIAL REWARDS of dramatic criticism do not, of course, compare with the remuneration given to leading actors. In the last week of its run at His Majesty's *Edward, My Son* took £3,052. (This, by the way, is the highest sum ever taken by a straight play in a London theatre at eight performances.) Robert Morley, playing the leading part of Lord Holt, was paid 9 per cent of the gross takings. Even when it was at the Lyric, a smaller theatre, it continued to take about £2,270 a week for well over a year. If £200 a week may be accepted as suitable remuneration for a leading actor in a West End success, it may safely be said that few critics are as well paid. On the other hand, their remuneration does not fluctuate like a player's, and half a dozen theatrical failures make no difference to their bank balance.

An actor who is not a star, but who builds up for himself a steady reputation as a supporting featured actor, may, once he is solidly established, count on an income of roughly £2,000 a year. A successful dramatic critic can call such a man a financial brother, even perhaps a little brother. Dramatic criticism is, in fact, one of the best paid branches of journalism. To offset this is the consideration that the number of dramatic critics' jobs available is very limited.

But the true reward of dramatic criticism, as of every worthwhile job, is in the work itself. The conditions under which it is done are pleasant. To finish the day by going to a theatre, where one will be certain to be seated near to people one knows, is like dropping into a club. And there is always the chance that one may see a masterpiece of writing or of acting, or even of both together. The hope is, in the nature of things, practically always disappointed, but it is never quite eradicated, and the sensation when it is fulfilled is wonderful. Then the dramatic critic feels an almost irresistible (though nearly invariably resisted) temptation to join in the applause that convention forbids him on the ground that he should not disclose his judgment until he has delivered it in his paper.

The profession of actor has, in its day, come in for a good deal of scorn. Shakespeare himself winced at the thought of being an actor.

*Alas! 'tis true I have gone here and there,
And made myself a motley to the view,
Gor'd my own thoughts, sold cheap what is most dear,
Made old offences of affections new.*

Lesser men than Shakespeare—

D

Augustine Birrell, for example—have shared his scorn. The artist, the novelist, the poet, the composer may abide by the judgment of posterity, but the actor cannot appeal to this judgment. 'No record of his art,' says Birrell, 'survives to tell his tale or account for his fame. When old gentlemen wax garrulous over actors dead and gone, young gentlemen grow somnolent. Chippendale the cabinet-maker is more potent than Garrick the actor. The vivacity of the latter no longer charms (save in Boswell), the chairs of the former still render rest impossible in a hundred homes.'

Now this, of course, is where the dramatic critic comes in. For the dramatic critic is the amber that preserves the histrionic fly. He preserves, not so much an actor's reputation, as some impression of what caused that reputation. The fame of Edith Evans's Millamant would have persisted only as a vague memory but for the words of my great predecessor, James Agate, when he said that her face was like a 'city in illumination.'

We can still to some extent share the experience of Partridge when he saw Garrick in *Hamlet* jellied with the act of fear at his father's ghost, since in those pages Fielding was writing as a dramatic critic should, and as few do. We can still hear some echo of Kean's Othello when Hazlitt says that 'the tone of voice in which he delivered the beautiful apostrophe "Then oh, farewell!" struck on the heart like the swelling notes of some divine music, like the sound of years of departed happiness.'

And again with Hazlitt you can still see the last two minutes of Kean's Richard III. 'He gave to all the busy scenes of the play the greatest animation and effect. He filled every part of the stage. The concluding scene, in which he is killed by Richmond, is the most brilliant. He fought like one drunk with wounds: and the attitude in which he stands with his hands stretched out, after his sword is taken from him, had a preternatural and terrific grandeur, as if his will could not be disarmed, and the very phantoms of his despair had a withering power.'

The representation of an actor, or for that matter of a man of action is

> Momentary as a sound,
> Swift as a shadow, short as any dream,
> Brief as the lightning in the collied night . . .
> The jaws of darkness do devour it up.

Unless the jaws of that darkness can be stayed, the player's performance, as soon as it is given, begins to slip down into a dim abyss of oblivion. To rescue him from that abyss is the critic's task and privilege. But for Plutarch, the words of Alexander, when urged to fight in the dark at Gaugamela, 'I will not steal a victory,' would be forgotten. The soldier is only a legend without the historian. The historian of the actor is the dramatic critic.

*It all happened a long time ago, in a world where mammas
were cold to unknown young men who neglected to change
for dinner (even if Lord X didn't bother) at the winter
sports hotel.*

The Most Miserable of Men

by DESMOND MacCARTHY

'O F all men,' said the youth sitting in the far corner of the
railway carriage, gazing into the setting sun, 'I am the most
miserable.'

We were alone in the compartment and he was talking to
himself; when I rustled my paper he took no notice. His lips
continued to move, but now inaudibly. His worried young face looked
intelligent and amiable: I liked him.

'I hope you won't think me intrusive,' I said (at the sound of my voice
he came to himself with a start), 'but if you feel like it, I wish you would
tell me what prompted that tragic exclamation?'

He started and flushed. 'Tragic what? What did I say?'

'You said you were the most miserable of men,' I replied in a matter
of fact tone. 'It's most unlikely I can help such a man, but it might be
a relief to him to talk about what is on his mind to someone he will never
see again.'

After a long pause he said shyly, 'I am ashamed.'

'Confession makes us all feel we are superior to ourselves,' I said. 'There's nothing like it for reviving self-respect.'

'I am too ashamed,' he repeated, smiling a little.

I came over to his end of the carriage, leaned across and touched his knee: 'You will forgive me?' We were silent and ceased to look at each other.

The rhythmic trantle-trantle of the unhurrying train was soothing to us both. Outside in the landscape the sun had gone down, and my companion, having now no dazzling disc to gaze into, fell to prodding the seat opposite with his stick. He was considering himself, I guessed, in a searching though, perhaps, no longer tragic light: I liked him very much.

'You see . . . The fact is . . .'

I caught his eye. 'Oh! I *can't*,' he exclaimed desperately, bringing his heel down on the floor of the carriage with a bang.

'How long ago did it happen?'

He seemed rather relieved at the question. 'Three years, about.'

'Three years. And you are still the most miserable of men?'

'No, oh, no! That's only what I said. I don't often think of it at all; but when I *do*—it's absurd—I often say that to myself. It's become a habit; though I don't always say it aloud,' he added smiling.

'Well, I'm glad you did this time,' I answered, 'for now you can get it off your mind and it will not come back again—at any rate, not so excruciatingly.'

He laughed, this time almost gaily. 'The truth is, now I'm evidently going to tell you all about it, what embarrasses me is that it is such a *little* thing.'

'There!' I cried, 'there you are! You're half cured already. Go on. Go on.'

'Well, will you believe something first? Really believe it? I'm *not* a snob; I mean I'm not, and never have been, such a snob as many people. I don't boast about my fine acquaintances; I'm not such a fool—now, at any rate. And I swear I never did really or very seldom; and then only in a way, don't you know that, that, that . . . But hotels have, or rather *had* (Heaven knows I'm cured!) a simply beastly effect on me. And,' he went on, stooping forward with a frown of agitated eagerness, 'I'm *not* a liar; I mean, of course, what anybody would call a liar; I don't lie much. But these hotels! I've thought a lot about them, as you will soon be able to imagine, and I've made out a sort of psychology of hotel-crowds. You see, in an hotel everybody loses everything that distinguishes and explains him or her; everybody is anonymous. There these people are, cooped up together, eyeing each other, wondering about each other, sneering at

each other, or approaching each other with the stiff comic caution of
mistrustful dogs.   Everybody who hasn't an obvious badge is an unknown
quantity.   Everybody gossips and guesses about everybody else, and the
result is everybody wants to flourish his or her credentials.   That is the
prevailing atmosphere, and it is odious—I speak with the bitterness of
one who has been infected.   A sensitive person in hotels inevitably
becomes misanthropic; I know I do.   One's fellow human beings are
simply awful in hotels.   When they come down day after day to breakfast, lunch and dinner; when you watch them over the paraphernalia of
tea in the marble hall, munching to music, you think to yourself, "This
is too much!   Here are these pigs with their noses in the trough again!"
Of course your own mouth is full, but they look so disgustingly dull and
useless—and so you do, no doubt.   They don't know how to spend
half their time—nor do you.   And with these *tu quoques* whispering in
your own ears, the impulse to distinguish yourself in the eyes of anyone
who seems just a little nicer than the others becomes irresistible.   In
short, you are pushed into becoming a snob of one kind or another.   And
now for my adventure, which has made me,' and this time he laughed
quite heartily, 'the most miserable of men.'
   'I shan't laugh again,' he added gloomily.   'It really is a painful
story.
   'I was travelling to a much frequented spot in Switzerland, a place
famous for winter sports, where a friend of mind was to meet me two days
later.   During the last stage of the journey I fell in with an English
family, and shared the same carriage.   We soon made out that we were
going to the same place and to the same hotel.   The family consisted of
a father, a kindly, modest, straightforward man, a mamma with a manner,
a girl whose looks pleased me extremely and a perky censorious Public
School boy.   I had better tell you I myself was in my twentieth year.
   'Father and daughter both seemed to like me at once, but Mamma was
proof against all my attempts to interest her; and when she did respond
at all, it was with a non-committal smile, all the easier to read for being
so gracious.   The father, the daughter and I were in those delightful
spirits peculiar to a first morning abroad—and you know how quickly
people make friends when they are childishly happy.   The boy was at
the age when he hates to show elation, and when the sight of a sister
making an impression on a young man (for some unknown reason with
which, nevertheless, I believe I sympathize) is irritating.   But even he
thawed over our second breakfast in the train.   His mother, however,
mostly kept her face to the window, smiling on us in a preoccupied way
from time to time, and rubbing away the frosted breath from the glass to
get a clearer view of the steep snowy hills and pine woods as they passed.
Sometimes, with a little ejaculation, she would single out something for

admiration, but with all my alacrity I was always too late to share her pleasure.

'I think I divined at the time that she was capable of reading her husband a lecture on the folly of making friends in the train with young men one knows nothing about, and that she wished me to feel that she regarded our further acquaintance as strictly conditional. Indeed, I must have felt that challenge in her from the first, and inwardly resolved to overwhelm her with my credentials, for only from having taken unconsciously some such resolve can I account for my subsequent impulse and behaviour.

'Well, towards evening we arrived at our destination. This was a long lake in a barren Alpine valley, with a large straggling timber village beside it. Black figures were still pushing about like water spiders over the surface of the ice, and still more people were plodding their way in file, or in knots, towards the gold-windowed barrack-like hotels on the slopes. The stars had begun to point above the mountains; and to draw such air into the lungs was like swallowing a draught of glittering icy water.

'My new friends wanted me to get into their conveyance, for, as I say, we had engaged rooms at the same hotel; and she whose presence had begun to infuse a subtle exhilaration into the scene, called out to me there was "plenty, plenty of room." Her voice in the dusk sounded magically kind and clear. But even if her mother had not proceeded to fluff herself out over the seat, they might have been cramped; so I waved my hat and drove alone, through the wooden snow-thatched village up to the hotel.

'The circular door of The Imperial admitted me to a hall of which not only the atmosphere, but the vegetation, was apparently tropical. On my way across the marble floor towards the gilded lift, I noticed couples swinging nonchalantly in rocking-chairs side by side among palms and flowers. There was a big group laughing and talking round a flaring fire: girls, in knitted jerseys, holding skates, girls in evening frocks, men in dinner jackets, and men still in their stockings and boots. The sting of frost was on all their faces, and their voices had that pleasant resonance which comes from having spent the day in the open air. At these sights the sense of the adventure of gregarious life got hold of me, and while I was unpacking I was filled with that delicious excitement (remember I was twenty) which gets so much weaker as one gets older—" Oh, what delightful things *may* not be going to happen to me next!" Then I opened the window and stepped out on to a balcony. The air was cold, the sky a limpid sable blue, and there, sure enough, were the mountains! If you had asked me, while I was unpacking, what was the most exciting thing in the world, I should have said: "Oh, meeting people and expecting one doesn't know what!" But on the balcony such adventures seemed superficial, or, at any rate, a mere garnishing to life. Dinner or no dinner, I felt I must go *out*. It was near *table d'hôte* time, and the assembled crowd in the hall made me feel self-conscious. I made for the door like a man catching a train. Somebody laughed. But the next moment I was running down over the snow, gloriously happy.

'The lake was as dark as agate, and so smooth it seemed a shame to scratch smoothness so exquisite. Tiny crystal splinters ran before me on the ice, and sparkled in the moonlight. And the undulating ringing of skates—how pleasing that eerie sound is to the ear! Every now and then I would stop to listen to it, chirping and shivering away across the silence, till it touched the frozen banks and stopped. Out I flew through capes of darkness into bays of moonlight, curving this way and that, with that effortless steadiness in motion which makes a skater feel more like a gull than a man; till, suddenly, I felt as though I had been alone a very long time. I thought of the hotel and turned to shore; and as I turned, far away on the dazzling white moonlit bank from which I had started, I saw a small dusky figure. It was a girl putting on skates. Even before I recognized her I knew it was my friend of the journey, whose voice had sounded so friendly all those hours in the train, who smiled more than most people and yet seemed graver than most. I struck out swiftly. We met and hailed each other. Of all the words in the English language, I believe "Hullo" is the most useful. "Hullo! Isn't it glorious!" we both exclaimed, and off we shot on separate ways to curve and recurve across each other's paths, saying, as we passed, things like: "My left ankle's weak," or "Just look at the mountains," or "I couldn't resist coming, could you?" Then away again we went. It excited me almost to laughter to think that she had felt the same impulse as I. Suddenly she called to me that she must go in; it was an intolerable shame, but they would be anxious about her, and she would be scolded as it was. I cannot remember what we said on the way back. It couldn't have been much, for we ran. But I have not forgotten the laughing face she turned to me from behind the gilt cage of the lift before she suddenly levitated and vanished upwards to get ready for *table d'hôte*.

'That lengthy meal was so near completion and I was so hungry that I decided to go straight in without changing. The newest arrivals were placed at the end of one of the long tables which was not yet full; and as I came in, trying to make my boots sound as little as possible on the parquet floor, I noticed that my seat would be beside my travelling companions. The father was nearest the end, the mother next above him, and the boy beyond her. So if I took the obvious chair she, when she came down, would sit beside me. I saw at once, from the look Mamma gave me, that my not having changed for dinner confirmed suspicions; and I thought that even her husband looked forward to our conversation soon showing the people opposite that I was not one of his party.

'By way of explaining why I was not properly dressed, I said that I had not been able to resist going down to try the ice and had stayed too late. This statement produced something like consternation. Papa put his pudding-spoon down suddenly instead of into his mouth, and I heard the mother say to her son: "George, run up at once. I must know what on earth Agatha's doing. Tell her to come down immediately. It's disgraceful; dinner is nearly over." But George did not budge. Then, turning to her husband, she said: "Do you mean to say you let that child go out at this time of night by herself after I told her not to?"

' "Did you see my daughter on the ice?" said her father to me, using his napkin and looking guilty.

'I was in the middle of telling them how she had come down after I had been there a little time, and how we had returned together, when in she came, rosy and smiling, and settled down—with perhaps just a little too much the air of nothing whatever having occurred.

' "I'm very late. Oh, Dad, it was too lovely. Mr —— was there. He'll tell it was worth missing all the courses for, though I *am* hungry."

' On me the effect of her voice was to make me think I might be looking as though a good deal had happened! And I made matters worse by turning at once to speak to her, and then, when our eyes met, forgetting what I was going to say.

'Well, after *that* I felt I must forthwith make the running with Mamma or she would see to it that their places were changed next day. From conversation in the train I knew the name of the county town where they lived, and by good luck I had stayed twice at a house in its neighbourhood for balls. My memory for people now served me in good stead.

'I was able to say "yes" repeatedly to the question, did I know the so and so's? The effect of all this on Mamma was—well, she became not only gracious but positively competitive, mentioning people and country houses herself with an ostentatious unostentation which made her children uncomfortable. "Oh, Mamma," I heard Agatha once murmur, "you know we only met them over the hospital bazaar."

'I liked Agatha for that; I sympathized with her deeply. But I was too intent upon my object, too flushed with my progress—possibly also with the Burgundy I was drinking—not to push on. I became confident, gay and satirical. I asked if the county beauty, Lady Georgina, was still as good as new. This led to Mamma asking me—and as she spoke she swept the strangers opposite into the conversation with a comprehensive glance—if I knew Lady Georgina's father, Lord X, a nobleman of the first importance. "Yes," I said, "I was driven over one afternoon to Thornton Abbey." That was true, only its enviable possessor happened to be, as a matter of fact, absent. I was proceeding to give my impressions of that grand and beautiful home when my attention was distracted by the behaviour of an elderly gentleman in a dark tweed suit immediately opposite. He had just finished and he was pushing his chair rather noisily into the table. I looked up and caught his eye. He was staring at me, I thought, with an odd, hostile intensity. Conversation had stopped for some yards along each side of the table. Yes, he was going to speak—and to me!

' "May I ask, sir," he was saying loudly and slowly, "if by chance I have the honour to be numbered among your numerous acquaintances?"

' "No," I replied rather jauntily, "I am pretty certain I never saw you before."

'He paused.

' "Well, I am Lord X," he said. And dropping his napkin on the table he turned his back and left the room.

'I have blushed with anguish at the recollection of that moment, which I suppose heartless people would describe as "an awkward pause." To me, it was a silent explosion. Then I heard Mamma, who had turned crimson, go off into a long loud artificial trill of laughter. Murmuring something about "impostors," she shook the crumbs off her lap and, summoning her family, swept towards the door. Everybody else was getting up. *Table d'hôte* was over; just a few people were cracking nuts at the far end of the table.

'But the girl on my right had not got up. She was pretending to finish her dinner. I know she looked at me twice; but I could not look back— please, please remember I was barely twenty, and very self-conscious at that. Not a word could I utter. Presently, she too (I heard her chair and her footsteps) went away, while I went on eating and drinking like a pompous automaton.

'I had to wait for the lift. In the hall there was a great deal of laughter, for the story was already travelling from group to group. I think I bore the titters, grins, and being looked at pretty well. Upstairs in my room, I went to the window; but now the snow mountains were as dull to me as sugar loaves. I soon went to bed, and, contrary to expectation, slept like a top. When my eyes opened the next morning I felt that something extremely unpleasant had happened, before I remembered exactly what it was. When I did, I saw my self-respect depended on two resolutions: to wait for my friend and not to change my hotel meanwhile. But I purposely came down late for breakfast to avoid the family who, as the next meal showed, *had* moved to another table. I also bore with apparent equanimity that wretched boy who would read out society paragraphs from the papers whenever I was in earshot, adding "old friends of mine," or "the dear duchess" as the case might be. Nobody asked me to join in any sports except one young woman who evidently did so out of curiosity so I practised figures by myself on the more secluded parts of the ice. When my friend did turn up he noticed at once that I was depressed. I left him in the smoking-room the night he arrived, and the next morning at breakfast he told me he had promised to make up one of a skating four. I saw he had heard the story, which was still having a success. He lunched with his partners, and a jolly noisy party they were. We did not meet all day. Before dinner he came into my room, and, after watching me dress in silence, he said, "I had no idea you were such a first-water snob." We agreed there was not much point in our spending the vac. together. We had a glum dinner. I went off the next morning to the South of France, which I could not afford—but I wanted to get away from snow mountains.

'There!' he said. 'And now I've told you why I am "the most miserable of men." You see it was, after all, only a tiny little thing.'

We both laughed.

'Pon my word,' he added, 'I believe I shall never think of it again.'

The train was now slowing up in front of a station. 'I've got to change here,' he exclaimed, hurriedly opening the door. We shook hands and I handed out his bag. Presently he came back to the window. Once more his young face wore a look of concern. 'I say,' he said, 'I hope you don't think I was an awful muff to mind so much. You see, what has bothered me most ever since was my having taken no notice of that girl when she stayed beside me alone in the dining-room. You've listened so nicely. You do understand, don't you?'

'Perfectly,' I assured him.

'That was the only moment I was really a coward,' he added.

The train began to move. He waved his hand gaily. 'Ain't I lucky to have had such a lesson young?' he said grinning.

'Stop!' I cried. 'What's the name of the people?'

'The people?'

'Yes, the family.'

'Dyce.'

'Agatha? Blue eyes you said? Agatha? Quite blue?'

He nodded.

'She's my niece,' I shouted. 'Mrs Dyce is my sister. You *must* see her; she's a perfect dear.' The train was drawing away faster. 'Not my sister,' I shouted, 'I don't mean her—haven't kissed her for nine years. You will meet . . .'

He had trotted nearly to the end of the platform, when suddenly a cloud of steam from the engine hid him from view.

I threw myself back in my corner. 'That may be very satisfactory, very,' I thought. ' . . . I do like him.' But the next moment I sprang up again—I had forgotten to ask him his name.

The Islanders are pouring across the Channel again, showing, as Sir Osbert Sitwell has pointed out, that post-war revival of the 'old instinct for travel of the British peoples, as much a part of their insular composition as is their poetry.' Mrs Nicholas, who ministers notably to that instinct in her 'Sunday Times' articles, writes here of an unforgettable year spent in Apulia.

A Year In Apulia

by ELIZABETH NICHOLAS

THE English, when jaunting in the sunny south, can be divided into two classes; those who do not like the heat and those who do. The first class is miserable most of the time, because a temperature above that usually encountered in an English May prostrates them utterly. The second class, to which I belong, is miserable unless there is a real, full-blooded sun, a blinding, scorching, searing sun, which comes dry to the skin and hard and clear and without mercy.

That is the sun for me, and with it I want a lonely, rock-encrusted coast where the sea is lively and very, very cold. When I bathe, I want to cry gratefully from the water, it is marvellously cool. I do not want to cry, bravely, it is quite warm, really. That is the cry of the bather round the English coast, and it is not for me. What pleasure is there in bathing if one is frightened lest the water be cold? The right approach is fear lest it be too warm and no relief from a grilling sun.

I want these things, and I want a copious supply of wine, which can be bought from a musty, cool cellar and poured from barrels into bottles, and cost no more than a few pennies. I want to sit beneath an umbrella on the quay of a small fishing village and watch the boats bobbing about on the water, while clams and oysters and sea urchins are opened for me and placed on a thick, blue china plate with half a lemon. I want olive oil, and olives, and fruit warm from the tree, and cooks who understand herbs and spices and the use of the grill. I want, also, to be far from my fellow islanders. To get these things I am prepared to forswear the 'cleanliness' so dear to the heart of the English. I will stay in a primitive pub which may, for all I know, be infested with what Baedeker calls disturbers of repose. I will do without a tiled bathroom and modern plumbing and constant hot and cold. I will eat from a wooden table or even a dirty table cloth. I will close my eyes to the state of the kitchen, and I shall be very, very happy.

It is for these things I remember Apulia. I remember the small and dark and noisy trattori with a quite absurd degree of nostalgia. I remember them, as I remember the long, sun-bleached coastline, the oleander and the cacti struggling together beside the dusty road, the vines and the carnations and the figs, the clear green sea and the crumbling baroque buildings, and I feel for them the warmest affection. Northern Italians are very right when they dismiss the Apulian people as loutish, ignorant, and of a dishonesty which passes beyond the realms of what is reasonable and right. But they are utterly wrong, I am convinced, in dismissing Apulia as a dreary place too, unworthy of attention. For it is an unspoilt, simple and very lonely countryside, untouched by the vulgarity which has laid hold of Capri, and Sorrento, and Amalfi.

This southern Adriatic coast of Italy is indeed unlike Rome or the north. It is more African, more barbaric, slow, and lazy, but it is beautiful too. The coastal towns, Mola, with its slim and graceful white baroque tower, and the cream and sienna houses of Monopoli, dominated by dim and elegant baroque churches, are all the better for being the home of hard-working fishermen, and not playgrounds for tourists. Polignano is also lovely, with a white enclosed square, and houses flush with the cliffs, and oleander trees everywhere. There was a restaurant in Polignano, a black market restaurant of course, where fish were brought dripping with the salty waters of the Adriatic and displayed on a tray for the customer to choose as he wished. Chickens were fried or most cunningly blended in a casserole, pastas were mixed with curious herbs, and the wine had a deep and satisfactory body to it. It was a good restaurant this, run on medieval lines; the women of the house did the cooking and invited guests into the great stone-flagged, dome-roofed kitchen to choose food from vast pots and pans. A curious air of solemnity hung over it: it was rather like going to church. Rushes covered the floor, unmasked torches provided light, and the two narrow windows gave straight on to the sea. The outer wall of the house, in fact, was a continuation of the steep, smooth sea cliff.

There was a terrace over the Adriatic, where the guests sat on what looked like a Roman sarcophagus and sipped vermouth while the dinner was cooked. Carnations sprayed over the walls, and the waves smacked hungrily against the rocks below, and the water of the sea had a thick, sweet look, which was both beautiful and strange. People sang of course; in the distance their voices were clear and true, and they sang nice, hackneyed songs from *Bohème* and *Butterfly* and *Traviata,* which no longer seemed sugary and trivial but very right and proper and faithful to the mood.

Sometimes we dined on the terrace, still listening to the sea and the thin, sweet voice of a young boy across the rooftops and the chatter of the women as they bent over their pots.

Our pleasure in these evenings was, I am sure, very conscious, and that is why, maybe, it is so firmly fixed in memory. It was incongruous and unreal that we should be dining with friends, on a warm and pleasant night in Italy, when a war had been going on for nearly five years, and not many miles from where we sat was a front line and gunfire and death.

Perhaps it is for this reason, too, that I remember the colour of Apulia. The red earth and the green harvest, the pink and blue and gold houses, the sea, purple and alien in winter and smooth green in summer, the flowers, the cyclamens and the oleander, the violets and the carnations and the crocuses and the irises which flowered, most mysteriously, in the soft rain of autumn. There were the trees too, the great Italian trinity of the fig, the olive, and the vine, which gave the people their sustenance of fruit and wine and oil. The tortured symmetry of olive groves covers a great deal of the Apulian landscape. They are everywhere, climbing the mountains on terraced walls, spreading over the plains, dotted here and there beside a farm house, stricken against the skyline in a remote valley. Always the olives: and the vines and the fig trees, great, tangled, sprawling fig trees, their branches clamped against the white walls and the fruit dripping and thick and rich. And everywhere the vines. Cut back raw against the winter soil, and heavy in the summer; and in autumn the leaves would ripen to the colour of wine and turn purple and black and full.

THESE ARE THE THINGS WHICH make Apulia, and with them the oil presses and the wine bins and the figs drying on a sack against the wall. They are there, naturally, part of the landscape; the capital and the reward of the husbandman, they achieve, in some strange fashion, a very fine dignity. It is pleasing to watch the Apulian peasant, bent backed and toiling in the fierce sun of summer, and know that he will himself drink wine from his grapes, chew the dried figs from his trees and eat pasta cooked in the oil from his olives. There is a hard and good simplicity in this, which is a pleasing contrast to the commercialized approach to life so common amongst those who live in more favoured parts of Italy.

Because the heat of Bari was intolerable at nights, we acquired, in a manner possible in time of war and occupation, a small villa some five miles down the coast. It was set back from the sea and enclosed in a large garden with a high stone wall. A caretaker and his wife lived in outhouses at the back, and they had turned over most of the garden to food crops. Corn grew sturdily, and in it an occasional errant carnation or iris, left over from the days when the soil was planted with flowers.

There were tomatoes too, and aubergines, and potatoes, and a lemon tree propped against the wall. A great fig stood in the courtyard to the side of the villa, spreading a grateful layer of shade, and here we sat and ate the good meals old Clementina cooked for us.

She was a very remarkable woman, toothless, wrinkled, encrusted with dirt of years, yet she was, I suppose, less than fifty years old. Her husband was her senior by more than thirty years; he had married her when she was in her thirties and had long since given up hope of finding a husband. She was very devoted to him, and very grateful. He is a good man, my husband, she would say. He could make children when he was nearly eighty . . . And we realized, with astonishment, that the small boy who we had thought was a grandchild was indeed Clementina's son.

We would drive down to this villa at night, along the coastal road, and as we got away from the town the air would become cool and it would smell of orange blossom, and fruits, and flowers. We would twist uneasily in our dusty, sweaty clothing and think of the sea and the warm pools of rock-enclosed water. As soon as we arrived, we would strip and cover ourselves in blankets and walk down the garden, over the sharp volcanic rock, to the water.

The sea, so light and clear and green by day, was heavy at night. It lay still in the moonlight, and a little sullen, and it never broke into waves as it came up against the rocks. It would come against them slowly, in a long swell, and the water would rise up against the white face of the rock and sink back reluctantly. The water was black and forbidding, and as we dived into it it broke into phosphorescent splinters, and our bodies would appear monstrously distorted, pallid like the belly of a fish, floating easily in the tide.

These moonlight bathes are another thing I shall remember always about Apulia. At midnight the sea was warm and the rocks still held the heat of the midday sun. When we had washed the dust and dirt of Bari from us we would climb out on to the rocks and sit, wrapped in blankets, and smoke; and sometimes we would see, in the distance, the green and red lights of a little ship heading towards the occupied coastline of Dalmatia. It was strange to know that the enemy lay across this placid stretch of water, and that the small ship, lights dim and flickering, was carrying fighting men to alien territory, that in a few hours they might be carried to a war, while we lay on our canvas beds in the villa and listened to the grasshoppers racketing outside, and smelt the heavy sweetness of the carnations beneath the window.

THERE WERE OCCASIONS, TOO, WHEN we went further afield. We went south, down the coast road, through Polignano and Mola and Monopoli and all the familiar coastal towns, where the houses were washed white and blue and pink, and hid, as we knew, scenes of almost indescribable poverty and squalor. We hardly noticed the vivid colour now, we were used to it, we accepted the gaily washed houses, the deep green of the sea and the crimson oleander as part of the landscape, and unexceptional. We were sated with this sort of thing, we were sick of the coast, we wanted the hills.

We headed for Alberobello and the trulli country, where there were low mountains and narrow twisting gorges, and a most admirably ordered way of life. The trulli house is a strange erection, like an oast house, round, with a conical roof painted with cabbalistic signs. No one, I think, knows their origin, how they came to be built or why. But there they are, clusters of them, for trulli houses spawn like a primitive cell. When the occupiers need another room they build another round house somewhere on the circumference and knock a connecting hole in the wall. They are very serious people, these inhabitants of the trulli country, tidy, frugal, and utterly different from their neighbours on the coast. They made a good wine, and were hospitable, and we would eat picnic lunches in their gardens, cheese and black bread and grapes and fennel, and it was good to be away from the disagreeable people of Bari and sit in the sun and look at the hills again and a sweeping landscape. Nothing good ever came out of a plain, in my opinion, and it was always pleasant to get away from the coast and see the trulli houses and walk up a hill when the sun had dropped and the harsh fierceness of the afternoon changed to evening.

Further still was Lecce, a town of superb baroque houses and a down-at-heel hangdog atmosphere. In Taranto we would eat clams and sea urchins and oysters, defying the urgent importunations of American friends, who swore they would kill us. In the fish market we would sometimes see the night's haul of octopi be emptied on the quay, and as we sat and picked at our clams and toyed with a glass of wine the dull thud would come to us of an octopus being beaten heavily on stone, in preparation for the table. An octopus needs to be beaten a good long time before it is tender, but it can then be eaten raw. It is good raw, but it is better fried crisp and golden and taken as an hors d'oeuvre with a light white wine.

These things we did in the summer; and when autumn came it was unexpected, and very chill. The rain came suddenly in October, and with the rain all the dried-up watercourses filled themselves and moistened the earth, so that the flowers which had been stultified by the summer drought came up again. Spring flowers, like cyclamens and anemones and violets and freesia, and it upset the orderly mind most sorely that there should be spring flowers in October, when the vines were brown

and tawny, like old wine, and the fig leaves had turned golden and
dropped from their stems.

The winter was hard and very cold, and there was snow. The Adriatic
curled itself into angry festoons of spray and smashed balefully at the
stone harbour. The landscape was grey and the olives and vines were
black against the frozen soil, and it was difficult to remember the summer
heat, and the colour, and the sea green and calm and without malice.

But if the winter was hard, it was not long. In February the sun was
back, cool and pleasant, and it had no wickedness in it. The flowers,
tireless in their activities, came out again. The white rocks along the
coast had been swept clean and salty by the winter seas, and the leaves
of the olives had been purged of dust and shone silver and smooth.

One day I went northwards a little, beyond Santo Spirito, and parked
the car off the road. It was April, and the war, clearly, was almost
over. Soon, in a week or two, I was going back to England; the year
in Apulia was almost over.

I walked for a little way up the track, beside the sea, and saw that the
grass was threaded with violets and freesias. Clearly, the winter too,
was over. The last winter of war, I thought, we have had six of them,
and that is the last.

The sun was warm, and the sea was very quiet and still, pressing gently
against the familiar rocks, swirling, without anger, in the bubble holes
which pitted the volcanic mass. I sat down in a comfortable niche and
put my face to the sun and wondered if it might tan me before I went
home. I had a book with me which had just come out from England,
Philip Guedalla's book about the RAF in the Middle East: I read a
little and remembered the long war in the desert, and Cairo, and
Palestine, and the sand and the dust and the steaming, sickly heat, and
thought it was over now, and would never come again.

After six years, the possibility of a pacific world was startling. I considered the idea while I watched a fishing boat moving out to sea, the
chug of her engines beating slowly through the still air. In a few days,
maybe, the whole ocean would be open to her again.

I tried to imagine this wild and primitive and beautiful country in
peace. I tried to imagine it emptied of jeeps and trucks and petrol
dumps, of piled ammunition and soldiers and barbed wire, and airfields.
It would, I thought, be immeasurably improved. Until that moment I
had known Apulia as a background to war. Now I saw it as it would
be once again, silence coming back to it, and emptiness and the calm
deliberation of the changing seasons.

I knew then that one day I would come back to Apulia; what had
been good and beautiful in war could not fail to be even more lovely
in peace. I would come back.

The One in the Window

by Olive Cook & Edwin Smith

TODAY, AS IN the past, the shop forms part of the fundamental furniture of every town and village. The bustle of buying and selling strangely animates the spirit of bygone ages which hovers about the pilastered doorway, the graceful bow window, or the robust sign of many a long established store; and where change is imperceptible, as in the harness and drum shops shown in these pages, the atmosphere of the past is even stronger. But however curious or ancient its shell or its trade, the shop is essentially a mirror of contemporary life and society, accurately reflecting every fluctuation of taste in what is either necessary or desirable. The ways of countryman and townsman, the pleasures of the rich and the poor, the sophisticated and the snobbish, the connoisseur and the amateur, all the endearing ingenuities and fatuities of our time are revealed in the shop window. From the diversions, more numerous than are pins in drapers', offered to our gaze, a few of the more forgotten and unusual have been chosen as the subjects of the following photographs.

THOUGH THE CHAIN store threatens to oust the individual shop, there are many active survivals of the days when shop, home and owner were undivided. The shop in East Street, Weymouth (right), is a charmingly unselfconscious example. Messrs Fribourg and Treyer flaunts its 18th century aspect in the hurry of the Haymarket, while Green's of Sudbury, despite its pennyfarthing, keeps pace with the times by flanking its pilasters with petrol pumps.

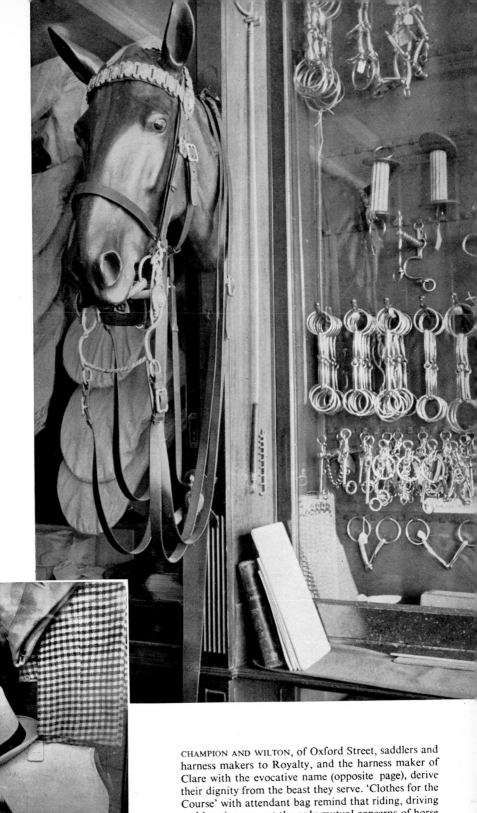

CHAMPION AND WILTON, of Oxford Street, saddlers and harness makers to Royalty, and the harness maker of Clare with the evocative name (opposite page), derive their dignity from the beast they serve. 'Clothes for the Course' with attendant bag remind that riding, driving and hunting are not the only mutual concerns of horse and human.

THE REFINEMENTS of display are not essential in shops which supply our basic needs, yet it is in such domestic establishments that a flair for arrangement is most often expressed, varying from the quiet symmetry of the Lewes Maypole Dairy window to the Ashwell butcher's brilliant façade of shaped box, hanging flowers, bull's head and gilded lettering.

HUMAN HAIR SPECIALIST, theatrical costumier, undertaker, antique dealer, haberdasher, toy boat maker, manicurist and doll's hospital. . . .

. . . . THESE ARE a few of the many displays that make the shop window
the town's first free entertainment.

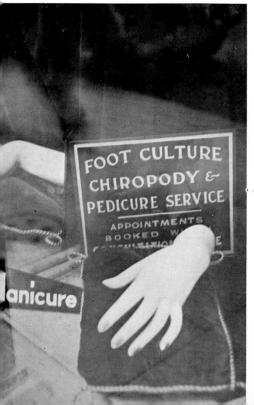

A CORNER OF Mr Meier's shop in Cecil Court illustrates the poetic atmosphere which may invest a haphazard collection of antiques. The cameos on the opposite page come appropriately from Cameo Corner, Museum Street. These small carvings in relief originated with the Egyptian scarab and have taken many forms, but they are particularly associated with the enthusiasm for classical antiquity which was characteristic of the Renaissance and again of the 18th century. The classical themes executed here in onyx, agate, shell, coral and opal all belong to the later period. The blue and white Wedgwood medallion of an angel is an example of one of the most charming of the many substitutes for cameos.

CONTRARY TO MODERN practice, which transforms an entire façade into a
showcase, the pharmacist's of Bath concedes half its area to a front which
not only frames flatteringly, but which is politely, properly and profitably
related to the city it serves. Though not itself ancient, the optician's sign,
one of several in London, is a diverting survival of the shop sign, once
essential and universal.

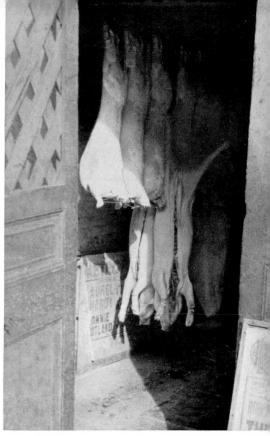

THE COSTUMIER'S BUSTS, perturbingly related to the butcher's carcasses and the eagerly assenting glove lasts, remind us that 'putting everything in the window' is a dictum well derived from shops.

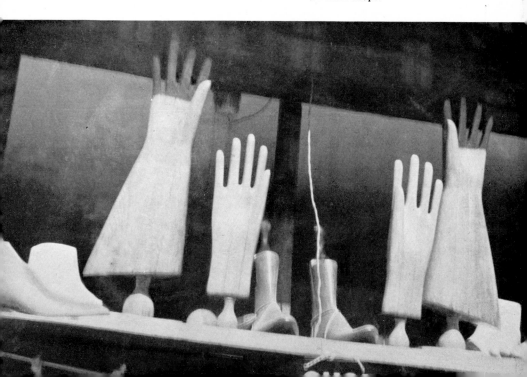

AGE AND TRADITION, whether of the objects offered for sale or of the establishment itself, are qualities in shops so appealing to the imagination, so hallowing to the object or service, as almost to suspend the idea of commerce. The enchanting jugs are Pratt ware (c. 1790–1810), the plates are Bristol Delft and the bowl Lambeth Delft of mid 18th century, from Allbrook's of Cromwell Place.

THE CHAMBER MUSIC and the military fanfares of other ages sounded on these instruments. A violin by Petrus Guanerius, a Stadler guitar and an early 17th century viola da gamba in the shop of Hill and Son, New Bond Street, form a contrast to the regimental drums from Henry Potter's of West Street, adorned with images which match their violent music and accompanied by the warlike mace, banner and sash.

AMONG THE COMMONEST methods of displaying merchandise is that of filling window or showcase with a number of similar or identical objects. The orderly company of walking sticks, the unexpected galaxy of brass fenders in Pratt's, Brompton Road. . . .

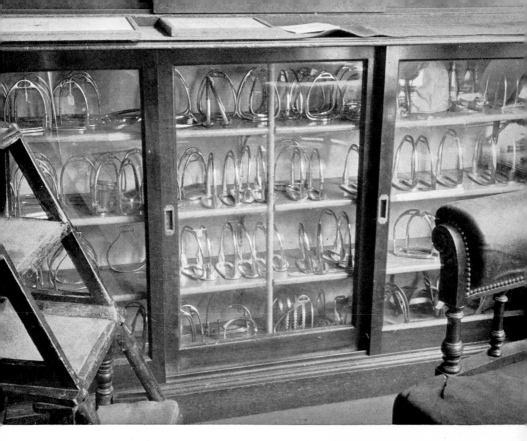

. . . . CHAMPION AND WILTON's massed stirrups, the rows of plates,
cups and candlesticks in Shapland's of High Holborn, even the window
of costermongers' tickets, exemplify the fascination of repetition.

THE COLLIER'S LIFE.

No. 1.

He works down below in the
dark, dreary pit,

So that folks like us round
the fireside may cheerfully
sit,

Tho' he toils in the mine, far
from Heaven's glorious light,

And his face may be black,
yet his big heart is white.

THE COLLIER'S LIFE.

No. 3.

The stranger, astonished, at
once turned from the inn,
When outside a cry rent
the air,
The pit is on fire and the
night shift's below;
He flew to the pit shaft,
but ere he got there,
The lads from yon brightly
lit house had arrived,
All eager to go down
below,
The stranger, amazed to
himself then said,
"Ah, the miner I'm
getting to know."

THE COLLIER'S LIFE.

No. 4.

Next morning at day
break he trod to the
pit,
What spanides co-labour
and wives
Of those who so bravely
to rescue their mates,
Without fear most wil-
lingly gave their
lives,
And he thought to him-
self as he passed from
their midst,
Old England of them
should be proud,
And think of the widows
when paying a wage,
And a pension to their
be allowed.

POSTCARDS AND PRAYER rug hang close to the glass of the shop window and dazzle the eye with small arranged units of colour. Though no two things could differ more in origin or worth each has been shaped by tradition. Of the cards, the recently published Welsh women at tea, the Wedding Day wishes and Southend Esplanade assure the survival of the popular fantasy embodied in the Victorian and Edwardian relics. The design of the early 18th century Ghiordiz rug, found in Perez of Brompton Road, is prescribed by religious custom. The central form, always strictly observed by the weaver, is based on the mihrab or prayer niche of an Islamic mosque, and the green of this panel and of the outer border is the sacred green of Mecca. When the call to prayer is sounded the rug is laid upon the ground with point directed towards Mecca.

ANTIQUE SHOPS ARE of two kinds. Museum-like precision characterises establishments like Spink's, where the T'ang dancer was displayed. The Tanagra figurines kept company with the medieval St. George at Mr Meier's, Cecil Court, where delightful chaos stimulates the desire for acquisition.

RELATIONS: A TOY theatre, set for *Aladdin*, from Benjamin Pollock Ltd. of Adelphi; a French clock, c. 1851, with a tight rope walker who dances the hours, from Wells of Beauchamp Place. Butterflies and moths, of which the largest is a chimaera from New Guinea, from R. B. Janson of Great Russell Street; and Victorian glass paper weights from Lorie's of Wigmore Street.

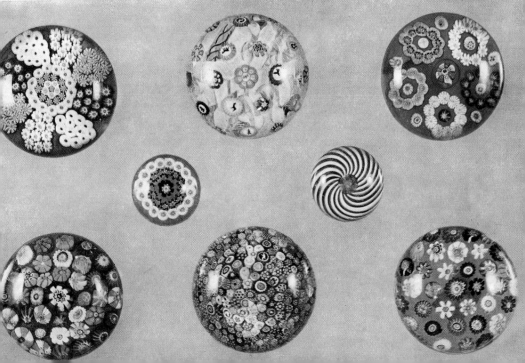

NOTHING IS SO fantastic or so remote that it cannot be offered hopefully for sale. Do you need a lion or a doll from China, an angel and birds from Sweden, a cake like a castle (Buszard's, Oxford Street) or a clock in mother of pearl like an Hotel de Ville (Wells, Beauchamp Place)? Size is the sole limitation to your choice. If it's smaller than the shop you will find one in the window.

MEERSCHAUM, FOUND FLOATING, soft and white like sea foam, in the Black Sea, is the material of these carved pipes from Astley's of Jermyn Street. The darker tones result from the penetration of smoke to carefully waxed portions. Sometimes the connection with tobacco is obscure: the legs of the lady at the top, for instance, are disguised cigarette holders.

The Gold Salt Cellar

photographs & commentary by Edwin Smith

ONE OF THE KEENEST SUBSIDIARY PLEASURES to be obtained from a work of art is in the attempt to relax its essential remoteness by probing the details of its origin: why and how it was made or upon what irrelevant human naughtiness its author was meanwhile engaged. The vision ultimately craved by this curiosity, that of the artist vividly employed about his masterpiece, is rarely evoked; the data available being seldom more than will establish the object's date and authorship.

The golden salt cellar of Benvenuto Cellini (1500–72), lately in London with the Vienna treasures, is a rare exception. It was originally commissioned in 1539 by the Cardinal of Ferrara, who, Cellini tells us in his Memoirs, *'ordered me to make the model of a salt cellar; but it was not to be after the usual pattern of such things.'* To Cellini's irritation, the Cardinal asked advice of 'two men of letters.' When it was given the Cardinal *'turned to me and said "Benvenuto, my friend, these designs please me so much that I do not know which of them to choose. So I leave the decision to you".'* Preambling characteristically, Cellini said, *' "I cherish the children born of my own art. Therefore, the first design I will show you . . . shall be my own work".'*

'WELL, *first I made an oval, a good deal more than half a cubit long*' (the cellar is 13½ in. long by 10½ in. high), '*and on this, with the idea of showing the embrace of the Sea and the Land, I made two figures, somewhat more than a palm in height, sitting with their legs intertwined, just as you can observe long arms of the sea running up into the land. The sea was figured by a man with a richly carved ship . . . arranged to hold a quantity of salt.*'

'THE *Earth I had represented as a woman, the most beautiful and graceful I could fashion or even conceive of. Near her I had placed a richly adorned temple, on which she rested her hand. This I intended for holding the pepper. In her other hand was a cornucopia*' (Cellini's memory is here at fault) '*decorated with every lovely ornament imaginable. . . . Then I awaited the Cardinal; and when he came with his two distinguished friends, I displayed my work in wax.*'

' "THIS *is something that would never be finished in the lifetime of ten men*",' cried one. ' "*And as for you, most reverend monsignor, you may desire it, but you'll never have it. . . . We spoke of practical things; but his design suggests what could not possibly be carried out*".' . . . The Cardinal said the undertaking was too elaborate for him. '*Then I—said, "Most reverend monsignor, I declare to you that I have every hope of carrying out this work for its destined possessor; and each man of you shall see it finished a hundred times more richly than the model.*

Indeed, I hope time may be left me to do much greater things than this".'

IN 1540 Cellini entered the service of Francis I of France. Soon after, Cellini tells us, the King wished for a fine salt cellar, '*so he asked me to make him a design for one, and without delay. I answered, "Your Majesty will see such a design much sooner than you expect"*' and after a rapid visit to the workshop '*I brought back with me a wax model, which I had already made at the request of the Cardinal of Ferrara. . . . When I uncovered it, his Majesty exclaimed in astonishment, "This is a hundred times more divine than I could ever have imagined. The man is a wonder! He should never lay down his tools"*.'

THE King provided 'one thousand old gold crowns,' and before 1543 it was completed *'all of gold, worked with the chisel. . . . The Sea was sitting above the group in proud and noble attitude; and all round him were different kinds of fishes and other marine creatures. The water was represented by waves exquisitely enamelled in its own colour.'*

'WHEN *I set the piece before him, the King cried aloud in astonishment, and could not look at it long enough. But he told me to take
it home with me again. . . . I did so, and at once invited some of
my good friends, and we dined together very merrily, the salt cellar
being in the centre of the table. And so we were the first to use it.'*

'THE *whole stood on a base of black ebony ... which was surrounded by a shallow gorge decorated with four gold figures in something more than half relief representing Night, Day, Twilight, and Dawn. Four other figures of the same size were meant for the four chief winds. They were carried out partly in enamel, and with all the exquisiteness you can imagine.'*

The High Street, 1750–1950

text and drawings by
WALTER AND LEONORA ISON

THE FOLLOWING PAGES illustrate three stages in the development of a
High Street of our own devising, compounded of actual examples with
some inventions. With the help offered, the history of architectural taste
is easily read in the buildings lining the High Street of any ancient town.
Of course, the general idiom will be tinged with the local vernacular ;
there will probably be no more than a few masterly passages, if any ;
and the many interpolations will require some degree of expert elucidation.

Many features of a purely regional character appear in the earlier
buildings, but a more general acceptance of orthodox classicism becomes
apparent as the 18th century progresses. One is able to trace the various
influences of successive leaders of architectural taste, from Wren,
Vanbrugh, and the Palladians, onwards to Adam, Holland, and Soane,
and thence to the Gothicists of the Victorian era. And at this point,
perhaps, some warning might be uttered against a too ready acceptance
of local tradition, which is always willing to find a great name to attach
to any building of merit.

G

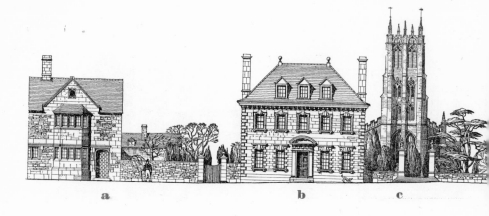

a   b   c

a   A STONE-BUILT HOUSE of about 1620. The wide bay with its low windows, divided by stone mullions into a series of narrow lights containing leaded casements, the prominent gable and steeply pitched roof, the Tudor arched doorway and late Gothic moulding of the string-courses, are all characteristic features of house design which persisted in country districts until well into the 17th century. Many houses of this description grace the towns and villages of the limestone area.

ture and segmental pediment, is well designed but too emphatic for perfect accord with the fenestral pattern, which is excellent. The ground-story windows are elaborately dressed with architrave, pillowed frieze and cornice, broken by rustic blocks, while those above are more simply adorned with eared architraves and triple keystones. Long and short quoins with chamfered joints strengthen the angles of the front, rising from the plinth up to the block cornice which underlines the high roof of stone tiles.

b   THE STREET FRONT of the Rectory, a house of about 1740, is a highly accomplished work of the English Renaissance school, with Italianate details applied to traditional building forms. The door case, of Doric pilasters supporting a triglyphed entabla-

c   THE PARISH CHURCH, dominated by a 15th-century tower, exhibits most phases of Gothic architecture in its fabric, while in the churchyard, umbrageous with yew and cedar, are gravestones carved with all the funereal symbolism of the mason's art.

d   e   f   g

d THE SCHOOLHOUSE, with two lofty stories surmounted by a high roof, has a front of charming composition in the vernacular Renaissance manner of about 1720, a style which derived from Dutch prototypes rather than Italian. The central doorway is enriched with a triangular pediment which is broken to receive an armorial cartouche, the arched windows are framed by moulded architraves with plain imposts and keystones, and the angle quoins rise to a coved crowning cornice.

e THE STONE FRONT of this house, dated 1707, is fairly typical of much Cotswold building of that time. The symmetrical composition is excellently patterned and the pedimented door case is impeccably classical, but the proportions and subdivision by mullion and transom of the casement windows give

them a 16th-century character. The manner in which the coved cornice is stopped short of the angle quoins and returned against the wall face is a further evidence of the builder's imperfect grasp of classical idiom.

f THIS HOUSE of about 1680 shows an earlier stage of the transition in styles then progressing. Mouldings and features of classical derivation are introduced, but the form of the gable, the low mullioned windows, and the steeply pitched pediment of the door case prove this house to be the work of a mason bred in the Gothic tradition of design.

g THE TIMBER-FRAMED medieval house, with each successive upper story 'juttied' forward, is a picturesque feature of our old towns, too well known to call for any description.

h   i

h ALTHOUGH THE HOUSES forming this mid 17th-century group are basically similar, with a stone-built ground-story supporting a timber-framed superstructure, their plastered fronts have undergone some changes. The 'Queen Anne' front of the left-hand house shows the sash-windows, at first divided into small panes by heavy glazing bars, which began to supersede the casement shortly before 1700. Another structural and decorative feature much used at this time is the boldly projecting modillioned cornice of wooden construction, which served to contain the boxed gutter. Various stages in the development of the shopfront are also to be seen, from the medieval arrangement of shutters falling forward to form a stallboard, protected by a pent roof on brackets, to the bay-windows that were brought to such perfection during the latter part of the 18th century.

i THE IMPOSING INN is an early Georgian building of brick with stone dressings, dating from about 1730 and reflecting something of the influence of Vanbrugh's highly personal style. Large in scale and almost aggressive in character, it was designed to impress the traveller with its importance. The three-storied front is divided into three bays by giant pilasters, with pedestals, rusticated shafts, and Ionic capitals, each pilaster being surmounted by its entablature of which the cornice only is continued across the bays, and a high pedestal parapet serves to conceal the roof.

j THE TOWN HALL, a stone building of 1750, is an excellent specimen of a small public building designed in the English Renaissance style. The simply treated arcade

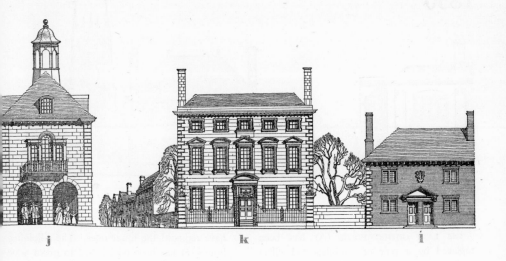

j   k   i

of the ground-story gives access to the market hall within. The council chamber on the first floor is lit at its end by a venetian window, dressed with the Ionic order, which opens on to a stone balcony with a wrought-iron railing. A modillioned cornice underlines the stone-tiled roof, from which rises an octagonal cupola.

k   THIS STONE-FRONTED MANSION of about 1730 has much of the finesse of mature English Palladianism, a style brought to perfection by the architects of Lord Burlington's following. All the elements used in the composition have been most carefully considered and related, and the designer's adherence to Italian principles of design can be seen in such features as the emphasising of

the first-floor windows with pediments, and the replacement of roof garrets by an attic story of which the windows are introduced below the main cornice. The house is set back from the street, within a forecourt enclosed by a wrought-iron screen between stone piers.

l   ALMSHOUSES, being monuments to their founders' piety, and from the nature of their planning, were usually given the architectural importance due to a minor public building. This is a late 17th-century example, built of brick with stone quoins, wooden window frames and door-hoods, and a modillioned eaves-cornice below its tiled roof. The general design and details are characteristic of the work of Wren's followers.

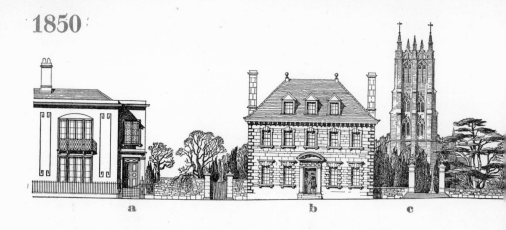

THE LATE GOTHIC HOUSE (A) has been replaced by a pair of semi-detached villas designed in the 'Grecian' taste of the early 19th century. Elegant proportions and a sparing use of sharply defined details are keynotes of this style, and the incised lines ending in frets are only one decorative feature reflecting the influence of Sir John Soane's remarkable mind. The ample windows, with their large panes and delicate bars, can be contrasted with those of the early 18th-century Rectory.

WHILE THE RECTORY (B) and the Schoolhouse (D) are unchanged, some small alterations have been made to the early Renaissance house (E), where sashes have been inserted into the upper windows and projecting bays

have replaced the lower ones. The adjoining house (F) has been demolished to make way for a dissenters' chapel, an 'Ebenezer' dated 1820. This has a stone front of essentially classical composition, dressed with 'Gothick' detail. Its two tiers of windows express the galleried interior, and an appropriately 'ecclesiastical' note is given by the pointed arches, the panelled buttresses terminated by open pinnacles, and the crenellated parapet. There are many delightful buildings in this highly artificial style which have been maligned by criticism from the wrong standards.

THE HALF-TIMBERED FRONT of the medieval house (G) has been plastered over, and new sashes and casements have been inserted into the windows.

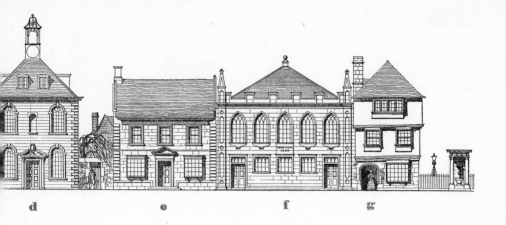

d   e   f   g

BELOW: TWO OF THE HOUSES in the group (H) on the left of the Inn were rebuilt shortly after 1790, as the beginning of a uniformly designed range of houses. This was the undertaking of a speculative builder who failed, like so many of his fellows, during the financial panic of 1793, when all over England buildings were abandoned in all stages of incompleteness. The fronts were designed in the manner made popular through the widespread influence of Robert Adam, for so long the arbiter of architectural taste. The general material was brick, with the fan ornaments over the first-floor windows, and the string-courses and cornice carried out in some such production as Liardet's Patent Stucco, while the mask keystone and imposts of the archway were standardised castings in Coade's stone, both very popular decorative materials of the time. The balcony railings were in wrought-iron with moulded lead enrichments. The elegant shopfronts, often of serpentine contour, illustrate the high degree of interpretive skill achieved by the carpenters, who invariably worked to the detailed designs provided by the numerous pattern-books available.

THE ASPERITIES OF THE INN (I) have been softened by clothing the brickwork with a coating of oil-painted stucco, and the addition of two tent-roofed verandahs with 'Grecian' railings, while the windows, like those of the Palladian house (K), have been reglazed with larger panes and more delicate bars.

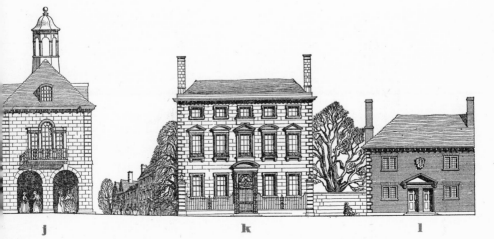

j   k   l

a   b   c

THE REGENCY VILLA (A) has received an addition in reinforced concrete construction designed in 1935 by a sincere and efficient architect of the 'avant-garde,' who has allowed himself to be misled by Keats's dogmatic utterance on truth and beauty. Although there are such cases of faith in a contemporary idiom outweighing all other aesthetic considerations, they are fortunately rare. The obverse of this medal is seen in the new Municipal Offices (I) that have replaced the outmoded Inn of 1730. The High Street front forms an extension and duplication of the Town Hall design, and it is probable that this meticulous copy has only been made possible by some sacrifice of the building's efficiency.

THE CHARMING RENAISSANCE Schoolhouse (D) has been destroyed to make way for a Victorian Gothic single story building of uncompromising ugliness and inconvenience,

for, while the leaders of the Gothic Revival produced many fine and remarkable works, this style was apt to degenerate into something mean and depressing in the hands of the less inspired architect or builder.

WHILE THE CHURCH (C) has escaped any violent restoration, the Renaissance piers at the entrance of the churchyard have made way for a pseudo-medieval lych-gate, and the Rectory (B) windows have been deprived of their glazing bars, a regrettable change but one easily remedied. The two brick houses (H) have suffered some changes, such as the removal of glazing bars from the windows and the alteration of shopfronts. A particularly deplorable example of 'Shopfitter's Modernistic' has displaced one of the lovely Georgian bow fronts.

THE PLASTER-FRONTED "Queen Anne" house

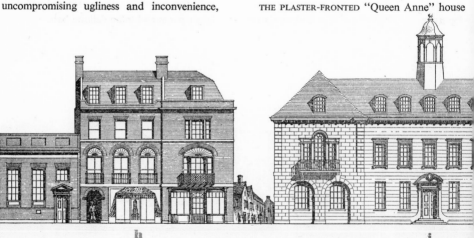

h   i

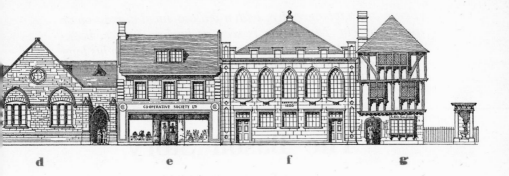

d   e   f   g

(H) has been replaced by banking premises, with a brick and stone front designed in the style deservedly called 'Banker's Georgian' and always recognisable from the exaggerated proportions of the essentially domestic elements used in its composition.

THE MEDIEVAL HOUSE (G) has been restored to the full glory of its half-timbering and latticed casements, for such romantic features are of great value to the promotors of 'Olde Tea Shoppes,' but the fine early Renaissance house (E), holding no such appeal to sentimentality, has been ruthlessly maltreated to provide window display space for the local Co-operative Store.

THE PALLADIAN HOUSE (K) now belongs to the electricity undertaking, and the fine ironwork screen and stone piers to the forecourt have been removed. Although display win-

dows have been inserted into the ground-story, this alteration has been made with a reasonable show of good taste and sympathy for the older work.

POSTSCRIPT

OUR FINAL DRAWINGS have shown a somewhat disturbing picture, for good buildings have gone from the scene while bad taste has marred the beauty of others. Now, however, it is probable that any further destruction will be strongly opposed by the various societies whose mission it is to preserve our scenic and architectural beauties. A section of the Town and Country Planning Act has been designed to prevent the haphazard demolition of any building which is good in itself, or forms an essential part of a group, so that there is some reasonable hope for the conservation of those delightful ensembles that still remain in many of our High Streets.

j   k   l

Being an autobiography, with a philosophical digression or two, wherein Mr Bason is seen as barber, tipster, book-seller, A.R.P. warden, civil servant, not to mention his long reign as king of autograph hunters and prince of cigarette card collectors, the whole forming a very remarkable document indeed.

The Bason Story

by FRED BASON

I HAVE had the honour of appearing in volumes 5, 6, 7, and 8 of this annual. Perhaps you will recall that in my first contribution I gave you the low-down on my high-up friend, W. Somerset Maugham. Next I told you of some of the pleasures and trials of being a SATURDAY BOOK contributor. My 'Who's Who' in volume seven gave pen-pictures of celebrities I've met in my long reign as the king of autograph collectors. Last year you read—or should have read—'Basoniana.' This time at the request of Leonard Russell and numerous other people I am leaving out my famous friends and writing about myself.

Now you know jolly well that I'm not a high-class literary bloke. I'm merely a cockney who does a bit of writing when it's too cold for him to take his barrowload of second-hand books out into the gutter. I'm a writer from sheer necessity, and at any gathering of literary celebrities I feel like a blooming fish out of water. So please bear with me if I do a little rambling and don't keep to strict chronological order.

I was born at an early age and have lived all my life in Walworth, a slum district of London, ten minutes from Big Ben and fourteen minutes from Bow Bells; and when there is any quiet in Walworth you can hear the chimes. Thus I am a veritable cockney. I do not feel particularly proud of the fact, but on the other hand I am most certainly not ashamed of it. I was an only son, and came into the world when my parents were in their forties. My childhood was particularly lonely and unhappy, so let's skip it. Some old geezer told parents at a school prize-giving at Croydon the other day that it was important their sons should do the sort of work they liked; it did not matter what money they earned, because there would be no very rich and no very poor in the near future. I wish he'd told this to *my* parents the day I left school at 14—it would have saved me over a year of jobs I didn't like. My father was a master jobbing harness-maker, but he wanted me to be a carpenter, whereas my mother, thinking of a nice *clean* job for me, wanted me to be a barber! And my mother got her way.

How I Became a Barber

TWO DAYS AFTER I FINISHED my schooldays there appeared in our local paper, the *South London Press,* an advertisement for an apprentice for a local barber's shop; and my mother commanded me to go with her to see about it. Weedy-looking specimen though I was, I got the job: I was to be lather boy and work me way up—though God knows where 'up' was! Wages, 7s. 6d. a week and tips, hours, from 7.30 in the morning until 'when the shop was empty at night.' Actually the door shut at 8, but there was always a shopful of customers when it closed, and these had to be polished off and polished up and then the place had to be cleaned before I could push off—and that meant it was seldom earlier than nine that I left that so-and-so barber's shop! Dirty faces, filthy noses, decayed teeth—that was my lot in life for six months. The air was foul, and I breathed hair-clippings for more than twelve hours a day —and for the most part the conversation was just as foul.

A great many of our customers never thought of washing before they entered the shop—my lather would clean as it moistened the beard, and when I handed them the towel to finish drying their chins they'd rub their faces as well and so have a wash! You'll realize that I'm writing of twenty-five or more years ago. Today, with laundry so expensive, barbers are more particular. And the assistants are far more independent nowadays and would refuse to shave a dirty man.

I had a half-day's holiday on Thursday, when we closed at one o'clock, but on that day I had to go on hands and knees and thoroughly scrub out the shop, and so it was usually 3 o'clock when my half-day started. On Sundays I had to work from eight till one, but here again though we closed the shop door at one there was always a shopful of customers who had come across from the pub just a few minutes before our closing time for a Sunday shave (which lasted many of them a week).

Did I learn to become a barber? No fear! I had set my heart on becoming a bookseller; books had been my companions in childhood, I was always a bookworm, and even a worm will turn. After six months as a lather boy I had a razor in my hand for the very first time, and I made such a bloody mess of the job on an old geezer's chin—he had volunteered for a free shave—that the boss grabbed the razor and told me exactly where I could go to . . .

Now, I thought, I shall be allowed to buy and sell books for me living. But oh dear no! Dad had his say, and he took me to a carpentry factory in the next district; and what with telling the boss I was a brainy boy, giving him a cigar, and fixing him up with a cert winner for that day's racing (which did win), he persuaded him to give me a trial.

My Dad

ON A CERTAIN VERY MEMORABLE DAY when I was about twelve my dad had his first, last, and only big win at racing. He won exactly £200 on a Lincoln and National double. But to tell you the truth it caused more trouble than it was worth, because for the next thirty years he chased the rainbow of another big win, and it for ever evaded him.

When he brought the £200 home in notes and silver my mother cried: it seemed to mean something akin to security. Dad promptly made some purchases to celebrate the occasion: a diamond ring, which cost about ten pounds, for my mother, and for me a 15s. scooter; and there was a huge basket of fancy fruit all tied up with pink ribbon that must have cost a fancy price. The rest of the money he put away in a biscuit tin at the bottom of the kitchen cupboard—a matter of some £180.

But not for long. In five days he had lost the whole sum, and on the sixth day he asked mother for 5s. to tide him over till someone paid a bill for harness work he'd done!

A mugs' game, all right. When my dad died at 78 he left behind a crowd of friends and 14s. 9d. Betting kept him and us poor.

How I Nearly Became a Carpenter

I HAD NO OBJECTION TO CARPENTRY as a career, but I went into it with the idea that some day, when I could please myself how I made my living, I would make bookcases and bookshelves and so save myself a great deal of expense when I opened my own bookshop. My mother said it would be a nice healthy job—such a change from the barber's shop. It was a change, but it wasn't healthy. They put me to work at the wrong end of a planing machine, covering me with chips and choking me with sawdust: I had to pull the planed planks out and stack them into neat piles. My wages were 21s. a week for twelve hours a day. We had a half-day on Saturday and the shop closed at one o'clock, but I had to stop behind and put the chips and sawdust into sacks—and if you've ever tried to hold open a big sack with one hand and shovel chips into it with the other you know it's a blooming tricky job; with someone holding out the sack we could have done it in half an hour, but alone it took pretty near two hours.

During the four months I was there, at no time was I taught even the rudiments of carpentry. Looking back I reckon all I learnt was the use of a straight left, how to rough-house when your opponent was too tough and tons above your weight and something of the handicap of horses.

It was while I was at this woodwork factory that I went full tilt at my hobby of autograph collecting as a means of escape; I got the autograph of Marie Lloyd at the Camberwell Palace of Varieties at the close of my first month as a carpenter. I remember how reluctant I was to go up and ask for it—my clothes were so torn and shabby, and even after a vigorous wash and brush up I wasn't free from sawdust. But having at last found the courage I said I was sorry I wasn't poshly dressed. Marie was very nice indeed and called me a 'little man' and 'dearie' and said clothes didn't matter a bit, it was what they covered that mattered most. When I repeated the conversation to my workmates the next morning (and with pride showed them her signed photograph) they had a great laugh, but I'm sure Marie didn't mean it that way.

In the end this job caused me to collapse—and through a long illness I still heard the roar of that confounded planing machine. Fortunately they didn't keep the job open for me; and when I was well again I was at a loose end.

Now I'd always been a bibliophile in my own small way, and at least three-quarters of my very slim pocket money went on books. I had an uncle living in Wandsworth who kept a book-china-old clothes shop, and most Saturdays I walked from Walworth to Wandsworth (about five miles) to buy books from him; he also allowed me to dive down the waste-paper sack and take home any books I needed from it. My folks, however, wouldn't believe that bookselling was a *real* job for a beginner. Dad wanted me to take up carpentry again, but by heck I'd had enough of it. For a while I did dead-end jobs, but I suppose they both saw eventually that I'd set my heart on becoming a bookseller and my own boss, so I was told to give it a try. If I failed, however, it was back to carpentry . . . That threat alone inspired me to make good.

As My Own Boss

A JUMBLE SALE WAS ADVERTISED outside a church off Coldharbour Lane, Brixton. Admission was 2d. With 11s. 8d. capital and a sack I went to that sale on a Saturday afternoon, and the vicar's wife charged me 8s. for 28 books that I chose myself. Somehow I felt jolly pleased with the deal; now I had some stock, and 3s. 6d. for expenses. Taking the books home in the sack made me sweat, for I'd chosen the fattest and biggest from the miscellaneous collection on the stall. All day Sunday I spent cleaning up my wares—and I was so inexperienced that

I even used boot blacking to make some of them look nice and shiny! Those that wouldn't shine I washed with soap and water and a large scrubbing brush. I can't remember the titles all this time afterwards, but I know some were theology and that others were bound volumes of magazines, and there was a book on astronomy which fascinated me. On Monday morning off I went to Charing Cross Road lugging some 15 or 16 of my treasures, and—what luck!—I fell into very kind and gentle Jewish hands and was able to sell out at a profit. With the confidence of inexperience I took all my books carefully out of the sack, laid the sack out, placed the books on it like a row of soldiers, and asked the bookseller to pick out his needs. He chose six. At first he refused to make an offer, but as I hadn't the slightest idea what to ask I said I would accept the best offer he could honestly make as I desperately needed the money. Whereupon he showed me a 10s. note and asked if I'd be quite satisfied with that. I said 'Oh yes, sir!' And he handed it over. As I was putting the rejected books back into my sack he gave me an extra 6d. for calling him 'sir!' It was a lesson I never forgot—that politeness pays. I asked him where he thought I could sell the rest of my wares, and he named a shop across the way. Again it was a Jew and again a kindly Jew; he chose only one book and paid the 4s. I had the impudence to ask.

After that I had a run of bad luck; no one seemed to want the few which remained—they were probably junk. I had made a profit, but I did so much want to sell out so that I could go home with absolute and undeniable proof that I *could* make a living as my own master as a seller of second-hand books. At last, off Seven Dials, I found a furniture shop with a row of books as a sideline. Taking off my cap, I asked if I could display some jolly nice-looking books I had for sale. Permission granted. I turned the sack upside down and out fell my wares. 'They are pretty nearly all real leather—*leather* sir, not just paper things!' The man called me 'a funny kid' and said he'd give me a real paper ten shilling note for them if I'd give him the sack as well and run to the corner for the *Evening News*. I said I'd get his paper gladly, but I couldn't part with the sack because it was my dad's and thus on loan, and in any case I hadn't any other means of transporting my stock. We compromised: I got his paper, and also some bread and cakes, and posted a letter.

I don't know whether he made a profit on those books, but I do know that after 25 years as a seller of books I still call on him—yes, and frequently display my stock on a sack as I did when I was 15. On this my first venture at bookselling I got 24s. *Twenty-four shillings!* And I'd sweated my guts out lugging huge planks of wood around for 21s. a week! Bookselling, evidently, was the life for me.

My Own Library When I Was 16

1. *Swiss Family Robinson* (School prize), ruined in fire 1942.

2. *Adventures of Sherlock Holmes* (Birthday gift from Uncle Charlie) blitzed, 1942.

3. *Liza of Lambeth,* by W. S. Maugham. (Very battered—but I still possess it 28 years later!)

4. *Pears' Encyclopaedia* (Kept it for 10 years and then replaced it with a more up-to-date edition).

5. *Boxing,* by Tommy Burns (Sold this in 1943 to Johnny Best, boxing promoter).

6. *Bits from an Old Bookshop—A Bookseller's Memories* (Still have it 28 years later).

7. *Barlasch of the Guard,* by Seton Merriman. (Sold it profitably some years later.)

8. Volume of the *Strand* Magazine for 1896. (Eventually made up a 'run' and sold them.)

9. *Street Guide to London.*

10. *Walker's English Dictionary,* 1830. (Beautifully bound.)

11. *The World's Wit and Humour,* Volume 5 (American. Published by the Review of Reviews, 1906).

12. *Hide and Seek,* by Wilkie Collins (Battered yellow-back).

Love in the Slums: a Digression

IT IS THE GENTLEMAN'S PLEASURE and privilege to pay the bill when he takes a lady out for the evening—but not in Walworth; the rules of etiquette there don't work out quite like that. You find a girl and you suggest the flicks, theatre, or posh dinner up West—and if she is no one's steady bird she says O.K. If she pays half of the expenses of the night out you know it's all temporary and you have no claims on her at all.

Well, you have your date and see her home. If she doesn't indicate that a kiss is required you just shake hands and suggest another date. If she's enjoyed herself and you've pulled no fast ones she may say O.K. and name time and place. At this second meeting, if she doesn't keep you waiting for more than half an hour consider you are in her good books! And if she's there right on time consider she's friendly towards you! Now if at the close of this second date she again insists on paying her half then just consider that you are still on appro and being sorted out and picked over. She may this time say that there's no harm in a kiss, so you give her a hearty one or not according to what sort of night you've had in her company. Were you bored? Did she get fidgety when you talked about yourself? That kiss of yours will tell her lots—and maybe more than you intended it to tell! If the next date is in the after-noon or early evening and it's still light, folks see you together, and it's a move up for the affair. If she takes your arm on this outing she's getting warm! Now after the stroll you suggest the pictures, and she doesn't mind if she does—which means she will. You pay and bang goes 3s. 6d. of your pocket money. Now on the way home what happens? Does she talk of paying her half? If she does, then let her, for she's still very cautious—and this may go on for months! But suppose she makes no suggestion whatever of paying her share and suppose that near her home she stops and of her own free will kisses you and is obviously prepared to linger in that amiable frame of mind. Then, boy, you've clicked! She has accepted you—she is your steady and you'll have the great pleasure of paying for all her entertainment till she finds a better beau with more of the ready, or gets tired of you, or you yourself have a bust-up and find another piece of homework more to your liking. If you look after her well you will probably have the supreme pleasure of keeping her for the rest of her natural life!

Me—I haven't got a steady—wish I had. But I know the rules, for I went all through these routines in my twenties.

How I Became a Tipster

RATHER PRECARIOUSLY, BUT ALWAYS just managing to make both ends meet and to give my mother a reasonable sum for my board and keep, I pegged away at book 'running'—i.e., buying books from one source and running them to another and selling as quickly as possible so as not to be cluttered up at home with unsaleable books—for about three years. Then by sheer good luck I got in the good books of a famous author and of a famous variety star. The author specially autographed copies of his first editions, and I was then able to sell them at anything from six to ten times the price I would have got for them unsigned (oh no—it wasn't a racket. The author not only knew what I was doing but wrote longer inscriptions than usual so that I could ask an even better price). As for the actress, she was a darling. At 18 I had a certain cockney charm which greatly amused this American star, and she made me a sort of mascot.

With the money I got from the sale of the autographed first editions I was able at last to obtain capital enough to open a bookshop. I thought my life ambition was achieved—my own master in my own bookshop, all in four years! But I had failed to reckon with the vital fact in bookselling that you can't wait for stock to come to you—you *have* to seek it fresh all the time. My shop was in New Church Road, Camber-well, and because it was barely 5 ft wide I called it the Little Bookshop.

After a while I found I was not making such a good living here as I'd made from book-running, but I refused to close down and return to the sack on my back. Then—was I lucky!—I got friendly with the American variety star. As soon as I closed my shop—and I closed it sooner than I should on most nights—I changed into my best suit and spent the evening as her head cook and bottlewasher. I adored her. I'd gladly have died for her. She was about 28 and was earning over £200 a week. I was 18. She took me everywhere as a sort of pet lamb to follow Mary! My mother met her on a couple of occasions and they had heart-to-heart talks. I never knew what was said, but evidently it was all right by both of them.

My heart's delight was popular in all manner of society, and at one midnight party we met a famous trainer of greyhounds. Somehow or other he and I got on like butter on toast—swimming pals after a couple of whiskies; and at the suggestion of my star, who said that the trainer was to help me if he could, we came to an arrangement that if I phoned a certain number at a certain time of day three times a week, I should receive information of a greyhound who was 'on the job' and bar accidents would win.

Now the folks in my neighbourhood were all for a bet on the dogs—the motor coaches for the evening trips to the dog-tracks started outside my bookshop door every night. I therefore gratefully grasped this gilt-edged opportunity of presenting them, for a small fee, with at least genuine information of genuine 'triers' (for not all dogs in a race try to win every time). The next day I phoned, and a dog's name was given to me. Should I bet on it myself? No—betting had ruined my father. I got a large sheet of white paper and in dense black charcoal I printed these words:

LADIES AND GENTLEMEN

Allow me to present to you the name of a dog which will, I assure you, win tonight. Its name is . . . Put your shirt on it. But don't forget tomorrow who gave you this very valuable information.

This sheet of paper I stuck in the front of my window, and all day long I drew people's attention to it. When the coaches began to fill up around 5.30 outside my shop I went alongside each *calling out the name of the dog!* All this was rather rich, seeing that I hardly knew one end of a greyhound from the other and had never seen a greyhound race or visited a dog-track in my life!

The dog was in the 8.30 race. I closed my shop at 6.30, went home, had tea, changed my clothes, wrote five or six letters, and at 8.15 was back at the shop. At 8.40 I phoned to the track, and one thing I remember vividly about that phone call is that my hand trembled as I held the receiver. I learnt that my dog had won by $\frac{1}{2}$ a length and that

H

the price was expected to be about 7 to 2 (i.e., put 2s. on to get 7s.—3½ to one). At 9.15 a boy came along with a penny greyhound result sheet. I gave him 6d. and wanted no change. It told me that the correct price was 3 to 1. Refusing to wait for the light of morning, I put up a big notice at once:

> *What did I tell you? I said it would win and it has at 3 to 1. Now don't forget the man who didn't bet on it but gave you the tip. And watch this window for more information!*

They didn't forget me—I received just over £4 before midday the next day, and many bottles of beer, several packets of cigarettes, a nice bunch of flowers, and two seats for a show at the Lyceum.

The long and the short of it was that being a tipster was *very* profitable until my source of information dried up. And it did dry up. You see, I soon had a huge following, and, seeing that they so frequently won, larger and still larger sums were invested, until the price of the dog was being killed, and the owners of the dogs that my friend told me about were unable to get fair odds.

In the strange manner that Fate laughs at all of us, I got a signwriter one day to change the sign above my shop-front from the LITTLE BOOKSHOP to the GREYHOUND BOOKSHOP (see Clegg's *Directory of Antiquarian Booksellers* for confirmation), because I was doing far more business as a tipster than I ever did as a bookseller. On that very day when the new name was painted up in flaming red letters, I went to the phone for my information—to be told that there was no more information for me ever. The man said he had expected me to put a fiver or tenner on and thus build myself up a little stack of money, but he had not expected me to broadcast the information to all and sundry and spoil the market. He further said that I'd been a little fool, and he warned me never to reveal his name, or his boys would come over and bash me into nothing! The truth was, he did me a very kind action, but it all went wrong because I'd always promised myself never to gamble on anything other than books.

So there I was, left high and dry. For a week I tried to forecast winners on my own, but I knew so little about form that only one won out of five selections, and that at a price which did not cover the losses of the other four. My clients drifted away, my run of luck was over.

Then for two or three weeks I gave no selections at all and set my mind to work to find a system whereby I could forecast with more certainty dogs that would win. Eventually I did find one which enabled me to forecast at least seven winners out of every ten selections! And what is more, it *still does*.[1] My clients returned, and for many months all was

---

[1]My system was to tip only dogs who were last-minute substitutes, by comparing overnight probable runners with the actual runners. When these substitutes were first or second favourites in the betting forecasts, they became my nap selections.

rosy. But this time I insisted on 10 per cent of all my customers' winnings, plus 1s. for the actual selection. After several successful months I managed to save a nice round sum, and then I did what I'd always wanted to do: I closed up my shop, went abroad for six months, and had the first good holiday of my life—the time of my life! No one will ever take away the memories of that wonderful holiday—it was the wisest thing I had ever done up to then.

I returned to England with less than 10s. in cash, and started all over again at my home at 152 Westmoreland Road as a book-runner. The circle was complete. I was back where I started.

How I Became a Cigarette Card King

RETURNING TO EARTH AND scratching up a living from it after a luxury cruise wasn't easy. True, I had round about 600 books of medium value, but I was stumped for ready money. Now since I was 15 I had been not only an ardent collector of autographs and signed photographs, but also of cigarette cards (i.e., those cards that used to be inserted in packets of cigarettes and were usually in series of 50), coins, stamps, and matchbox labels. Invariably all my treasures were housed in the wardrobe and my clothes chucked about anywhere—and there wasn't a table or a chair that didn't have boxes of cards or what have you underneath it!

I now set out to make a sideline business by selling cigarette cards. In those far-off days I had only three competitors in the world who made a living in this way; and right from the start I touched lucky. Owning myself about 200,000 cards, I was able to interest a wide public in carto-phily—the posh word for collecting cigarette cards—by means of short articles in all manner of magazines and journals—*Pearson's Weekly, Tit Bits, Everybody's,* the *Leader,* the *Exchange and Mart,* and so on. My articles were pioneer efforts and brought me within a very few weeks an exceedingly large mail. It seemed that thousands and thousands wanted one or two odd cards to complete sets. As people frequently offered me 1s. for a single card, I broke up my own sets and made a very good living out of it. One of my articles in *Pearson's Weekly* brought me over 200 requests for more information on values and varieties, whereupon the editor asked me for a short article on cards every week, agreeing to pay me £1 extra for every 50 genuine inquiries I answered from his readers. For five years I wrote on cards, and went from *Pearson's Weekly* to *Tit Bits.* I continued my 'Cigarette Card Box' weekly feature until about six months after the beginning of the war, when cigarette cards ceased to be put into cartons.

I have already recorded in an earlier volume of this book that two weeks before the war started I travelled to Germany alone, and with no knowledge of German except 'No,' 'Yes,' 'I love you,' and 'Please sign my book,' to try to get Hitler to swop fag cards with me. I knew that he collected them and supervised all new issues, which for the most part were for the greater glory of Germany. I took with me 200 choice English sets, but I couldn't get near him. I contented myself with buying several thousand sets of German cards, and returned to England the day before war was declared. The first incendiary bombs to fall in Westmoreland Road gutted the room in which all my cartophilic treasures were housed, and those that were not burnt were soaked with water. Irreplaceable treasures! When the fire was out I went up again to see the ruins of a lifelong collection, and I sat and cried my heart out. When later I made a claim for about a tenth of the true value of the cards, autographs, and stamps, the Government people laughed at me, and I did not receive a single penny compensation. Lizzie, my landlady, got about a quarter the value of the home she had lost—she settled for a cash sum down without waiting, as the money was needed for replacements. For three years we had no roof and only half a front wall to 152. More bombs, or blast rather, destroyed the back kitchen and ruined autographed photographs which I had put up on the walls to keep my courage up and remind me of the good old days. Later I moved the remainder of my treasures to the basement, and blime, we then got flooded out by stopped-up drains, the water pouring in and making a further mess of my remaining cards! Today I possess about 5,000 cards—all that remain of a collection once $1\frac{1}{2}$ million strong!

So ended my reign as a king of cigarette card collectors and dealers. It was one of the busiest periods of my life; I might have made a fortune if the war hadn't come. During the war I was a full-time A.R.P. warden in Walworth; but I was badly injured, and after six months in and out of various hospitals and convalescent homes I was discharged.

It Took Me Twenty Years to Get it: Interlude

ONE OF THE VERY FIRST BOOKS I ever sold was on the art of making patchwork quilts. I remember it so well because, having paid 3d. for it as a sheer gamble, I was utterly astounded when I was offered the enormous price of 15s. for it within a few days. I was so astounded that when the lady paid over her fifteen bob I gave her 2s. 6d. back for luck! I had looked at the nice coloured pictures in the book and promised myself that some day when I was rich I would own a patchwork quilt in all the colours of the rainbow, and that it would cover my bed.

In the days when I had money to burn I would willingly have paid £10 for a genuine Victorian patchwork, but I never saw one in all my travels. Then one day I saw on a barrow a brown paper parcel, and curiosity made me open it. It contained some 2,000 six-sided two-inch wide patches, some sewn in long lines to each other, some loose. I got them for a reasonable sum, and for two weeks Lizzie (my landlady, Mrs Keep) and I sat for hours joining patch to patch. Then she backed the whole with some blackout material, and I now have a real patchwork quilt like those I saw in the book twenty years ago. And do you know where I found this uncompleted genuinely early Victorian collection of patches? In my own home road, Westmoreland Road, Walworth.

Uncivil Civil Servant

IT TOOK FOUR DOCTORS, A Red Cross Commandant, a titled lady and the welfare officer of Southwark to get my honourable discharge from the A.R.P. as unfit for further duties. There was no 'working a ticket': once in the A.R.P. you stopped there till you were practically dying on your feet! It was such a thankless task that anyone in their right senses preferred the Army. For about a month after my discharge I did nothing —at least, nothing that I can remember save chop wood in my backyard and cry for God knows what reason.

But with the help of a kindly doctor, some treatment, and a good deal of will to get better from myself, I did slowly mend, and I was mending when I was called before some tribunal formed, it seemed to me, just to see what I was doing to help the war along; for I was the only one in front of that body of hard-faced women and pukkha sahibs with military bearing and aged dials. They fired questions at me and I got all flustered and tongue-tied—and after about ten minutes of wasn't I ashamed of myself for doing nothing to help the poor Poles, Czechs, and what not I broke down and cried. So they made me a Civil Servant. I was ordered to go to one of the Ministries to be found a 'light' office job.

I really can't remember that at that Ministry I was allowed to do a single thing which helped the war effort. Persons on the staff—and they were mostly over military age, or invalids, or mothers with families, or throwouts from the Services—had a certain little amount of work to do, and if they didn't rush it they could just manage to make it last nearly a day, what with breaks for 11 o'clock tea, well over an hour for lunch, tea again at 3, and preparations for departure at about 5! And they jealously guarded their little section of work in case the chief saw them doing nothing and transferred them to a much busier section in a less pleasant office in a not so congenial district.

When I arrived on the scene for my light office job it was so light that it consisted practically of addressing a few envelopes, repairing and re-labelling a few more, seeing that everybody had nice white sheets of blotting paper to doodle upon, and making myself as inconspicuous as possible, so as to be in no one's way. A child of ten could have done all I did in my year as a Civil Servant. The hours dragged, I got piles from sitting inactive for hours; so I bought some twopenny exercise books and filled in my time writing articles, which appeared in magazines all over the world.

All the same, I can honestly say that I never neglected the little bits of work I was given. I merely speeded it up and went back to journalism. Everyone was exceedingly kind to me—too kind. They just didn't bother about me at all. Sometimes I was told to lose myself for the afternoon as there was to be an inspection of the staff: I suppose they thought I might blurt out a few uncomfortable truths. I did after a while protest that I could do lots more than make office files and repair envelopes, and I wasn't sorry to find myself transferred to the stationery department of the Ministry. I assisted here in ordering and sending out rubber stamps. We almost became rubber stamps! Then I was transferred to Pens and Inks with a kind man as my boss, but it was all pretty futile, and I made it my business to get the sack.

All the time I was working in this Ministry I spent my entire lunch times buying books in and around Charing Cross Road. My wages were very good, and I always had at least £2 a week to spend on books. Knowing that when the war was over I should return to my own job of bookselling, I stocked up my home with the best books my money would buy.

Finally, the Ministry gave me the option of being transferred to a branch many miles from home or the sack—and as I was begging for the sack I was delighted when I got it.

So ended my career as Civil Servant.

Those Lantern Slides

I HAD, OF COURSE, TO REPORT to the local Ministry of Labour in Walworth Road that I was available for work, but I begged them to let me return to bookselling, for I could have got dollars for England by selling my books in America. But oh dear no—I had to do work of National Importance! So they sent me to the London County Council, at County Hall, where I was taken on as a temporary clerk in one of their innumerable departments.

Here I became nothing more or less than an errand boy. I was given fiddling filing jobs, made to get the newspapers and run messages—anything except the clerical work I was paid to do. So one day I took the law into my own hands and went to another office and saw and spoke to a really real L.C.C. official; when I left he promised to see what he could do to help me. I told him that I was able to make first-class toys from oddments like cotton reels, matchboxes, and old tin cans; that I was an authority on the art of toy-making and had written books (*Toys for*

Nothing and *More Toys for Nothing,* published by Hutchinson) and articles on the subject over many years, besides broadcasting several times in the Children's Hour on how to make good toys at no cost whatever. A week later I was transferred to the equipment supply department at Stockwell, and through the kindness of several officials I was eventually given an office all to myself where I invented and made good toys for children out of salvaged oddments. These toys were put on display in another large room so that teachers calling for equipment could examine them and go back to their schools with fresh ideas to keep children interested and amused. The six months during which I made toys were the happiest of all the war months for me. I was doing a job I loved doing, I was practically my own boss, since no one disturbed me—all they wanted was results, and in those six months I made over 200 first-class exclusive toys. My work was play, for I loved it; but work it was, because every toy had to be conceived in the simplest way possible. It is easy for a handyman to make a battleship from matchboxes, cotton reels, and paper, but I had to plan so that a child of eight or nine could make it.

As a result of all this pleasurable work I got fit and well in mind and body—my nerve came back. In six months I gained 8 lb. in weight, and was returning fast to my normal 8 st. 4 lb. when the axe fell! There came to Stockwell a very big noise in the L.C.C. to make readjustments and cut down the staff; and he of course saw the roomful of toys I had made. On finding out that I had been engaged for temporary clerical work and most certainly not as a toy-maker, he very soon put a stop to my activities, and within a week I was transferred—not to clerical work, oh dear no—to the lantern slide department, and there for four or five months I did up lantern slides, replacing their broken glass fronts and framing them with black tape. It was no longer the red tape of the Civil Service, it was the black tape of the L.C.C. Hour after hour I sat at a tiny table in a draughty top-floor room mending those confounded little slides—thousands of them! Take off the broken fragments of glass (broken in cartage from one school to another, though why they were never packed in padded boxes beats me), get out a square of glass to cover the actual glass slide, put the two together, and then bind with gummed black tape. And this went on for hour after hour. I couldn't take any pride in the work; a boy of 14 or 15 could have done it—and for all I know now is.

Then the war finished, and as I was one of the last to arrive I was naturally one of the first to go. I hope I left behind friends who think of me occasionally.

I am grateful to Stockwell, for it was there I returned to good health.

The Circle Completed

I HAD TO REPORT TO THE Labour Exchange that I was 'free,' and again I begged them to let me lodge my insurance and employment cards with them and return to my former profession of antiquarian bookselling. But the man I saw was reluctant to release me. 'I see,' he said, 'that you are a bookseller. Look, there's a proof-reader's job going at Lloyd's Shipping Registry. Here's a card of appointment—go after the job at once.' Well, what the hell proof-reading has to do with bookselling God above knows. However, I went to offices in Southwark Road to be given a trial. I had, of course, done a little proof-reading for my own books when the galley sheets were sent me, but proof-reading for Lloyd's huge Shipping Registry was an entirely different matter. The type was mostly small Bible size, and most of the 'readers' were old men with 50 years' experience and union cards and big magnifying glasses! I lasted exactly one day. Someone had to check the proofs I'd checked, and although I found an odd full stop or comma out of place, this expert found dozens of errors I'd overlooked! I got 18s. for my day's pay and a terrific headache.

Back I went to the Labour Exchange. The same man served me. Would I care for a job as a jobbing gardener or assistant editor of a boys' 2d. coloured comic? 'No!' I said. 'Let me see the boss of this Exchange.' Eventually I saw the boss and he said I could most certainly return to bookselling at once. A charming man—I wish now I'd bought him the best cigar in London. Free, free! No more to be directed to this job and that; free once again to become a book-runner at 38 as I was at 15! The merry circle was complete—I'd got absolutely nowhere in life! True, I knew a great deal more about books and was unlikely to use boot polish to clean them with. True, I had a very nice stock of good-class books, I knew their values, I had a few pounds in the bank to tide me over the blank period. But all in all I was starting out all over again.

Having a Go at Shelley

FOR FOURTEEN YEARS I WROTE and wrote and no one paid the slightest attention to my writings. True, they hit the target and I got paid for 90 per cent of them, but that was because I chose obscure magazines and never dared to show my wares to the better-class and more famous journals. But now I have been discovered. Editors commission my work, I get a steady fanmail, and I am able to earn enough to pay for my cigarettes the whole year round out of my wages for words! I haven't exactly arrived, but the train is slowing up and although the platform is in a fog it's somewhere there in the distance . . .

So, greatly daring, I joined the Society of Authors.[1] I've paid my subs

[1] I resigned after a year because I considered it *impudent* to continue—I'm no author.

and I feel happy to be in such a posh do with eminent literary blokes. One of them called upon me recently. He said he wondered what I was really like—I felt like something out of the blinking zoo. I was only medium pleased to see him because he was to some degree patronizing; but he said I ought to improve my education—and he's the third bloke to tell me that inside a month!

When he'd pushed off I thought over what he'd been saying and decided I'd have a bash at this improvement of the mind once again—recently I did have a go at Einstein's books and try to understand relativity, but I couldn't make head or tail of what he was writing, so I gave it up. Then I explored the drawings and doings of Aubrey Beardsley, but he seemed to be a genius who went wrong somewhere, and although I could see that he had a dandy eye for line I preferred Arthur Rackham any old day. So I gave up art.

Then I thought I'd have a basinful of Shelley, and I get hold of a nice little edition, slip it into my pocket, and jump on a bus and go over to the Regent Palace Hotel lounge. Here I get a comfortable chair, a welcome smile from a clean-looking waitress, and a shandy all for 1s. 2d. Then I open Shelley at page one to find the first do is called ' The Daemon of the World.' I don't know what a daemon is, but I'm having a go! And it starts, 'How wonderful is death, Death and his brother Sleep! One pale as yonder wan and hornèd moon, With lips of lurid blue. The other glowing like the vital morn, When throned on ocean's wave It breathes over the world; Yet both so passing strange and wonderful!' Well, I can't get the hang of it, so I read it out loud—'How wonderful is death,' etc. There is a geezer sitting right next to me and he looks round startled and amazed. But I don't care, on I go mumbling the words to myself. Then a bloke in evening dress comes up and says, 'Excuse me, sir—are you feeling well?' I say I'm feeling all right in a way, but I'm having a go at Shelley. 'Ah,' he says, melancholy-like, 'I'd keep off sherry if I were you.'

The One-Legged Man

I ALWAYS WRITE OF WHAT I see and know. I leave fiction to others. Having said that, I will tell you of a ghost I saw. Take out a map of England: you will see the tiny village of Langstone, near Havant, in Hampshire, opposite Hayling Island. Langstone is at the foot of the tall bridge leading to Hayling Island. Dear friends of mine at the Petersfield Bookshop loaned me after my illness a room above a storage place close to an old windmill that had been converted into living quarters, where I could stay and look after myself and get well in peace and quiet.

You go up the main street of some twenty tiny houses from the mill, pass over the main road (Havant–Hayling motor-bus road); facing you then is a quiet shady lane leading to wide marshes and smooth mud (little sand) for miles. At ten one morning I went down this lane on my way to catch the bus to Portsmouth. It was a bright day and the birds were singing. I was happy. Then suddenly it seemed as if all was silent. I stopped. I felt uneasy. In front of me, not more than twenty feet away, there lay on the ground a naked man, and he had half a right leg—a stump above the knee. He was old—I would say well past sixty —and bald and awfully thin. I walked forward slowly, and I was afraid. There was silence in that lane. I looked around, thinking I should need help; there was no one about at all. I walked nearer and was within three or at the most four yards—the distance of an ordinary room— when the man vanished. He didn't fade away, he simply vanished. But I saw that man with my own two eyes on the ground stark naked—and I say that I saw a ghost.

G. Bernard Shaw and Me

FEBRUARY 1, 1949. IN THIS month's *Chambers' Journal* there appears the article by me entitled 'The Romance of a Book-Runner' which I mentioned in last year's SATURDAY BOOK as being accepted by them. They had it exactly thirteen months before they printed it. But it wasn't an unlucky thirteen—oh no, to be sure!

February 17, 1949. A letter from John M. Dickie, editor of *Chambers' Journal*. *Dear Mr Bason: You will be interested in the enclosed post-card which came in for you today from Ayot St Lawrence, on the behalf of G. Bernard Shaw. I hope you will be able to help, and to your advantage. Yours sincerely.*

The card from G. B. Shaw *via* Dr F. E. Loewenstein, Remembrancer to Mr Shaw, says that I am the man they are looking for, and asks me to try to get out-of-the-way Shaw items, such as Press cuttings, programmes, leaflets, pamphlets.

February 20. Me to G. Bernard Shaw, c/o Dr Loewenstein: *Blime gents, I reckon I ought to put up a coat of arms or something, book-runner to G. Bernard Shaw! Lor Luvva blooming duck! Alas, I can't help very much at the moment because all I have got in the way of Shaw interest is Press Cuttings, first edition, 1909, for which I require the sum of 7s. 6d. (I trust it isn't too expensive) and three programmes—first-night ones; they are a little unusual and for them I ask the sum of 2s., which isn't a bit expensive—plus postage, a tanner, which makes 10s. I hope G.B.S. considers this a fair and honest price. I send these four items right now. And if he or you don't want any of them I wonder if Mr Shaw would do me the honour of autographing one item personally to me; I promise faithfully never, never to sell it. I would keep it as a souvenir of a real red-letter day in the life of a very ordinary book-runner. No offence intended by this request, I assure you. I promise you I will do my best to get more Shaw items but, of course, I am unable to guarantee results because, you see, book-hunting and leaflet-hunting is all a matter of luck. But believe me, I will most certainly try.*

March 2nd. My copy of *Press Cuttings*, published Constable, has been in my possession for about seven years waiting for someone to pay me 7s. 6d. for it. Now G. B. Shaw has sent it back to me with the following amazingly long and generous inscription in his own handwriting. On the half title: fifteen lines of 110 words: *The Lord Chamberlain banned this play as too personal to General Kitchener, not recognizing that Mitchener is a caricature of the Duke of Cambridge and quite unlike Kitchener. He even objected to Balsquith as offensive to Arthur Balfour and Herbert Asquith, though the compound Balsquith was in* Punch *almost every week. A club had to be formed, and the play presented as a private entertainment of its members. The members received tickets on payment of their entrance fees. Later on the play was licensed with the two names changed to Bones and Jones, the ringmaster and the clown of the Christy (Negro) Minstrels established then in London. G.B.S.* Inscription on the title-page, also in the noble handwriting of G.B.S., consisting of 10 lines of 42 words: *This, the first and only separate edition, was discovered 40 years later by Fred Bason, snapper-up of such highly considered trifles, and autographed for him by the friendly author G. Bernard Shaw of Ayot St Lawrence on March 1, 1949.*

So my copy has in all 25 lines consisting of exactly 152 words (I wonder if Mr Shaw, with his witty mind, intended it to be the same number as my humble home—152?). Be that as it may, this copy stays at that address; it's not for sale at any time or at any price. This is one book I jolly well *won't* sell—so there!

Afterthoughts

LEONARD RUSSELL introduced Nicolas Bentley to me, and he in turn introduced me to a firm of publishers; and with Mr Bentley editing my awful English I believe my diaries for the past 27 years are to be published. Glory be!

I WANT TO RETURN to Funchal in Madeira and see if I can recapture the joys I found there in my twenties. I also want to find out whether the girls *did* turn to fat!

I AM ALWAYS delighted to hear from readers, and I promise to reply to everyone in time. But please—*please*—you must provide me with a stamped addressed envelope. The address is 152 Westmoreland Road, London, S.E.17.

Confessions

Kassemoff

NINE

distinguished

men & women reply

to a 'Saturday Book'

questionnaire

1

by ELIZABETH BOWEN

What has been your greatest personal deficiency in life?
Laziness—what they at school called 'slackness.' Result: sins of omission.

What century or period is your spiritual home, and why?
Late seventeenth century in England—provided one had been 'fortunately' born. Should have enjoyed small country house life of that period, with what one takes to have been its mixture of tranquillity, formality, style, grace, and intelligence.

On what occasion have you been most frightened in your life?
By a V.1. Or when I thought a plane I was in was crashing. Also went through awful phases of sweating-fear of the dark in my childhood, when I had been reading ghost stories.

What was the most momentous interview of your life?
With my first publisher, Frank Sidgwick, when I was 23. I had gone to see him in response to a letter saying he was interested in my book of short stories and would like to discuss them. During the conversation the idea that the book really *was* going to be published dawned on me.

Where and when did you have the most memorable holiday of your life?
The first time I went abroad—as a child, in the summer of 1913. Night and day in Brussels; night in Cologne; journey along the Rhine by river steamer; rest of the time in Switzerland—Wengen,

in the Bernese Oberland. Nothing particularly exciting happened: it was the sheer new sensation of 'abroad-ness' which was exciting. A temperamental traveller's first taste, as it were, of blood.

Where and when did you have the most memorable meal of your life?

My first grown-up dinner party, at which I met an Archbishop.

Have you any pet reforms?

Income Tax. Under three headings—(a) adjustments for authors, (b) husbands' and wives' incomes to be taxable separately, (c) greater distinction to be made between earned and unearned incomes.

Are you urban or rural by temperament, and what is your conception of the ideal house or flat?

Rural. House in the country; enough but not too much garden. Friends within reach but not on one's doorstep. House should be, ideally, 18th-century: not too large. Countryside should be as quiet and remote as possible; and should have kept as far as possible its indigenous people and traditional way of life. Travel to or from the outside world should be not too difficult or expensive. Self-sufficiency, but not isolation, seems to me to be the ideal. It is probably well to have lived in a big city for some years at one or another time in one's life.

Are you a host or a guest?

Hard to say: I enjoy being either. Perhaps, on the whole, host.

To what do you attribute your success?

Power to concentrate when I *am* working. Good temper; in the main, good will towards other people. Power to throw things off.

What lessons has life taught you?

To allow other people to go their own ways. To discard extraneous wishes and concentrate on what I really do desire. To cut my losses.

Is there any other profession you might have been good at?

I should like to have been an architect. Or (if I had been a man) a barrister.

2

by IVOR BROWN

Is there any other profession you might have been good at?
A psychologist. (Any bluffer can be that.) Or a writer of advertisement copy, but that needs ability.

What has been your greatest personal deficiency in life?
Unwillingness to hit those who cannot hit back.

What century or period is your spiritual home, and why?
Periclean Athens (provided I was a free citizen) because then and there all the arts and sciences were young; so too was the most exact and beautiful of human languages.

On what occasion have you been most frightened in your life?
Frights cannot be measured arithmetically. All frights are frightful.

What was the most momentous interview of your life?
Two *viva voce* examinations.

Where and when did you have the most memorable holiday of your life?
Holidays, like frights, cannot be measured arithmetically. All holidays are memorable, sometimes because of continuous rain, bad food, and worse company, sometimes because of the reverse. My happiest have been in Scotland, Denmark, and Greece.

Where and when did you have the most memorable meal of your life?
Meals, like frights and holidays, cannot be measured and compared. On the whole, the further north you go the better the food. I have had the most pretentious, expensive, and worthless food in France, the best in Scotland (aforetime) and Scandinavia.

Have you any pet reforms?
Abolition of smoking in theatres. Compulsion of pedestrians to cross according to the lights.

*Are you urban or rural by temperament, and what is your conception
of the ideal house or flat?*

Being a normal human being, I naturally like both town and country
according to season. My ideal house or flat is one run by my wife.

Are you a host or a guest?

I consider myself a poor performer in either capacity.

To what do you attribute your success?

The alleged 'success' I attribute to mastery of the tricks of the exami-
nation system, i.e., low cunning in the concealment of my ignorance.

What lessons has life taught you?

Reading, writing, and almost no 'rithmetic.

3

by BERNARD DARWIN

Is there any other profession you might have been good at?

I don't think so. I have tried three others—the Law (both branches)
and the Army during the first war. I liked the Bar—the other two
I cordially disliked. As far as I can judge I was equally inefficient
at all three.

What has been your greatest personal deficiency in life?

A hatred of doing things in the nature of business and a consequent
inability to understand them.

What century or period is your spiritual home, and why?

The Regency period in the sense that it seems to me the most
romantic, but I sometimes wonder whether the romance is not a little
spurious and I doubt whether in fact I should have felt at home in it.

On what occasion have you been most frightened in your life?

Either when I observed Richthofen's Circus flying straight for our unprotected depot in Macedonia or when the bombs were falling very close to my head in the two Baedeker raids on Bath.

What was the most momentous interview of your life?

Probably in fact in 1908 when I went to see the then editor of the *Evening Standard,* who gave me my first job to write about golf. More vivid, however, is my first visit to Lord Northcliffe at Sutton Place, when he sat me down in a chair and asked me what I knew about except golf. I answered Dickens and murders, which proved quite a judicious choice.

Where and when did you have the most memorable holiday of your life?

My first visit to the South of France (a few years before the first war) with its waking up in the sleeping car to see the sun shining on 'a view like a classical landscape.' There was a quality of enchantment about it never quite to be recaptured.

Where and when did you have the most memorable meal of your life?

In the village of Baldja in Macedonia when a friend and I went to stay with the head man of the village, a splendid old Turk with beautiful manners, and sat on the floor to eat a duck of divine flavour, never to be forgotten.

Have you any pet reforms?

No. There is so much to be said for Lord Melbourne's 'Why not leave it alone?' I agree with Mr. Jellyby's advice to his daughter Caddy (in *Bleak House*), 'Never have a mission.'

Are you urban or rural by temperament, and what is your conception of the ideal house or flat?

I live and like living in the country but think I am urban rather than rural in temperament, being dreadfully ignorant of many country things. I have never acquired the art of standing and looking over a gate and am no good at village politics. The last part of the question depends much on whether you can get any servants or have the money to pay them. The ideal is therefore constantly shrinking. Granted the possibility I should vote for a small country house not very far from London.

Are you a host or a guest?

Unquestionably and almost shamefully a guest. I love staying with other people and have had many angelic hosts and hostesses whose arts, I am afraid, I have never been able to acquire.

To what do you attribute your success?

Such as it is, to having been able to do the only sort of thing I liked and was interested in and not having to do the things that bored me.

What lessons has life taught you?

When I was quite young I wanted to do nothing (except play golf) and have never ceased to be thankful that this was not possible. And I think it very important to have something you like to do and to go on doing it as long as you are allowed. At the same time I wish I had been interested in more things such as gardening and fishing before it was too late to learn. Finally, it is a good plan to have as many young friends as possible.

4

by STELLA GIBBONS

Is there any other profession you might have been good at?

Yes; granted permission to be always alone in the kitchen I could have been a cook, for cooking is the only thing besides writing that I do with competence. Lack of firmness would have made me an incompetent nanny, though the society of young children soothes and satisfies me, and we get on well together. Had I been born a man I would have chosen to be a religious pilgrim or an explorer or a sailor, but naturally I cannot say if I should have made a good one.

What has been your greatest personal deficiency in life?

Lack of method.

Procrastination.

A weak memory.

—in that order.

I

What century or period is your spiritual home, and why?

Although the menaces of the 20th century hang in the back of my mind as hell hung in the minds of mediaeval Christians and it takes all my faith to surmount them, I could not wish to live in the past, when children inevitably died of mastoid or diphtheria. But by temperament I am one of the more serious Edwardians; that is to say, moderately progressive, with a strong social conscience, a strong dislike of passion in politics, and a strong wish to live under a rule of 'sweetness and light' that has developed naturally from an education penetrated by the Christian ethic. So I would choose to live in 1902, the year of my birth. In 1902, the collective social conscience had developed so widely since 1870 that the intolerable burden of the suffering poor upon the individual conscience was beginning to be relieved. Some Victorian falsities had disappeared, and men and women had learned how to be friends. Most people still drew their pleasures from natural sources rather than from gadgets, drugs, and machines. Women could be good without being considered dull. Prettiness was not suspect. Propaganda, as a weapon, did not exist. Politics were a game, dirty perhaps, but amusing still. The scientists were still in leash, and England was still insular and still (outwardly, at least) honest. Yes, I chose 1902 —until I looked at a photograph of some National School children taken in that year, and then I decided that if the poor children of 1902 looked like that, I will choose to live today, when they look cheerful and sturdy. To me, the immense flowering of the collective social conscience almost makes up for the menaces of 1949.

On what occasion have you been most frightened in your life?

Munich Week, 1938.

What was the most momentous interview of your life?

Men have momentous interviews; women, even in this age, usually have momentous conversations. I count as memorable certain casual conversations in which the other person has said something that afterwards influenced my way of living. I remember the lecture, short, sharp, and unexpected as a spring hailstorm, given me in my youth by an older woman about taking from a young man without giving in return; and the one sensible remark I ever heard from an old aunt (now dead) who had lived in Italy: 'The English don't rest enough.' I remember the change in a priest's voice when I proposed that my banns should be called in his parish for a Lenten wedding—'That is a matter for yourself and your fiancé to decide,' and how (being a pagan in those days) I wondered at the severe tone without a clue to its cause; and the last dry remark of my history mistress when we all said good-bye to her on our last day at school: 'You, Stella, have what is called the gift of the gab and unless you put some solid knowledge behind it you will never do anything worth while with it.' But I do not think that one realizes such remarks were momentous until the wheels they set in motion have been revolving for some time.

Where and when did you have the most memorable holiday of your life?
In the June of a wet summer that had brought on the meadow flowers and made the marguerites larger than I ever remember them, I went by myself for a fortnight to a small house in Sussex belonging to my husband's family. It is made chiefly of wood, and when, after awakening peacefully at about eight o'clock, I went downstairs to make tea, the walls would feel still warm from the previous evening's long hours of sunlight. I used to pull *The Times* through the letter-box and put it unopened on the increasing pile in the hall, and after I had breakfasted in the garden or the sunny morning-room on toast and potted meat and tea, with the birds for guests, I would write until I felt hungry again and then eat fat mutton stewed with barley and washed down with milk, as if I were an Arab. Sometimes I rode slowly on a hired bicycle along lonely lanes where the Downs towered over me in the warm grey air, and once I found a deserted Jacobean mansion for sale; with the escutcheon above its door hidden in white roses, and in its overgrown gardens a spreading briar of minute scarlet ones that might have hedged in the Sleeping Beauty. I entertained company only twice; I went in to Brighton by bus once; and having made my bed at dusk, I would do the day's washing up every night while listening to sugary tunes on the old wireless set. I shall always remember this holiday above all others because during it I learned to my great surprise that I am not really domesticated, and also that the amount of sheer dullness I can take without becoming bored is practically unlimited.

Where and when did you have the most memorable meal of your life?
In another June, in Switzerland this time, at the end of the long pull up from Wengen to Wengenalp, I came to the lonely hotel whose terrace overlooks the Jungfrau, and with some difficulty made the people there understand a request for tea with bread, butter, and salad. I waited on the terrace, watching the clouds rolling down over the ridge to the left of the Silberhorn while the silvery light grew ever darker until all the peaks were hidden, and the waterfalls shooting over those titanic precipices glimmered as if it were already dusk. Soon a cheerful Swiss-German girl brought out a tray laden with: a slab of hard, pale, rich cheese; slices of almost black rye bread positively exuding nourishment and explaining by its substance the Biblical name 'staff of life'; four thick curled shells of

dewy butter; and a lettuce whose thin sappy leaves were filmed with oil, and vinegar sighing forth a memory of garlic. It all tasted delicious, but I remember it chiefly because to partake of it in that place was to eat Switzerland; so truly did the fresh simple flavours express the mountain wildernesses that man cannot debauch. Even the tea, the one exotic element, was thin and hot, like sunlight at ten thousand feet. It cost me the equivalent of three shillings, and my only regret is that in my hunger I ate it much too fast.

Have you any pet reforms?

I would like all advertising forbidden in the streets and buses and Underground except on specially built hoardings at intervals of a mile or so, the colours and lettering of the permitted advertisements to harmonize or contrast pleasingly with the surroundings (white and yellow near the green open spaces for example, and pink and black in streets of grey or smoke-coloured houses). If anyone complains that the advertisements of today replace the coloured pageantry of the past, I would suggest that the advertisers divert their talents to planning processions, such as the ancient Guilds had, proclaiming the virtues of Gummo and Phooeygen and the rest, the planners to work under choreographers skilled in the picturesque groupings of crowds. If the processions held up the traffic, so much the better; the carnage on the roads would be reduced.

I would also like to stop the publication of all newspapers and the broadcasting of all news except local news for five years, to give us time to calm down.

Are you urban or rural by temperament, and what is your conception of the ideal house or flat?

Rural, on the whole, but more suburban than either; I like the leafy privacy of quiet residential roads that are never lonely; and the sense of being poised between the pleasures of town and country. Deep country oppresses me with its insistent beauty, while to live in the heart of a city would be misery.

I am content with our own small modern house on the edge of London, but I would like one more room and a slightly larger garden. If I were a spinster I would like to live in a small stout wooden hut in a high Alpine valley.

Are you a host or a guest?

A guest, but not a frequent or a successful one. I am the worst hostess I know except at children's parties; ours have always been very successful because I enjoy them. Grown-up parties bring out the worst in me and therefore I avoid them.

To what do you attribute your success?

Enjoying the act of writing.

Luck.

Older peoples' kindness when I was young.

Trying always to tell myself the truth.

Having a just estimate of my powers.

Being a good listener.

Hard work.

Conscientiousness.

Self-control.

Not being cursed with a passion for fame or money or exhausting and expensive pleasures,

and

Being married to a man whose attitude towards my work is perfect.

What lessons has life taught you?

Passivity and patience.

5

by JOHN GIELGUD

Is there any other profession you might have been good at?

Doubtful.

What has been your greatest personal deficiency in life?

Moral courage—lack of it.

What century or period is your spiritual home, and why?

18th Century.

On what occasion have you been most frightened in your life?

I am frequently frightened, and surprised to find that fear varies so little in degree. One appears to feel as frightened by a small event as by a large one. It is only a question of how *long* the fear lasts

What was the most momentous interview of your life?
My first audition to enter dramatic school.

Where and when did you have the most memorable holiday of your life?
Venice, August, 1939.

Where and when did you have the most memorable meal of your life?
Restaurant des Pyramides, Vienne, France, 1937.

Have you any pet reforms?
Abolition of noise.

Are you urban or rural by temperament, and what is your conception of the ideal house or flat?
Urban. Small house. Privacy. Largish rooms.

Are you a host or a guest?
Host.

To what do you attribute your success?
Enthusiasm, vivacity, good health, good luck, single-mindedness, conscientiousness.

What lessons has life taught you?
To enjoy the present, resist wallowing in the past, and not to dread the future unduly.

6

by HERMIONE GINGOLD

Is there any other profession you might have been good at?
I have always imagined I might have made a really good spy. Fascinating foreigners and mink coats are right up my street (unfortunately only metaphorically speaking). I find consolation in thinking that a mink coat even when worn next to the skin must be very hot wear in mid-summer.

What has been your greatest personal deficiency in life?

Unspeakable laziness, and the belief that if you put bills unopened behind a picture frame there is no need to pay them.

What century or period is your spiritual home, and why?

The Naughty Nineties, because there was no National Insurance Card baldly stamped 'Female.' On reading over my card, I am startled to find that in the event of my being married, widowed, or divorced, I must notify the National Insurance Office at once. In the good old Nineties one's parents would have been the first to know.

On what occasion have you been most frightened in your life?

My greatest fear is to be trapped in a fire, and the first night I ever spent in a New York hotel was in a bedroom on the 60th floor. I couldn't sleep a wink for wondering how many sheets I should have to knot together to reach the street. This night is definitely awarded an H. certificate.

What was the most momentous interview of your life?

I haven't had any momentous interview yet.

Where and when did you have the most memorable holiday of your life?

A certain spring spent in a villa on Lake Maggiore some time before the war—no, not the Boer War.

Where and when did you have the most memorable meal of your life?

High up on an Alp at 12 o'clock at night while motoring through France. I was given wonderful soup, fresh trout, a good salad, and a bottle of wine. Imagine this in England!

Have you any pet reforms?

All persons to be medically examined before being allowed to buy theatre tickets. Those suffering from bronchitis, asthma, or any form of chest or throat complaint liable to result in fits of coughing during a performance should not be permitted to buy them.

Are you urban or rural by temperament, and what is your conception of the ideal house or flat?

Definitely urban. Must live within walking distance of the theatres. My ideal house would be made of elastic.

Are you a host or a guest?

Definitely a hostess.

To what do you attribute your success?

Fate inscrutable.

What lessons has life taught you?

The most important things in life are those trite three, health, wealth, and happiness, and you can't have too much of any of them.

7

by COMPTON MACKENZIE

Is there any other profession you might have been good at?
The only other profession in which I could have felt sure of being as successful as I have had the good fortune to be in my own would have been the stage.

What has been your greatest personal deficiency in life?
A dislike of saying 'no.'

What century or period is your spiritual home, and why?
The present, because I can add to the present so much of the past.

On what occasion have you been most frightened in your life?
Hearing the Jack the Ripper murders being shouted by hoarse throated paper-sellers at night.

What was the most momentous interview of your life?
Probably when I told the High Master of St Paul's School that I did not intend to win a scholarship at Oxford, and thus secured myself from any possibility of entering the Civil Service. I was fifteen years old at the time.

Where and when did you have the most memorable holiday of your life?
I have not had a holiday in the strict sense of the word since I left Oxford, but if I may count as the equivalent of a holiday the enjoyment of a job of work, I should say either my time at Gallipoli or the year I spent recently following the tracks of the Indian Army over three continents.

Where and when did you have the most memorable meal of your life?
In Paris in July, 1938, when as a member of the Saintsbury Club I was a guest of the greatest society of epicures in the world—The Club de Cent.

Have you any pet reforms?

The equalization of the rates for travel and freight—on the lines of the Post Office. In other words, the same fare whether you travel from London to Brighton or to Wick, and the same charge for a ton of goods irrespective of distance. Such a reform would distribute the population of Britain equitably, and ultimately, when extended, the population of the world.

Are you urban or rural by temperament, and what is your conception of the ideal house or flat?

I am rural by temperament. Apart from believing that no flat can be ideal, I cannot answer the second part of this question.

Are you a host or a guest?

I suffer from the delusion that I am a host, but I am informed by all those who ought to know that I am always a guest.

To what do you attribute your success?

Vitality, memory, sympathy, and hard work.

What lessons has life taught you?

This is the kind of Brains Trust question I deplore, but one lesson is the discovery by personal experience that the copy-book maxims of youth are true. Too many cooks do spoil the broth, stitches in time do save nine, birds of a feather do flock together, and one of them in the hand *is* worth two of them in a bush.

8

by A. L. ROWSE

Is there any other profession you might have been good at?

Politics, perhaps—if one could bear it. Publishing—certainly.

What has been your greatest personal deficiency in life?

Touchiness, rather than pride; impatience; a lack of sympathy for the second-rate, an *almost* total inability to put up with fools. Worst of all, an inexhaustible capacity to be tortured by human foolery.

What century or period is your spiritual home, and why?

The Elizabethan Age: for then life for Englishmen was at its most stimulating and all geared to creativeness, instead of the corrosive and denigrating criticism in every field of activity today, which destroys men's natural creativeness and frustrates their fulfilment in positive achievement.

On what occasion have you been most frightened in your life?

When I discovered by chance, as a young man, that in the room which I lived in and loved and had come to identify as my own, my predecessor had hanged himself. It took many years living in it to exorcize that ghost!

What was the most momentous interview of your life?

With the Board of the Drapers' Company, who made it possible for me to go to Oxford—described in *A Cornish Childhood*.

Where and when did you have the most memorable holiday of your life?

Berlin, 1931. Unforgettable. Agonizing.

Where and when did you have the most memorable meal of your life?

I don't remember meals as such—much.

Have you any pet reforms?

Reducing our sex-legislation to a rational basis, in conformity with the Continent. Hardly a pet reform; merely sensible.

Are you urban or rural by temperament, and what is your conception of the ideal house or flat?

Rural. An eighteenth-century country house, or seventeenth or sixteenth century: almost anything so long as not modern. I loathe the idea of life in the flat.

Are you a host or a guest?

Host. I don't like much ever being asked as a guest.

To what do you attribute your success?

Concentration, hard work, common-sense; a refusal to be deflected or discouraged by anything or anybody.

What lessons has life taught you?

Not to expect anything from circumstances or people; to expect everything of oneself; not to pay any attention to what people think, or pretend to think; not to think that one can influence anyone much; to stand up for oneself—for if one doesn't, no one else will. To be careful with money; to keep one's own secrets. To regard love and fulfilment as the best things in life.

9

by G. B. STERN

Is there any other profession you might have been good at?

I used to imagine I was a 'born actress.'

What has been your greatest personal deficiency in life?

I never had the slightest talent for physical proficiency; for anything like walking, climbing, jumping, swinging on horizontal bars, and so forth. I get tired easily, or my ankle turns, or I hold the thing the wrong way, whatever the 'thing' may be. In fact, I'm afraid that in movement I fatally lack swiftness of adjustment. My incredulous and (I can't help feeling) my touching delight when I found I was quite good at, for instance, managing a punt, or playing ping-pong, or (long ago) dancing a tango, showed that rightly or wrongly I over-valued any achievement right outside my own sedentary line. One always does.

What century or period is your spiritual home, and why?

'Oo!—I dunno' (*Kipps*, by H. G. Wells).

On what occasion have you been most frightened in your life?

In this answer, to make up for the last, I can really spread myself, because I have so often been more frightened than I have ever been before in my life. However, I'll first of all clear out of the way the things that have *not* frightened me more than they normally and reasonably might; and, in fact, where (I've been told) I've kept extra-ordinarily calm:

Air raids (in either World War); three major operations; the big Los Angeles earthquake when I was there in March, 1933.

Now for the occasions or moments which have most frightened me; choose any one out of these:

(a) Once when (heaven alone knows why) I was persuaded to climb a Dolomite; a Dolomite without a funicular; and found myself incredibly standing in dazzling sunshine and thick deep snow on top of a mountain (certainly with a glorious view of the whole range, which I would have been glad to give away with a pound of tea). For I was then faced by the unalterable fact that I had to come down again on my own two legs, and that there was no other way except by the skill and endurance which I did not possess.

(b) The few moments waiting before I had to go on the platform and deliver my first lecture in the U.S.A. to a large expectant audience, after I had seen hundreds of people drive up and enter the hall. I could hear their loud bee-hum as they sat there in front, confidently dependent on me alone for their entertainment. When I walked on, they would suddenly be silent. I had no colleagues, no allies, no prompter, as I would have had if I were an actress. And I said to myself: 'I can't do it.' Directly I started I was perfectly all right; I always am; indeed, more than all right, rather happy; knowing I could make them laugh and listen, and keep them amused and interested for just as long as I liked. Yet still and always I go through that agony just before; though perhaps never again quite as badly as on this first appearance. On the mike, I don't care tuppence; I simply can't understand a speaker with microphone nerves. After all, lecturing in the flesh, you can anticipate (vividly) seeing your audience at any moment get up and walk out on you in little bored knots and batches, yawning and resentful; but you neither see nor hear them abruptly switch off their wireless when they've had enough of you; and you read your speech, so the fear of amnesia is removed. Amnesia is a terrible fear, miles out of your own control; a total black-out in memory (H. G. Wells once spoke of it as a *white* black-out, and that's nearer how it really feels: a small area in your brain going all of a sudden white and blank).

(c) Which accounted for that ghastly moment when I was very young, about sixteen, I think, when I had conceitedly let myself in for appearing in a provincial music-hall to recite a long poem I had written myself, to benefit the victims of some catastrophe, I forget what. Dressed up as a midshipman, and rigid with fear, I strode smartly into the glare of the footlights, bungled my naval salute, recited about three lines—and dried up.

(d) Whenever I am lost, literally lost; lost—and alone. Two occasions I remember for their special quality of panic and horror. Once at Broadstairs when I was about five years old, the crowd around the niggers on the sands broke up and swept me along with them, away from Nurse and the others and safety. The obvious conclusion was that I should never see them again.

And about forty years later, the desolate and 'for ever' sensation of
being lost, knee-deep in snow, crossing Central Park; all paths
smothered and suffocated by snow; and not a soul in sight.

(e) Packed claustrophobically in a huge crowd during a heatwave in
Paris on that night of August, 1914, when France had declared war
against Germany. We were on our way home from Switzerland, and
this seemed as near home as we were likely to get; for there were no
porters, no conveyances, and apparently no trains ever again. The
crowd had gone mad with excitement; they were screaming
'à Berlin!' and manhandling any Germans they could lay hold of.
To be wedged helplessly in a crowd, and desperately longing for
home—these seem to add up to my worst sort of fear. (G. B. STERN,
frightened of, also: Wasps. Thick fogs. Oculists. Bad news.
Swans in a rage.)

What was the most momentous interview of your life?

Seriously, I can't choose; but on a flippant note I recall a fairly
momentous interview with an arrogant head-waiter at a restaurant
just opened; the wine-waiter (bothered by my questions) had summoned him to his aid, and he tried to crush me by the somewhat
startling statement that *white wine had no dates.*

Where and when did you have the most memorable holiday of your life?

Motoring through France on a wine tour at the time of the September
vintage in 1925. That is, if the most memorable holiday means the
most light-hearted holiday. It does, to me.

Where and when did you have the most memorable meal of your life?

At Zürich (I forget the name of the little restaurant) with Marguerite
Steen, on our very first evening abroad after the war. Our dinner
had that 'abroad' sort of flavour, perfect in food and drink and
atmosphere, which we had almost forgotten existed.

Have you any pet reforms?

'Pet'—what a funny adjective in this context!

Of course I have ideas on the subject of several reforms, political,
educational, economic, religious, or social; but I am by no means
a reformer by nature; an effective reformer should be both militant
and practical. Besides, any ideas that one might throw out impul-
sively in conversation should in cold print be well substantiated, all
facts verified, all scaffolding tested. Better leave it alone.

*Are you urban or rural by temperament, and what is your conception
of the ideal house or flat?*

I am urban *and* rural by temperament; and my conception of the ideal
house or flat must have a balcony or a terrace overlooking the sea
or river or at any rate water of some sort; that is, apart from its other
amenities; because I get a quite immoderate and unbalanced pleasure

by eating and drinking out of doors (as long as it isn't a picnic!).
I prefer Georgian or Queen Anne architecture; a garden with shade,
and fruit-trees standing in long grass and buttercups; a not too self-
conscious fountain, and one close-shaven lawn. And I like my ideal
house placed so that all the bedrooms have several windows (and
several views), and one can lie and hear bird-song in the early morning and, if possible, a waterfall when falling asleep at night.

This would look as though I were rural by temperament and not
urban; except that I also love the theatre; I'd badly miss intimate
encounter with a rich variety of friends who live in London and the
fun and surprise of unexpected meetings with friends who are not
there all the time. If I could have all these just as well in the
country or by the sea— You don't 'alf want much, Miss Stern!

Are you a host or a guest?

A guest, because unless invited to a meal, I needn't be there (wherever
'there' is) at the beginning; I can leave whenever I like, and well
before the end; and at a pinch, I needn't be there at all.

To what do you attribute your success?

Answer: Define 'success.'

What lessons has life taught you?

That you can't have everything. That you can't have it both ways.
That when you get powerfully indignant and all worked up over
something impersonal, you're pretty certain to find something deeply
personal right down at the root of it. That while one person may
walk away with the horse, another, as far as you're concerned, mayn't
even look over the stable door. That if you let yourself in for
something distasteful on the careless assumption that Wednesday
fortnight never comes, Wednesday fortnight always *does* come; there
is nothing more inevitable than Wednesday fortnight (I believe it
has sometimes been called the Day of Reckoning). That your own
friends are lovable, exciting, loyal, interesting, decent, companion-
able, witty, and attractive, but *why* are your friends' friends always
so frightful? (And, moreover, why do your friends think *your*
friends awful, when they're not?) That almost every platitude,
aphorism, proverb and axiom is dead true; probably it has only
become a platitude through its unsnubbable persistence in proving
itself true, over and over and over again. That if any one of us
could know exactly what any other one of us was thinking and
feeling nearly all the time, most of us would die of surprise.

This is only a very brief selection picked up at random from the
huge accumulated pile of lessons that life has taught me. Life
teaches me on an average about fifty fresh lessons a week . . . I
sometimes wish it would stop for a little while, and let me relax.

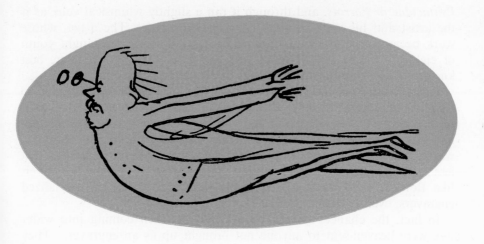

Edward Lear : a self-caricature

Two Great Bird Artists

by BRIAN READE

HE most ambitious ornithographical project ever realized was *The Birds of America,* a series of aquatints by an English engraver, Robert Havell, after drawings by the American naturalist John James Audubon. This series was published on a vast scale between 1827 and 1838. A plate from it depicting the white-headed eagle (or as it is frequently called in America the bald-headed eagle) is reproduced in these pages at less than a quarter of the original size. Benjamin Franklin once said, 'I wish the Bald Eagle had not been chosen as the representative of our country. He is a bird of bad moral character; he does not get his living honestly'—an allusion no doubt to the eagle's habit of stealing the prey of more industrious birds.

Audubon was born in Louisiana in 1780 of French and Spanish parents and was educated in Paris, where he received instruction in drawing from the Jacobin painter, Jacques Louis David. His enormous book, which contained well over a thousand life-size studies of birds in appropriate surroundings, was the last important work of natural history to consist of copper-plate illustrations. Even while it was in production a new phase of bird books opened with a series of lithographs, hand-coloured and brought out in parts from 1830 to 1832.

127

This series was Edward Lear's *Illustrations of the Family of Psittacidae or Parrots*, and through it ran a slightly whimsical vein, as if the artist and his subjects were on speaking terms. The artist, whose work became the prototype of a whole school, was a self-taught youth of eighteen, better known in middle age as a landscape painter, best known today as author of the books of Nonsense.

Edward Lear's reputation as a draughtsman of birds was confined to students of natural history, and it might have spread much further if his best prints had been republished. With his sure grasp of avian shapes and characters he brought new life into an over-stylized art; and what was even more to the point in those pre-photographic times, he saw that less inaccurate results were obtained when the artist was his own engraver, like Bewick, than when his drawings were interpreted by specialized engravers, even careful ones like Havell.

In fact, the chances offered by lithography, then coming into wider use, were heaven-sent to anyone not brought up as an engraver. They made it possible for a draughtsman's actual touch to be reflected in the plates. All that was needed was to adapt oneself to draw on lithographic stone, and that Lear managed with distinction. By 1832 he could claim to be the first artist of any consequence to use the medium for a book on birds, and the first Englishman to produce a book of plates devoted to a single family of birds.

During his early twenties Lear was engaged in making drawings of birds and animals belonging to the thirteenth Earl of Derby, and in preparing some of the lithographs for John Gould's *Ramphastidae* and *Birds of Europe*; but his ornithographical work came to an end in 1837 owing to bad health and bad eyesight. It filled a period in his life which he looked back upon affectionately, for it had been a period of hope and promise, and of happiness due in part to the friendship of Lord Derby's grandchildren, nephews and nieces, for whom he composed the celebrated *Book of Nonsense*.

If we turn to the Nonsense illustrations we find that the creatures there are dressed not in the costumes of the Victorian epoch when they came to life, but in those of Lear's own boyhood, before he knew what life was like. The forms are partly human, partly those of birds and animals, especially about the arms and legs. And if we turn to the self-caricatures he put in letters we shall find he liked to represent himself mostly as a sort of human bird in a shorthand idiomatic style that shows signs of the habits and the skill evolved in drawing birds. Some idea of the original application of that skill is given in the reproductions of a macaw from the *Psittacidae,* and of an owl and a pelican from the *Birds of Europe.*

The Red and Yellow Macaw

Edward Lear

White-headed Eagle ? Male

FALCO LEUCOCEPHALUS

Fish Hawk Yellow and Cat

▌. Audubon's 'Birds of America'

The wrinkled sea beneath him crawls;
He watches from his mountain walls,
And like a thunderbolt he falls.

TENNYSON

The White-headed Eagle: from J.

HE clasps the crag with crooked hands;
Close to the sun in lonely lands,
Ringed with the azure world, he stands.

Above : The Pelican

Edward Lear

Left : The Barred Owl

Edward Lear

Of the great Bottle Man hoax, and of mid-18th century rakes, and of their successors the Macaronis, whose twin passions were their wardrobes and their wagers

A Man in a Bottle

by RONALD FULLER

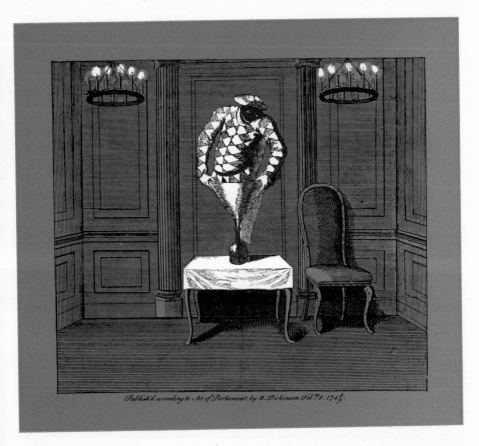

Publish'd according to Act of Parliament, by B. Dickinson Feb.ʸ 8. 1745.

N Thursday, January 12, 1749, an odd advertisement appeared in the newspapers. At 6 p.m. on the following Monday, the Little Theatre in the Hay-Market, where the comedian Samuel Foote held his famous 'Tea-Parties,' was to be the scene of a mysterious performance. A 'Person,' it was stated, would ('without equivocation') get inside an ordinary tavern quart-bottle and, after being firmly corked up, would sing songs, play the music of every known instrument on a common walking-stick and allow himself to be lightly tossed from hand to hand. Later in the evening he would emerge from his bottle and conjure from the grave the spirits of any dead relatives with whom members of the audience wished to have ten minutes' conversation.

On the evening of the 16th, a prodigious crowd filled the theatre and waited for nearly an hour, 'without a single fiddle to keep them in a good humour.' The buzz of excited talk became shriller; the walls re-echoed to catcalls and the hammering of canes, the floor to angry stamps. At 7 o'clock a fellow parted the curtains, bowed deeply, and announced that the audience would have its money returned if the Bottle Conjuror failed to appear. Some wag shouted that the conjuror would get into a pint bottle for double prices; and excitement became frenzy. A lighted candle was thrown down upon the stage. At the same moment part of one of the boxes collapsed, and a young man fell with it into the pit. Terrified of fire, the audience fought for the exits, but the mob which in the mid-18th century seemed to materialize from nowhere at the sound of a scuffle surged in huzza-ing from the streets and began breaking chairs and tearing fittings from the walls. They burnt the theatre curtain on top of a bonfire of furniture; crowds collected to watch the blaze, and the pickpockets were busy. In the confusion the theatre takings disappeared, and the fat Duke of Cumberland, fleeing in a panic from the 'battle of Bottle-Noodles,' lost his gold-hilted and gold-tasselled sword.

The Battle of Bottle-Noodles was something more than a nine days' wonder. No one guessed who had been at the bottom of it, though during the next three weeks several suggestions were made in letters to the Press. One, signed S.M., stated that the Bottle Man had been kidnapped from his coach by two rogues of the Gun Tavern. Another described how he had entered his bottle in order to show his patron how the trick was done. Whereupon the patron whimsically corked the bottle and slipped it into his pocket. 'He is still in the gentleman's custody,' wrote this correspondent. 'He uncorks him now and then to feed him and let in some air.' But long confinement seemed to have damped the Bottle Man's spirits, and he sang and played on his walking-stick no more.

During the remainder of the month, various prints and advertisements appeared: *The Bottle Conjuror's Reflecting Mirror, or One Fool Makes Many, Folly Triumphant, The Bottled Heroes, or Madness and Folly à la Mode*. In *English Credulity, or Ye're All Bottled!* a masked Fiend emerges from a bottle, while Folly in cap and bells surrounds with a rope several great personages of the day, including the swordless Duke of Cumberland. A week or so later Don Jumpedo announced that he would, for a small fee, publicly jump down his own throat; while on

January 27, Dr Benimbo Zammampoango guaranteed ('without equivo-cation') to remove his bowels, wash them, and return them to their accustomed place (boxes 5s., pit 3s., gallery 2s. and 1s.).   And then, a few months later, the joke was forgotten; and the joker himself dead.

He was John, second Duke of Montagu, Knight of the Garter, Master General of the Ordnance, Master of the Great Wardrobe, Fellow of the Royal Society, and Colonel of the Queen's Regiment of Horse.   He was also son-in-law to Sarah, Duchess of Marlborough, who noted that he liked 'to get people into his gardens and wet them with squirts, to invite people to his country house and put things in their beds to make them itch, and twenty other such pretty fancies.'   He was famous for his love of frolic and his poker-face; and he possessed, to a mild degree, most of the characteristics of the Rake.

THE RAKE OF THE MID-18TH CENTURY had a colourful ancestry.   His predecessors had been those Sons of Belial who, under flamboyant names, had whooped in packs up and down the midnight streets of London, slitting noses, breaking the heads of watchmen, or rolling belated women about in barrels.   But by 1750 he had become less of a terror, if not less of a nuisance, than the Mohocks of the 'twenties.   He is represented in contemporary pamphlets as a young man of birth, wealth, and elegance, fresh from the Grand Tour of Europe and loosed on London. He was usually to be found at Marybone or Vaux Hall, aggressively drunk from ten in the morning onwards, pursuing every woman within range ('for I do love the little rogues hellishly!')   He lost huge sums at the faro tables of the *Savoir-Vivre* or playing hazard at the Cocoa-Tree. With a crazy exuberance he amused himself with wagers, impromptu races down Pall Mall or Fleet Street in sedan chairs, or donkey races in the Tyburn Road.   He swaggered outrageously, larding his speech, like Bobadil, with 'tall oaths': 'The devil take the hindmost is always my way of travelling. The moment I dismounted, down dropt Dido, by Jove: and here am I alive and merry, my old boy!'   At nightfall he sallied forth in full cry, with packs of his fellow Bloods and Nerves, rounding up stragglers and burying them under cabbage leaves at Covent Garden, unhooking shop signs, or fighting the hackney coachmen, who used to cruise patiently up and down the streets removing helpless nobles from the gutters and driving them safely home to an inn.   If his money was not all spent in gambling or fantastic wagers, it went on the Seraglios, on Burgundy at White's or Bung-Eye in the gin-shops.   Then, according to the moralists, he fell into the hands of the usurers of Tower Hill, and ended up penniless and exhausted in gaol.

The qualifications for becoming a full-blown Rake or Blood, as dis-tinct from the mere Baby-Buck, were wealth and breeding.   Those who possess power without responsibility can hardly avoid feeling superior to the run of people, who must work to live; and one way of showing superiority is by the practical joke, which is also a gesture of contempt. *'Ye're all Bottled!'*   The common Cit was an inferior being, and to 'roast' him now and then was not only an amusement but a necessity, like fox-hunting: it kept the vermin properly under.   So the pranks of the young Rake usually took the form of the Hoax, though the word was not used till towards the end of the century.

In 1740 four young Bloods of quality had dressed up as highwaymen, held up a coach and killed one of the ostlers in a struggle.   Ten years later London was terrified by a crazy trooper who prophesied the city's total destruction in an earthquake; and two sparks knocked at doors up and down the streets, calling out in a Watchman's voice: 'Past 4 o'clock, and a dreadful earthquake!'   Seven hundred coaches were counted streaming past Hyde Park into the country, and enterprising dressmakers sold earthquake gowns for those who wished to sleep in the open parks till the scare was over.   The 'wicked' Lord Lyttelton advertised his own death and circulated copies of a mock last will and testament; Hellgate Barrymore used to leave coffins lying about, with macabre dummies in them, or with Hooper the prizefighter dressed as a clergyman at his side would march a band of revellers about the streets of Wargrave in their

THE ILLITERATE MACARONI.
of 21 Learning his A.B.C.

shirts. The Man in the Bottle was one way of snapping one's fingers in the face of convention.

The Hoax was one way; another was by blasphemy and the Black Arts. The Rake was associated in the popular mind with tales of dubious clubs and the kind of orgy known as Nameless. But Rationalism, the Royal Society and Defoe's *History of the Devil* had turned the black Master of the Coven into Old Nick, the churchyard bogey, and even the Hellfire Rakes of the 'fifties were only playing at a schoolboy Satanism behind a cloud of rumour.

One of the more notorious hoaxes of the century, when Jack Wilkes introduced a horned and soot-covered baboon into the secret rites at Medmenham, broke up the Hellfire Club in 1763. The members of it were, for the most part, public figures who could not afford a too scandalous publicity. What had brought them together was the free-masonry of travel. The education of the wealthy was finished by the Grand Tour, and year after year young men met in Paris or Rome or Constantinople to argue about art or to discuss the latest extravagance of fashion. It is not surprising that they should have formed clubs like the Divan or the Dilettanti; nor that the exuberance which expressed itself in strange rites and practical jokes should express itself also in clothes. It was the Grand Tour which created the Macaroni Club.

John Hawkesworth, in 1753, distinguished eight degrees between the Greenhorn and the Blood, between the fool who could not open his mouth without a 'Rat it!' or a 'Zookers!' to the Joyous Spirit, whose frolics finished with the brothel or the gaol. One of these eight was the Jemmy, or Jessamy, the jasmine-scented fop, the next step in whose evolution was the Toledo-sworded, tavern-gambling Smart. As the uproarious violence of the Rakes declined, the Jessamy emerged, mincing, in their wake.

He called himself, in 1760, a Macaroni; and with those other Bucks whom he had known in Naples he formed the Macaroni Club. The word was a symbol for wit, taste, travel, and polite learning. The Club was the arbiter of the fine arts and Genteel Sciences. Above all, it was the arbiter of Fashion.

The habits of smashing windows, invoking the devil or making loud noises at night had always been accompanied by a passion for dressing-up, sometimes in Oriental costume, sometimes in elaborate disarray. But while the Bloods had displayed their personalities chiefly by their pranks, the Macaronis displayed theirs chiefly by their clothes. They tripped about the streets with a peculiar pointed strut, like dancing-masters; but they preferred to lounge at street corners, for they hated exercise.[1] Not

[1]*Boswell :* You are a delicate Londoner—you are a Macaroni; you can't ride.
Johnson : Sir, I shall ride better than you. I was only afraid I should not find a horse able to carry me. *Life* (ed. Hill), 1887, V, 84. (Aug., 1773.)

THE RIDICULE.

for them the shrill Halloo, the chase of the fleeing Watchman, the brick through the dark window. Their existence was as elaborately pointless as a mechanical doll's. Horace Walpole spoke contemptuously of the travelled youths with curls and spying-glasses, and satirists referred to them as objects of the neutral gender. 'It talks without meaning, it smiles without pleasantry, it eats without appetite, it rides without exercise, it wenches without passion.'

There were notable exceptions. George Villiers, whom Mrs Montague called the 'Prince of Maccaronis' was one of the heroes of the *Macaroni and Theatrical Magazine.* Others were Barrymore, Petersham, and even the remarkable Horne Tooke. No doubt many of the Macaronis concealed beneath silks and lace and expressions of unendurable boredom the spirit of Sir Percy Blakeney. But the twin passions of the true exquisite were his wagers and his wardrobe.

THE MACARONIS DID NOT BLOSSOM fully till the early 'seventies, and by 1776 the word, according to Fanny Burney, was no longer fashionable. At their height they were the scandal and delight of the caricaturists. They crowded the newly opened Pantheon in the Oxford Road, they yawned with ennui over the card tables of Almack's, they discussed the Genteel Sciences with lisps and drawls and simpers. Some, exhausted by the effort of speech, adopted the practice of humming continuously 'in a *Piano.*' They neither swore nor puffed clouds of tobacco, like the Rakes of the previous generation. The one was too great an exertion; the other would have spoiled their perfume, the jasmine on their handkerchiefs or, on their faces, Mr Giles's fine Compound, at a guinea an ounce.

No effort, however, was too great where clothes were concerned, and by the late 'sixties the Macaronis had already become the leaders of outrageous fashion. The pink satins, the lemon-yellow Jessamy gloves, the green silk stockings, the wigs stuck with jewelled pins—all these developed into such extravagancies that the human being behind the frills and ruffles, the saucer-like buttons and enormous buttonholes, could be but dimly guessed at. The wigs grew taller and more involved. Some of them were three feet high, all wreathed in powdered loops and swags and scrolls. From the Macaroni's pocket drooped the lace handkerchief; his right hand rested on a tall cane, festooned with golden cords and tassels; his face was patched and painted, his shoes invisible behind great steel or silver buckles. The crowning absurdity was the tiny hat perched on the towering wig:

> *Five pounds of hair they wear behind,*
> *The ladies to delight oh,*
> *Their senses give unto the wind,*
> *To make themselves a fright oh!*
> *This fashion who does e'er pursue,*
> *I think a simple toney,*
> *For he's a fool say what you will,*
> *Who is a Macaroni!*

Although they influenced fashion, invented the coloured stock, and even anticipated the trouser, the Macaronis did not last for much more than two decades. In the early 'seventies the events of the American War disturbed what Wraxall calls the 'general tranquillity of society'; by 1781 Charles James Fox, who had once been a leader of fashion, was wearing his threadbare blue frock-coat and buff waistcoat, and new ideas about equality eclipsed the old splendours. The gold-laced hats and frocks for morning dress, which had been the fashion of one generation, became the theatre-properties of the next, and men with heads cropped and powderless went about in mere pantaloons. For a while, in the early nineteenth century, Corinthian Tom and his fellow-sparks revived the hilarious frolics of the Bloods, whose last shadowy descendant was perhaps Gilbert the Filbert, exquisite for a brief moment before the first World War engulfed him.

The Rake was a phenomenon which appeared partly because of a London at once large enough to contain the world[1] yet small enough for a man to know all the Somebodies by sight, and partly because of an England still ordered under the rigid hierarchies of wealth and breeding. He began to disappear when London grew too big for him, when wealth and power shifted to the commercial middle-class, and when the idea of corporate responsibility took a firmer hold on men's minds. Possibly also the development of the Public School helped his extinction by canalizing the need for noise, exercise, and personal display in the tasselled caps and coloured stockings of the First XV. The words 'Blood' and 'Nerve' linger to this day among the fossils of schoolboy slang.

Whatever the cause, the Rakes have disappeared. And if they had been no more than noisy toughs or mincing epicenes, there would be little reason to mourn their passing. But they were much more than merely that. Among the anonymous rowdies were men of culture and imagination: great public figures, like Wilkes or Charles James Fox: patrons of the arts: men of taste, who, with a magnificence not since equalled, laid out those elegant gardens and built those Palladian mansions whose grandeur and serenity seem today an ironic commentary on the uses to which so many of them have been put. The huzzas, the pot-house songs, even the most monstrous imbecilities of Dandyism, were expressions of an intellectual as well as of a physical energy, an energy which found its outlet in the solemnities of politics as vigorously as in the frivolities of fashion.

The Practical Joke, I have said, was one way of proving superiority to ordinary folk. It should not be forgotten that a number of these rakes and rowdies were, in fact, superior; and had no need to prove it. Too much has perhaps been said about their pranks and follies. In reading of their crazes for what Mrs Montague called 'fat-headed Pagodas,' for embellishing their grounds with 'Hermetick Retreats' and their lakes with carved Sea-Gods 'entwined on their Ouzey Couch,' one sometimes forgets the splendour of the great terraces of Boughton, which was the miniature Versailles of the Governor of the West Indies. And the Governor of the West Indies, the trusted and responsible servant of King George, was that Duke of Montagu who so successfully pulled the world's leg on January 16, 1749, at the Little Theatre in the Hay-Market.

So that to see such men as him only as freaks or buffoons, or to judge and condemn them for their frolics without remembering their qualities, would be to turn them into caricatures, would be in fact not less foolish than to try to fit a whole human being into a tavern quart-bottle.

[1]Horace Walpole's World, that is, which (he says somewhere) was 'very amusing last Thursday evening.'

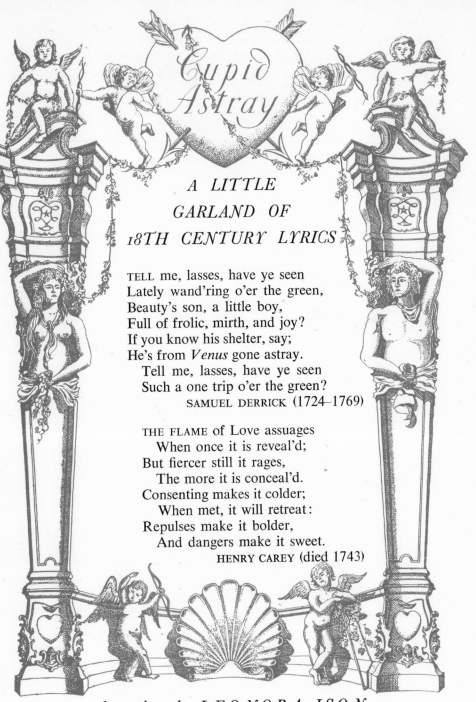

Cupid Astray

A LITTLE
GARLAND OF
18TH CENTURY LYRICS

TELL me, lasses, have ye seen
Lately wand'ring o'er the green,
Beauty's son, a little boy,
Full of frolic, mirth, and joy?
If you know his shelter, say;
He's from *Venus* gone astray.
   Tell me, lasses, have ye seen
   Such a one trip o'er the green?
       SAMUEL DERRICK (1724–1769)

THE FLAME of Love assuages
   When once it is reveal'd;
But fiercer still it rages,
   The more it is conceal'd.
Consenting makes it colder;
   When met, it will retreat:
Repulses make it bolder,
   And dangers make it sweet.
       HENRY CAREY (died 1743)

decorations by LEONORA ISON

THE FAN

FOR VARIOUS purpose serves the fan;
 As thus—a decent blind,
Between the sticks to peep at man,
 Nor yet betray your mind.

Each action has a meaning plain,
 Resentment's in the snap;
A flirt expresses strong disdain,
 Consent, a gentle tap.

All passions will the fan disclose,
 All modes of female art;
And to advantage sweetly shows
 The hand—if not the heart.

'Tis Folly's sceptre, first design'd
 By Love's capricious Boy,
Who knows how lightly all mankind
 Are govern'd by a toy.

ROBERT LLOYD (1733–1764)

On Some Snow
that melted on a lady's breast

THOSE ENVIOUS flakes came down in haste,
  To prove her breast less fair:
Grieving to find themselves surpass'd,
  Dissolv'd into a tear.

ANONYMOUS

(From Steele's *Poetical Miscellanies*, 1714)

Song

I SAW *Lucinda's* bosom bare,
  Transparent was the skin,
As through a crystal, did appear
  A beating heart within.

The beating heart transfix'd I saw,
  And yet the heart was stone;
I saw it bleed, and by the wound
  I thought it was mine own.

But O! when I perceiv'd it was
  Enshrin'd within your breast,
I knew 'twas yours: for mine, alas!
  Was never yet so blest!

JOHN SMITH (circa 1713)

139

A Nosegay for Laura

COME, YE FAIR ambrosial flowers,
Leave your beds, and leave your bowers,
Blooming, beautiful, and rare,
Form a posy for my fair;
Fair, and bright, and blooming be,
Meet for such a nymph as she.
Let the young vermilion rose
A becoming blush disclose;
Such as *Laura's* cheeks display,
When she steals my heart away.
Add carnation's varied hue,
Moisten'd with the morning dew:
To the woodbine's fragrance join
Sprigs of snow-white jessamine.

Add no more; already I
Shall, alas! with envy die,
Thus to see my rival blest,
Sweetly dying on her breast.

THE REVEREND FRANCIS FAWKES (1720–1777)

SONG

WHENEVER, *Chloe*, I begin
  Your heart like mine to move,
You tell me of the crying sin
  Of unchaste lawless love.

How can that passion be a sin,
  Which gave to *Chloe* birth?
How can those joys but be divine,
  Which make a Heav'n on Earth?

To wed, mankind the priests trepann'd
  By some sly fallacy,
And disobey'd God's great command,
  Increase and multiply.

You say that love's a crime: content:
  Yet this allow you must,
More joy's in Heav'n when one repent
  Than over ninety just.

Sin then, dear girl, for Heaven's sake,
  Repent and be forgiv'n;
Bless me, and by repentance make
  A Holiday in Heav'n.

PHILIP DORMER STANHOPE, EARL OF CHESTERFIELD (1694–1773)

SONG

THOUGH, FLAVIA, to my warm desire
  You mean no kind return;
Yet still with undiminish'd fire
  You wish to see me burn.

Averse my anguish to remove,
  You think it wond'rous right
That I love on, for ever love,
  And you for ever slight.

But you and I shall ne'er agree,
  So, gentle Nymph! adieu!
Since you no pleasure have for me,
  I'll have no pain for you.

ANONYMOUS

(From Lewis's *Miscellaneous Poems by Several Hands*, 1730)

SONG

SEE, SEE, she wakes, *Sabina* wakes!
  And now the sun begins to rise;
Less glorious is the morn that breaks
  From his bright beams, than her fair eyes.

With light united, day they give,
  But different fates ere night fulfil;
How many by his warmth will live!
  How many will her coldness kill!

WILLIAM CONGREVE (1670–1729)

142

CHLOE

Chloe's the wonder of her sex,
 'Tis well her heart is tender;
How might such killing eyes perplex,
 With virtue to defend her?

But nature, graciously inclin'd
 With liberal hand to please us,
Has to her boundless beauty join'd
 A boundless bent to ease us.

   GEORGE GRANVILLE, BARON LANSDOWNE (1667–1735)

AN EPITAPH ON A GALLANT LADY

O'er this Marble drop a tear,
 Here lies fair *Rosalinde*.
All mankind was pleas'd with her,
 And she with all mankind.

   THE HON MRS MARY MONK (died 1715)

143

Of Toby Jugs, otherwise Toby Fillpots, of the Staffordshire potters who first manufactured these characteristic expressions of 18th century English life, and of their long hold on the public.

The Surprising History of the Fillpot Family

by JOHN HADFIELD

The King Hal Toby Jug

ONE of the pleasures of studying or collecting works of art is to relate them to the social history of their period. Ceramics, particularly, have always been rich in allusion to contemporary customs, personalities and events. And in no field of ceramic art is the relation closer than in Staffordshire pottery—a subject of popular interest today, but one which has had comparatively little attention from the historian.

Early Staffordshire pottery was far from being a *fine* art. It was the product of people who made things primarily for use, and who were for the most part simple, uneducated men, isolated from metropolitan and cosmopolitan influences. Their wares owed little to conventional art forms, except for the occasional influence of 'foreigners' like Voyez. Most of their models expressed the rustic and provincial life of their times. They were made for sale to farmers, shopkeepers, innkeepers, and the lesser gentry. Staffordshire jugs, figures, and chimneypiece ornaments are a much more faithful reflection of their period than the sophisticated pieces of Bow and Chelsea porcelain, which were often derived from Continental models and designed for the cultivated taste of 'persons of quality.'

The early history of the Staffordshire potters, apart from Wedgwood, is still largely hidden in obscurity. Many chapters remain to be written —perhaps never will be written, since the potters themselves were so often 'small men' who left no records of their work and little documentation of their wares. It is impossible, however, to appreciate their achievement fully without some knowledge of their background.

Much of the land in the Potteries was from early times split up into small holdings, which gave security of tenure and unusual opportunity for initiative. As Lord Wedgwood wrote in his book on *Staffordshire Pottery and its History,* 'these early master potters were handy men of many trades. They made their pots in sheds at the "backsides" of their dwelling houses, alongside the cow-shed. They dug their own clay, often in front of their own front doors. The Wedgwoods at least owned and dug their own coal . . . It was a peasant industry, carried on by the family, among the pigs and fowls.' Shaw, in his *Staffordshire Potteries,* describes the manufactory of Thomas Whieldon, one of the Grand Old Men of the craft, as 'a small range of low buildings, all thatched.' He goes on to say that Whieldon's early productions were 'knife hafts for the Sheffield cutlers: and snuff boxes for the Birmingham hardwaremen, to finish with hoops, hinges, and springs; which he himself usually carried in a basket to the tradesmen.'

In 1754 the highest wage paid to the workmen was eight shillings a week. The whole community was isolated and self-contained. The first Josiah Wedgwood recorded that early in the century there was only one horse and one mule kept at Hanley, 'no carts scarcely in the country, coals carried upon men's backs.' The industry developed greatly in size and output during the century, helped by the cheap water transport of the Trent and Mersey Canal, which was completed in 1777. But even in Victorian times (and later) the people of the Potteries were famed for their independence. They were suspicious of strangers, jealous of their secret processes. Their lives were lived in a remote world, circumscribed by the chapel, the ale-house, the pot-bank where they worked, and the uplands where they repaired with their whippets.

From this secluded, unpromising field, far from the fashionable world of Court, coffee-house, and basset table, came a profusion of delightful

L

ceramic conceits—figures, groups, jugs, animals, plaques—many of which have an originality of form, a freshness of conception, and a freedom of modelling that is often lacking in the products of the more famous factories of London, Bristol and the Continent.

PERHAPS THE MOST CHARACTERISTIC, as it certainly is the most popular, product of the Staffordshire potteries is the Toby jug. There can be few cottage homes in England—and very few taverns and alehouses—that have not housed a Toby or two in the last 150 years. And it has steadily appreciated in the estimation of the connoisseur until today a fine example of a Ralph Wood Toby Fillpot is the supreme prize of the pottery collector, and its value can run into hundreds of pounds.

And yet, how little we know of the derivation and introduction of the Toby jug! It appeared, at some time in the latter part of the eighteenth century, from the kilns of the Woods and Thomas Whieldon, and later was copied and adapted by others. But hardly any of the early models were marked, and their origin must largely be determined by their glazes.

Vessels in human form are, of course, to be found in almost all periods of history. Ewers modelled as heads or decorated with masks survive from mediaeval times, and in the seventeenth century the bearded Bellarmine jug, named after Cardinal Bellarmine, had wide currency. But the Toby jug is essentially an expression of eighteenth-century English life. A full-length but foreshortened figure, with a jug of ale in one hand and a cup or a pipe in the other, he sits, his rubicund face grinning contentedly, a sturdy, shrewd but comfortable John Bull—without John Bull's truculence. He is hollow, and holds a full pint of ale. He has a handle behind him (sometimes curiously shaped as a caryatid). The brim of his hat forms the rim of the jug, and the crown of his hat forms a lid.

Why the name Toby Fillpot? As recently as 1915 that pioneer in pottery lore, Frank Falkner, wrote in the Catalogue of *The Earle Collection of Early Staffordshire Pottery* that 'the name Toby, now quite a generic term, is probably adopted from Sterne's immortal Uncle Toby, the real hero of *Tristram Shandy*.' Uncle Toby undoubtedly became something of a proverbial figure, but although his name acquired in the course of time some loose association with Toby jugs it is doubtful whether he provided the origin of the name.

It is now generally believed that the name derives from a poem by Francis Fawkes (1720–1777), entitled 'The Metamorphosis, or Toby Reduc'd.' Fawkes was a clergyman who attained some fame as a translator of Anacreon and Theocritus. 'The Metamorphosis, or Toby Reduc'd' was first printed in 1761 in his volume of *Original Poems and Translations*. It is doubtful, however, if Toby Fillpot would have achieved immortality merely as a result of the publication of this book, for it had no very extensive circulation and was not reprinted. Toby owes his popular fame to the reappearance of the poem as the subject of an engraving, published by Carington Bowles, after a design by Robert Dighton. The jovial toper depicted in the engraving, with bulging paunch and stocky legs, a foaming jug of ale in one hand and a churchwarden in the other, is the prototype of all Tobies. The poem, as it appears below the engraving, runs as follows:

Dear Tom, this brown Jug that now foams with mild Ale,
(In which I will drink to sweet Nan of the Vale),
Was once Toby Fillpot, a thirsty old Soul
As e'er drank a Bottle or fathom'd a Bowl.
In boozing about 'twas his praise to excell,
And among Jolly Topers he bore off the Bell.

It chanc'd as in Dog-days he sat at his ease,
In his Flow'r woven Arbour as gay as you please,
With a Friend and a Pipe, puffing Sorrow away,
And with honest old Stingo was soaking his Clay,
His breath Doors of Life on a sudden were shut
And he died full as big as a Dorchester Butt.

His Body, when long in the Ground it had lain
And time into Clay had resolv'd it again
A Potter found out in its Covert so snug
And with part of fat Toby he form'd this brown Jug
Now sacred to Friendship and Mirth and mild Ale.
So here's to my lovely sweet Nan of the Vale.

Fawkes himself did not take full credit for this pleasant conceit. He describes it, in his book, as 'imitated from the Latin of Hieronymus Amaltheus.' Clearly, however, it was the lilt and homely joviality of Fawkes's verse which was responsible for the conceit tickling the public fancy. It became one of the popular songs of the day. It was introduced by John O'Keefe into his comic opera, *The Poor Soldier*, at Covent Garden in 1783. Subsequently it was sung with great success by John Johnstone and Charles Incledon. It was even quoted by Canning in the House of Commons during a debate on Catholic Emancipation.

How did Fawkes's poem come to the ear of the Staffordshire potter who made the first Toby jug? When? Which of the potters was it? These are questions to which it is by no means easy to find answers.

Mr W. B. Honey and other authorities believe that many of the potters took their models from popular prints; but it seems almost certain that

A Characteristic Toby Jug   *Martha Gunn, the Gin Woman*
BY RALPH WOOD   BY RALPH WOOD

the first Toby jug was made *before* Carington Bowles issued his print of Toby Fillpot. One or two jugs bear the mark R. WOOD, which is believed to denote the elder Ralph Wood, who died in 1772. Mr Wolliscroft Rhead, in *The Earthenware Collector,* suggested that the early Tobies made by Thomas Whieldon were probably made even before the appearance of *Tristram Shandy* in 1759. I do not know what evidence he had to support this statement. If we accept the derivation of the Toby model from Fawkes's poem we cannot admit of any true Toby jug being made before 1761, when the poem was first printed.

Whatever the early chronology may be, it is certain that the best 'pedigree' Tobies were produced by Whieldon and the Ralph Woods, father and son, between about 1770 and 1790. Tobies were also made by Hollins, Neale, Davenport, Walton, Pratt, and other potters. I would hazard the opinion, however, that only those of the Pratt type, with their vivid under-glaze mottling or zig-zag decorations in yellow and blue, can compare in quality with the early Whieldon and Ralph Wood jugs.

The merit of the Wood and Whieldon Tobies lies partly in their spon-

Lord Howe
BY RALPH WOOD

The Planter or Sailor Toby
BY RALPH WOOD

taneity and sureness of modelling, and partly in the unsurpassed purity
and softness of their coloured glazes. The range of colours was restricted
to those made available by metallic oxides—yellow (iron oxide), green
(copper oxide), blue (cobalt oxide), and a rich purplish brown (manganese
oxide). No red was obtainable. The metallic oxides were mixed with
a translucent lead glaze, applied with a brush, and fired at a high temperature. As a result the colour appears to be both *in* and yet *under* the translucent glaze. Vivid though it may be, it has a reticence of tone that is
never achieved by the harsh over-glaze enamels which gradually replaced
the under-glaze process after 1780.

The original Toby jug, whether made by the elder Ralph Wood or
Thomas Whieldon, quickly became a recognized convention. It was
reproduced in large quantities, with only minor variations of size or detail.
Yet although the model remained substantially the same the colouring
of almost every jug was different. Of the many variants of the original
Toby Fillpot perhaps the finest model—as it is one of the most costly
today—is that with a shield at the side, inscribed 'It is all out Then fill
him agian' (*sic*).

The popularity of the original Fillpot led inevitably to the invention of different types. Strictly, I suppose, they should not be called Toby jugs, but the name has acquired a generic meaning, and the variants that appeared before the turn of the eighteenth century belonged recognizably to the original Fillpot family.

Some of Toby's closer relatives are distinguished only by the style of their clothes. 'The Convict,' for instance, is much like his respectable fellows but has a broad arrow painted on his vest. Two very rare Tobies in the famous collection of Captain Price were conventional (if crude) in shape, but one held an open book instead of the usual jug or tankard and the other held a vessel of wine over a fire between his knees. Sometimes a dog—occasionally even a goat—reclines at Toby's feet.

It has often been assumed that Toby satirizes the gross, self-indulgent country parson who was a familiar figure of the times and was portrayed in Fielding's Parson Trulliber. There appears to be no justification for this belief, which probably arises from confusion with the well-known Staffordshire figures of the Vicar and Moses in the pulpit and the Parson and Clerk drunkenly supporting one another on their way to church. At least one Toby, however, has a particular resemblance to a parson. It has been called the 'Parson Toby' when the coat is black, and the 'Unfrocked Parson' when the coat is coloured. But the same figure is also known as 'Dr. Johnson.' There is undoubtedly a resemblance; and Johnson, after all, was a Staffordshire worthy.

Of the types which differ substantially from the original some are seated and others are standing figures. The 'Hearty Good Fellow,' who stands, slightly swaying, with one arm flung across his chest in a flamboyant gesture, is a popular traditional model, but his tree-stump background seems somewhat incongruous, his modelling is often weak, and I admit to a prejudice against standing figures. Surely an essential characteristic of a Toby should be that he sits, even if his seat, like that of Walton's sailor, is a chest labelled 'Dollars,' or a barrel like that of Ralph Wood's charming 'Lord Howe.'

The naval splendours of the age were reflected not only in the 'Lord Howes' and 'Rodneys,' but also in three distinctive and exceedingly rare figures called the 'Midshipmite.' These have a primitive quality that reflects that of the pew-groups of the first half of the century. No Toby is more enchanting than the 'Midshipmite' playing a fiddle. How far removed he is from the splendour of that other rarity, the famous 'King Hal,' a magnificent piece of pottery, decorated with pale blue, buff, and olive green glazes, which is supposed to represent George IV, when Prince of Wales, impersonating Bluff King Hal at a masquerade in Brighton.

Another jug which has more trustworthy associations with Brighton is the female Toby, which represents Martha Gunn, the 'gin woman,' who, as a bathing attendant at Brighton, used to dip Prinny in the sea when he was a boy. The Ralph Wood model of Martha Gunn, with Prince of Wales's feathers moulded on her bonnet and a gin bottle in her hand, is a lovely work of art, and, I believe, has the distinction of fetching the highest price ever made by a Toby jug at auction—six hundred guineas in 1918. (Collectors need not despair, however, as a perfect example of this jug was sold at Sotheby's in 1948 for the slightly less intimidating sum of £200.)

BUT THESE ARE THE FREAKS, the 'sports' of the Fillpot family. Let us return, glancing as we go at the quaint 'Royal Bargeman,' with his full breeches and a base moulded with a medallion head of George III, to the more homely types, such as the 'Thin Man'—a most decided personality—and the 'Squire,' a lean patrician figure, with pipe in mouth, seated in a corner chair (and, incidentally, more frequently faked than almost any other Toby).

Even in its early days, as these notes may indicate, the Fillpot family had several branches. Throughout the nineteenth century they multiplied, though most of the descendants were of inferior stock. In our own century the mass-producer, the imitator, and the deliberate faker have all added to the Toby population. Most modern Tobies have little to recommend them aesthetically, though a pair representing Mr Churchill and Mr Roosevelt will have a certain historic value in years to come.

There is nothing surprising, however, in the deterioration of the product as a work of art; the same process can be seen in almost all the applied arts. The fact remains that Toby Fillpot still maintains his hold upon the sentiment of the public.

Is mere quaintness the secret of Toby's popularity? Perhaps there is a deeper underlying appeal. It defies analysis, and, like the British character, is woven from many apparently disconnected strands. One strand might be traced back through the history of the English taverns and Toby's traditional association with the 'friendship, mirth and mild ale' of Francis Fawkes's poem. Another might take us into the folk-lore of the name Toby—through Sterne's Uncle Toby, whose influence on our story we have already noted, to Shakespeare's Sir Toby Belch, another 'thirsty old soul' (Toby is still a favourite nickname for the rotund and rubicund). Again we might venture into the obscure realms of anthropomorphic imagery. It is no new thing for man to make idols in his own image.

Perhaps, in the middle of that century which more than any other formed and fixed our national character, an unthinking Staffordshire potter happened to fashion in clay something that has since come to be regarded as one of the *lares et penates* of the British people.

Some Eighteenth Century Worthies

drawings & clerihews by NICOLAS BENTLEY

MRS THRALE

*It put Mrs Thrale
Completely beyond the pale
When she became the totsey
Of Signor Piozzi*

SIR JOSHUA REYNOLDS

'You're a wizard—by Gosh, you are!'
They said to Sir Joshua,
Comparing his Countess Clancarty
With the original old party.

LORD CHESTERFIELD

Lord Chesterfield
Thought it best to yield
To no form of vice
That was not quite nice.

LORD NORTH

Lord North
Was easily raised to wrath
If you were such a noodle
As to hum Yankee Doodle.

CHARLES JAMES FOX

Fox was all right
As long as he wasn't tight;
That is to say,
For the first half hour of the day.

CAPTAIN COOK

Captain Cook
Was told to sling his hook,
When he first attempted to land
On Tasmania's golden strand.

THOMAS GRAY

There was something slightly fey
About Thomas Gray,
As you might have assumed
From his meditations on the entombed.

*Concerning the musical comedy empire of Napoleon III,
which was set to music by Offenbach and dressed by an
Englishman, Charles Frederick Worth, who dressed
every queen in Europe except Queen Victoria.*

Monsieur Chiffon; or The Lad From Lincolnshire

by DONALD MacANDREW

WHEN, in 1848, the July Monarchy collapsed and Louis Philippe, the hated bourgeois King, fled in terror, Louis Napoleon, nephew of the great Napoleon, was on December 10 elected president of the Second French Republic.

But it was only a Republic so-called. In reality political chaos reigned, and the squabblings of Legitimists, Orleanists, Red-Republicans, reactionaries, revolutionaries, Communists drowned certain Cassandra voices which proclaimed that this place-seeker, true to his

Napoleonic code, was out to grab the French throne. Four years later, however, it was given to him.

So eager were most people to get back to work, and so weary of uncertainty were they all, that they voted for the devil they knew, sooner than face the unknown demon of Socialism. In December 1852 he who had been the chief spokesman of Republicanism was crowned Emperor, and absolute ruler, of France.

But Napoleon III knew that his position was a shaky one. The public had accepted him as Emperor to gain peace at the price of its political ideals, and unless it got it, and prosperity too, it would again split up into factions and turn him out. So he began to make concessions. Louis Philippe had been stingy. He went the other way. He transformed the dark, smelly, mediaeval Paris of Louis Philippe, with its tortuous lanes and rat-infested tenements, into a city of broad white avenues ending in vistas, tree-lined boulevards, gardens, palaces. Paris became the world's most modern city, a mid-nineteenth century New York. Louis Philippe had starved Paris of pageantry and spectacle. His successor gorged her with military reviews and processions: the *Cent Gardes,* all flashing swords and bobbing bearskins, galloping behind the Empress Eugénie's *calèche*; cannons booming; fireworks; fountains *en grandes eaux.* Paris became for the first time the pleasure city of Europe and even the hub of the world's trade.

The new boulevards and boulevard cafés were thronged with exotic foreigners, some of them making their pile from speculation, generally fraudulent, in connection with the city's improvements. The Court, too, was made up very largely of careerists. Napoleon III and Eugénie were cosmopolitan adventurers: naturally then, in their prosperity, former friends clustered round them. The French nobility avoided the Tuileries during the Bonaparte restoration, and European royalties, when at last they visited it, went away laughing. It was all so brand-new and glittering and parvenu, they said. For a moment they had stepped upon the stage of a musical comedy empire. It surely could not last long. The actors were opportunists making the most of their chances before the final, disastrous curtain fell.

Certainly the protagonists in the drama looked like characters in Opera Bouffe. The Emperor in frock coat and stovepipe hat, small, but with immense moustachios and imperial, was the typical comic-opera Frenchman of Tenniel's cartoons. His consort, 'the Spanish maypole,' with her sensational red-gold hair and swanlike grace, was a shepherdess, or a goddess, from Offenbach burlesque. Offenbach, the Frankfurt Jew, had composed the score to which galloped, waltzed, and can-can'd the whole operetta regime. His music (at least in the eyes of foreigners and of posterity) was the perpetual rollicking accompaniment to all the jigs and junketings—whether held in the Tuileries, the Mabille Gardens, or in the streets on *mardi gras*.

Its settings the musical comedy empire entrusted to Baron Haussmann. Though nobody today would deny the baron genius as a town-planner, the architecture of the monster palaces and hotels with which he flanked his boulevards seems swaggering and oppressive. The higher one looks the more does each seven- or eight-storied plaster façade burst into a florid jungle of ornament, Roman and Romanesque, Rennaissance, Rococo, Moorish. 'The Napoleon III style,' commented Zola—'the confused bastard of every style.' Haussmann and the *nouveaux riches* were letting their taste rip.

In matters of furniture and dress the Tuileries dictated during the early 'fifties. Apartments were decorated in the silk and boule and ormolu *Louis Seize* of the Empress's *salon rose*. Ladies wore the floating muslins and soft colours that Eugénie, mindful of her own transparent complexion, had decreed: pearl grey and Ispahan pink, Tèba, Eugénie blue. But as the 'fifties advanced certain daring spirits rebelled. They began to affect screaming macaw-like colours and jackets of mannish cut. 'The courtesan,' wailed a moralist, 'today sets the tone in everything.'

Who now should step forward and overrule the courtesans? What dress-designer of genius could marry, say, the fashionable magenta hue with reasonably good taste? In 1859 one Charles Frederick Worth, an Englishman born in Lincolnshire, supplied the answer.

CHARLES FREDERICK'S FATHER, a solicitor, had gained wealth and valuable business connections by marrying a woman of higher social standing and fortune than himself. But so disgruntled was old Worth with life in a particularly damp and foggy corner of England that he took to wildcat speculation with his wife's property—a thing one could do in those days. By the time Charles Frederick was eleven the money was all gone.

When the crash came the boy was obliged to quit school and work in a printer's office and his mother to swallow her gentlewoman's pride and become housekeeper to some rich cousins. Charles Frederick never forgave his father for causing his mother this humiliation. Though in after years he made him an annual allowance, he always refused to meet him or to hold any direct communication with him. Nor was his indignation entirely filial feeling for his mother. Another instinct was stirred. Unbecoming beyond words it seemed to Charles Frederick that a lady, a member of an old English county family, a Quincey of Quincey, should be reduced to drudging for a livelihood.

He was, it will be seen, a boy of a romantically-determined character.

M

Ladies, high-born and beautiful, were the lilies in the field of life for him.

When, after a year's misery at the Lincoln printing office, he became a shop-assistant at Allenby's, a big London textile firm—a job which he infinitely preferred—he spent all his leisure hours at the National Portrait Gallery and at Hampton Court Palace with a sketchbook copying portraits of Queen Elizabeth. She, as seemed only proper, was more gloriously attired than Solomon. And wherever she went she must have occupied a royal amount of space. Over her broad farthingale her painted velvet skirt spread for nearly a yard from either hip. Her heavy robe of state flowed the length of a staircase in her wake. Even now, at thirteen, Worth was having visions of one day himself designing huge stiff dresses for Empresses and Queens. And, since all his leisure was spent in solitude, he being too fastidious or, it could be said, too much of a snob to join the other shop assistants in their Cockney outings, these visions had scarcely appeared before they possessed him utterly.

Besides being a dreamer the lad had quick parts and business acumen, gifts early revealed and rapidly cultivated from his having been thrown on to the world while still a child. At fourteen he had become a cashier at Allenby's, sixteen found him in the selling department at Swan and Edgar's, while at nineteen, deciding to make a clean break with the past, he suddenly threw up everything and went to Paris. Only in Paris, he felt, could his taste and abilities find their full expression. He was fully confident that, once he had learnt French, and thoroughly Parisianized himself, his experience in dressmaking both as salesman and clerk, would, with his genius, soon float him to the top.

Paris and those richly dressed portraits of Queen Elizabeth were, he lived to tell his grandson, the two motivating influences of his early career. And of nobody who ever lived is it truer that outside his career he was nothing. Literature, sport, politics—even friends in other professions: all must go lest they disturb his dream of one day being Court-dressmaker to the whole world. Not till 1858, thirteen years after his arrival in Paris when he opened his own dressmaking house, did he allow himself to marry. Worth had met his bride-to-be three years before when he was head salesman at Gagelin's, the big silk mercers in the rue de Richelieu, where she was employed as a *demoiselle-de-magasin*—what we should today call a mannequin—and since it was Worth's business to sell the models she displayed, he and she were thrown together all day long. Between them they made Gagelin's sales gallop. Worth, now thirty, united outwardly boyish enthusiasm with remarkable powers of persuasion; while the distractingly pretty girl who moved like an angel gave the Indian shawls and casaquins in which Gagelin specialized a new elegance. Worth had persuaded the directors to add a tailoring department and fitting rooms to the establishment, and the idea was highly successful. When, in addition, he had increased Gagelin's, and his own, prestige by having a Court robe and train of his design included in the Exposition Universelle of 1855, the time seemed over-ripe to offer him a partnership.

But Worth, when at last the partnership was offered, refused it. He and a young salesman from another shop, a Swede named Bobergh, had decided to pool their resources—Worth's brains and Bobergh's recently inherited capital—and open their own *maison-de-couture*. Accordingly they leased an entresol in the rue de la Paix (not then, it should be explained, the *de luxe* shopping street of Europe, but a residential high-way hitherto untarnished by trade). And thus the House of Worth was launched.

As has been said, he married at the time the business opened. From the outset it had been agreed that his wife should be *demoiselle-de-magasin* in the new venture: the agreement was a kind of dowry on which the husband insisted. Though there could be no doubt of his love for the pretty, smiling French girl, or of her adoration of him, always he kept a professional eye on her points as a model for his new dresses.

One evening when the Worths were going to a public ball he produced an evening dress striped like a Dutch carnation and told her she must wear it. She refused—she would be so stared at, she said. The dress was pretty enough, but it was of satin, a material then only used for upholstery and the linings of carriages. Every other woman's dress would be of tarlatan, or of floating, cobwebby tulle. She liked new things, of course, after somebody else had introduced them, but she was too shy to be a pioneer. Worth was adamant. His wife wept and stormed and pleaded—and finally wore the dress. She was in agony throughout the evening, but she set a new fashion in ball dresses.

Shortly afterwards, when they were going to the Opera on a Patti night, he made a hairdresser bleach her head and cut her front hair and curl it in tiny ringlets on her forehead. He then placed her in the front seat of a box in full view of the auditorium. Every other woman in the theatre had her hair parted meekly down the centre and drawn madonna-wise over the ears . . . Next morning a boulevard journalist referred to 'Pretty Madame Worth and her Madame Récamier coiffure.' And the Récamier style became the mode.

But the most startling toilettes devised by her husband were those Madame Worth had to exhibit at the races. Among these was his *trotteuse*, or new walking crinoline, which she displayed on the Pré Catalan. This consisted of an overskirt of taffeta which could, by the pulling of an interior cord, be drawn up to reveal a vivid magenta petticoat with a hem only a few inches below the knee, while round the top of the petticoat the overskirt, like a theatre curtain, hung in alternate loops and tassels. The legs, encased in high-buttoned boots, emerged from the bell of the wide red petticoat like stamens from a giant fuchsia. With this Madame Worth sported a tiny rose-coloured parasol and pill-box hat. Every other woman, of course, wore a skirt down to the ground and a tall bonnet. There were stares and glares and giggles as poor Madame Worth paraded the course with her husband, he seeing to it that she demonstrated the working of the overskirt at least once every fifty yards. Yet the convenience of the short petticoat was even then per-ceived by some . . . Six months later, in December, the lake in the Bois was frozen. Suddenly in the midst of the hundreds of skaters appeared the Empress Eugénie, the Princess Metternich, the Duchesse de Morny, and Mademoiselle de Pourtalès, wearing fur toques, kilt-length skirts, Turkish trousers and fur-lined boots. Thus Royalty sealed the propriety of Worth's most daring experiment.

It was the Austrian Ambassadress, the Princess Pauline Metternich, who had imposed the new style on the Empress. If, initially, Paris and Queen Elizabeth were the inspirers of Worth's art, the Princess far more than poor, pretty, timid, smiling Madame Worth was the active feminine influence in his career.

IN THE CIRCLE of 'keepsake beauties' always surrounding the Empress, and selected by Eugénie moreover with care, since the whole must form a frame of brilliants to set off her own loveliness, the Princess Metternich, thick-lipped, brown-eyed and tawny, stood out curiously. She was not at all beautiful, certainly; her profile, we are told, was 'quite simian'; and her small, erect person in its vividly-hued garments resembled 'a barrel-organist's ape.' But she was sparkling, gay and insolent. She was also—except on that disastrous night when she tried to foist Wagner on to Offenbach-worshipping Paris—extremely intel-ligent. On the very day she arrived at Court, leaning on the arm of that handsome young husband whose diplomatic career she had made, she took the measure of the society in which she found herself. She felt that she with her Viennese gaiety could keep this shallow water dancing and scintillating.

And she did. Eugénie almost at once embarked on a headlong friend-ship with her, creating her *maîtresse de plaisir,* in other words Court jester. Some of the practical jokes that her '*chère* Pauline' staged seem depressingly caddish and silly to us, but this sort of lark was common form in 1860, and the Empress was amused. More pleasing are descrip-tions of the charades and *tableaux vivants* that Pauline directed. The first time that they had charades at the palace after her nomination, she substituted for the usual Biblical or mythological subject—some played-out *Toilette d'Esther* or *Jugement de Paris*—a street scene in which she herself, as a *cocher de fiacre*, with top hat, hands in trouser pockets, and cigar, entered singing, between puffs, an extremely *risqué* song. She went further yet. She engaged a can-can dancer from the Mabille Gardens and a *café chantant* singer to perform at the Tuileries and soon half the Court ladies were imitating the high kicks of Rigolboche and the sly innuendos of Therèsa. She loved to present bizarre novelties. And charming ones too. She retrieved her Wagner fiasco by presenting her countryman Johann Strauss, whose *Beau Danube* waltz immediately 'took.' And then there was Worth.

Worth was one of her earliest discoveries. A tremendous friendship immediately sprang up between them. It proved, moreover, enduring, being rooted, as they were gradually to discover, in a sort of consanguinity of mind. He and she, the bourgeois shopkeeper and the Austrian Ambassadress, met as artists, who, inhabiting far-apart but equally barren latitudes, were drawn to one another by mutual sympathy. For Worth, too, there was the lure, appreciative rather than snobbish, of the Princess's high aristocracy. For eccentric and insouciant though she was, and despite the perpetual cigar, she had at her command all the airs of a *grande dame*, not to mention a stentorian voice that could quell mutinies.

He did not harbour fatuous hopes of becoming her lover. He was a family man and she, who had enough personality to make any man she chose her grovelling slave, or any woman either, was deeply attached, and faithful, to her brilliant adoring young husband. He and she met on what may be called the plane of art (an elevation which did not prevent fitful squalls in the Worth *ménage* over that tiny, brown, cigar-smoking monkey woman).

For all that, the Princess's original motive in starting their friendship had been a practical one. She saw in Worth a dangerous rival in self-advertisement, a man who would infallibly get to the Tuileries before long with or without her aid, and who would supplant her there as arbiter of the mode. She determined to make herself his show-woman.

Worth's commissions at the Palace, then, were sponsored by the Princess. Soon a clique of Court ladies who spent all their time trying to keep pace with her were ordering frocks from Pauline's latest protégé. These, having too much money, nothing to do, and sawdust-filled heads, lived for fresh sensations, and since a new chignon or an opera cloak by Worth was always just that, there was fierce competition as to who should be first to parade it. Each of them would have stooped to anything only to do once what poor Madame Worth would have given worlds never to have to do at all. However, this success spelt release for her.   Never again need Madame Worth be pressed into the firm's service.   Henceforth her sultan could select one of his more striking-looking clients to exhibit each new confection.

Inevitably before long the Empress sent for Worth.   Her ladies had told her so much about him; would he make a dress for her?   She had already worn one of his styles for skating.   Today she was wearing another, for her skirts, like everybody else's just then, were distended by a sort of giant mousetrap fixed underneath them, and this, only three years since, had been a Worth patent.   Eugénie had worn the crinoline cage from its inception, had, indeed, initiated its vogue.   And here it may be well, before describing her interview with Worth, to explain how it was that she came to introduce it.

Throughout the 'thirties, 'forties, and 'fifties skirts had been growing wider and wider.   To attain the desired amplitude some eight or nine petticoats were needed, of which the upper two had to be starched to a board-like stiffness.   In addition panniers of horsehair were worn above the hips.   Doctors frowned at the mode.   The burden of stuff they said, and particularly the quantity of material bunched at the waist, made women with child faint, especially in hot weather.   Everybody knew, for instance, that the weight of the Empress's petticoats was to blame for her two miscarriages.

Here was a problem.   All Europe looked to Eugénie to set the fashion, and to fortify her reputation the utmost expansion of petticoat was necessary.   On the other hand Napoleon III wanted an heir.   What was to be done?   At last an English inventor had brought Worth a cashmere skirt mounted on extremely flexible steel frames.   The steels gave the fashionable spread without the superabundance of petticoats.   Apart from being hygienic the skeleton underskirt freed the legs for dancing: polka-ing, for example, need no longer be impeded by a thick wadding of linen clinging to the calves.   Worth improved on it, however, with his gored skirt swung from the waist and with its first steel only just above the knees.   By this a wider circumference was achieved than ever before. Naturally the silk mercers were delighted.   And Eugénie too.   Thanks to this invention she was able to wear a skirt twelve yards round the hem only a week before a successful lying-in.   Did she think today, three years later, when she summoned Worth to her presence, that she was to meet one who had been a sort of accoucheur at the Prince Imperial's birth?

Probably not, for she received him fully expecting to find him a cocksure young man in need of putting down.   Nor was she wholly at fault. Worth confronted her armed with a roll of Lyons brocade which he was determined she should wear.   The Lyons silk industry was declining— for ninety years there had been a craze for English fabrics, English

cottons. From the outset Worth had opposed this with all his revolutionary, and Francophil, ardour. He declined to use materials not of
French manufacture. Besides, the patterns woven into the Lyons
materials were the patterns he loved: big-flowered, traditional patterns
of the sixteenth century, as in portraits of Queen Elizabeth. So he did
what he could to give a new life to Lyons. His clients, fascinated by
the richly coloured silks that he displayed, purchased lavishly, but to
revive the ancient industry the great dress-buying public must be reached.
This meant securing the Empress's patronage.

Sartorially Eugénie was, except in the matter of the steel crinoline, a
conservative. She clung to her muslins and to what we today call 'pastel
shades.' So when the young man introduced, as he thought diploma-
tically, his Lyons brocade of cramoisie roses on dull gold, she smiled
and shook her head: 'I should look like a curtain,' she told him. '*Ah,
mais non, non, non, votre majesté.*' Worth was flattering but firm.
Eugénie polite but stubborn. Deadlock had been reached when the
Emperor suddenly joined them.

Eugénie at once appealed to him—unwisely. For the Emperor, always
defeated by his wife in their private tiffs, was quick to take advantage
of a third party's presence, and that a man's, to impose his will on her.
She must wear the Lyons brocade at such-and-such a forthcoming reception, he said; when trade so needed encouragement the Empress of the
French would wear the nation's products. And he gave the order. 'You
will revive the glory of Marie Antoinette,' he said to her. 'Marie
Antoinette was the last sovereign to wear silk brocade.' The flattery was
deft, for Eugénie, in her self-drammatizing way, identified herself with the
tragic Bourbon Queen.

When she appeared in the brocade dress at the reception there was a
chorus of adulation. Even Pauline, who was seldom guilty of overpraise,
complimented Eugénie on her likeness to Marie Antoinette. Within six
months the number of silk looms being operated at Lyons had doubled
and the output had quadrupled. Silk became the proper wear even in
the streets.

Eugénie created Worth *premier Ministre des Modes.* Soon the Czarina,
the Empress of Austria, the Princess of Wales, the Queens of Spain and
Sweden, and the black Queen of Madagascar were either visiting or ordering dresses from the shop in the rue de la Paix. Their patronage was
of course a magnificent asset, but Worth found royalties rather niggardly
and exacting. An order to dress an opera performance with Patti as
diva proved more remunerative. But the woman who bought more than
any five clients together was the red-headed English *demi-mondaine*
Cora Pearl. She, in one of her brief, bustling visits would stride through
the showrooms ordering dresses of any of the most expensive and bright-

coloured fabrics that happened, in her tearing haste, to catch her eye. All the Second Empire's preposterous chorus of lost ones were presently being habited by Worth.

LONG BEFORE 1870 THE House of Worth had swelled from a mere entresol to an emporium, *de luxe,* discreet, and occupying three floors. It ran along very gentlemanly lines. 'Handsome young men cravatted *à la Colin* stood here and there prepared to minister to the ladies' choice: but they did so in an easy nonchalant way without any of that terrible persuasiveness so characteristic of the *magasin des Nouveautés.* Again, passing to and fro were girls whose gowns, though black, represented the Master's latest creations in such wise that a customer had but to point to one of them to indicate what kind of puff or trimmings she desired. The first hand, elegant but tired-looking, was also there, welcoming the customers with great dignity.' Boxes of gardenias, making the atmosphere heavy, were placed in every fitting-room and reception-room, and on each step of the broad oak staircase. Upstairs in the exclusive *salle de lumière,* 'where the windows were hermetically sealed and the walls were all huge looking-glasses,' ball dresses and costumes for *bals masqués* were sewn on to their wearers 'by the light of a dozen gas-jets with movable shades.' Finally, there was the Master's private room, where at 5 p.m. Worth, in a velvet dressing-gown and fur cap, held court, dispensing Russian tea and cigars to the Princess Metternich, the Duchesse de Morny, and their crew.

'Worth was very amusing,' wrote one of his clients, 'and his popularity came quite as much from his personality as from his genius. He would look at me first for a long while without speaking. Then in an inspired and faraway voice he would say "Light gauze . . . silver grey . . . roses and leaves." And he would disappear. Then I had to go. The Master was engaged on his new masterpiece. To do him justice he never made a mistake with me. But no matter what I fancied I had to obey him. If he decided that I wear blue or green I had to do as I was told. He was a tyrant but we all adored him.'

' . . . Quite as much from his personality as from his genius': the Tuileries' ladies proved their love for him by dubbing him '*M. Chiffon*'— '*Faune des Toilettes*'—'*le haut baron de la couture,*' and, what with his Francophil tendencies Worth conceivably liked rather less, 'the Lincolnshire lad.' But it was all otherwise with their husbands. 'Whatever kind of a hermaphrodite is a man milliner?' the lions of the Jockey Club growled to one another. Worth to them was an unknown species. But they knew about his high prices, and how all their wives mobbed this self-satisfied-looking little man who had risen—so they averred—from a walk of life far below the sphere graced by themselves.

As to Worth, he wanted neither feminine flattery nor masculine sneers to think himself an ornament to any community. He was absolute King of Fashion. He looked upon lovely women as garden flowers in need of daily attentions from men, but like flowers they must also be helpless and let the gardener prescribe what was best for them. In sartorial matters, at all events, they must never be allowed a say. And this mingling of naïve idealism and masculine arrogance was apparent in Worth's manner. He was flattering and belligerent in turns, yet even his belligerence was unconsciously ingratiating. So was his round pink moon of a face broadly smiling above the stand-up collar and the much-too-tight frock coat. He looked so successful, so hugely pleased with himself; you saw it even in the outsize camellia in his buttonhole. It was impossible not to fall in with his rhythm. 'In every great artist,' he once told the Empress, after she had taxed him with his despotism, 'there is much of Napoleon. Me, I am a very great artist.'

His friendship with Princess Metternich, as has been shown, ran along firmer lines than his relations with his other clients. In all matters of taste, other than dress, she was a dictator as absolute as he, and her loyal subjects at the Tuileries, the Empress among them, bowed to all her whims. The only advice in non-professional matters that Worth ever listened to was the Princess's. Her quicksilver mind ran into all kinds of intellectual and artistic channels and, since she loved and revered Worth, she insisted on enjoying all her enthusiasms with him. Above everything she and her husband adored German music and the stage, and Worth developed a taste for concerts and serious drama from attendance at the Austrian Embassy. Nor, like the other Court ladies, did she pointedly ignore Madame Worth. She taught her to collect bibelots and introduced her to painters like Courbet and Corot. Thanks to her influence, their elder son was allowed to study in Corot's studio.

In return Worth designed for her 'the Pauline Metternich costume,' a two-piece dress in contrasting colours: allowed her to parade at Longchamps his first non-crinoline gown, with a train clinking all over with jet *passementerie*: and discussed with her his future projects. A frock 'embroidered all over with peacock feathers': a 'fretwork dress, scalloped, pinked and *decoupé*.' Dresses beautiful, preposterous, freakish.

WORTH CLOSED SHOP IN THE 1870 war, and next year, during the siege of Paris, transformed his workrooms into emergency wards to receive the overflow from the hospitals. The family lived in Havre at the time of the Commune, returning to Paris when peace was restored under the presidency of M. Thiers. Worth's reopened in 1874.

In 1878 Bobergh retired and Worth's two sons, after completing their military training, went into the firm; Jean, the artist, took over the designing department, and Gaston, who had studied law, managed the finances. They were hard-working, duty-loving young Frenchmen. They, their parents, wives, and later their children, all lived in concord in the house in the rue de Berri.

The firm now yielded £50,000 a year profit, dressed every queen in Europe except Queen Victoria, employed twelve hundred hands as against fifty when it opened, and maintained its leadership of fashion even after such rival *grands couturiers* as Doucet, Paquin, Felix, Redfern and Rouff had arisen. Yet his status as Grand Old Man of Fashion did not prevent Worth being discontented and irritable. He felt that he had lost his grip on the firm to which he had devoted all his youth. He was jealous of his sons. He disliked the new styles.

He was, it will have been remarked, a man with an extraordinarily adherent mind, one on which a very few early impressions had struck deep and indelibly. Long ago he had come to Second Empire Paris with his gift, and lo, those vividly hued crinolines woven out of his early dreams about Queen Elizabeth had proved to be what Paris was waiting for. Paris had advanced halfway to meet him then! But this *Troisième République* was another thing; these tight-fitting dresses of the late 'seventies and 'eighties were both suggestive and undignified. And the colours! Sage-greens and mauves inspired by two crazes from across the Channel, aestheticism and Kate Greenaway-ism, they were as drab as everything English. Worth disowned England. Except for a few regular customers at the shop, he avoided altogether the English colony in Paris.

Always his mind harked back to the Second Empire in the 'sixties, that fat and happy time. Well, the great aviary was deserted now. The Empress was in exile, Cora Pearl was banished, and the Princess Metternich in her native Vienna, galvanizing even the staid court of Franz Joseph into life. To the Empress and some of her ladies he sent bunches of violets every year. With the Princess, however, he still exchanged cigars and reminiscences, on the occasions of her flying visits to Paris.

Right up to the last he paid daily visits to the rue de la Paix: his sons endured them with commendable patience. The firm and his grand-children were his only interests. He adored the little boys. Indeed, his death, at the age of seventy-five, was the result of a chill that he caught one bitterly cold afternoon in March, when he had taken the children to the draughty Théâtre de St Martin too soon after his return from a holiday in Cannes.

'The Revolution of 1870,' he once said, 'what is it to the Revolutions affected by me? First I introduced and then I put an end to the crinoline.' And the boast is justified. For the crinoline is the social history of a decade. By it even more than by Haussmann's architecture or Offenbach's can-cans is the musical comedy empire remembered.

About the little owl Florence Nightingale rescued from some Greek urchins, and its remarkable character, and the book about it privately produced for the Nightingale family circle; the whole presented by Mrs. Woodham-Smith, whose biography of Miss Nightingale is now in the Press.

Florence Nightingale's Pet Owl

by CECIL WOODHAM-SMITH

'I HAVE a passion,' wrote Florence Nightingale, 'for the society of almost any kind of creature.' History has preserved the names of a number of personages who have shared a similar passion— Charles the Second, Byron, Elizabeth of Bohemia, the poet Cowper. Unexpected company for Miss Nightingale, but then there is so much about her that is unexpected. She has suffered a curious fate; her own fame has obscured her, and the real woman has become invisible behind the figure of the Lady with the Lamp.

The passion Miss Nightingale cherished for creatures was of an unusual kind. It had not its roots in frustration: the creatures whose society she enjoyed were not an old maid's children. She sought neither the flattery of unquestioning exclusive devotion nor an outlet for unwanted tenderness. It is significant that dogs played only a small part in her life and that she was devoted to the indifference and grace of cats, keeping them six and eight at a time. She had a taste for odd creatures, for chameleons, cicadas, tortoises, birds. The contemplation of their oddities, their 'strange ways of going on,' contact with the life which pulsed so urgently and enchantingly in their small peculiar bodies, brought her, she said, a sense of relief. While she was with them she felt herself to be drinking at the untainted source of life; the difficulties, the brutalities, the sufferings, and the miseries of the world momentarily retreated, and she was refreshed.

Physically she remained detached. She was not a woman with the urge to touch, she had none of the common feminine desire to pick small creatures up. Though she was deeply fond of children, especially small children, she did not caress them. She enjoyed them at a distance, attending with infinite patience to their well-being, liking to see them happy, sitting for hours observing their behaviour without wishing to intrude or interfere.

Of all her pets the one she loved most was a little owl she bought in Athens in 1850. She was then passing through a period of great difficulty; she was already thirty and for years she had been struggling in vain to persuade her family to allow her to leave home and train as a nurse, for years too she had been trying to find courage to dismiss the most eligible of all her suitors to whom, though she knew that for the sake of her destiny love and marriage must be renounced, she was deeply attached. In the autumn of 1850 she had a breakdown and went abroad with her friends, Mr and Mrs Bracebridge, to winter in Egypt and Greece. As always in her darkest hours she turned to 'creatures' for consolation. She travelled up the Nile with two chameleons, who slept on her bed, and she was 'so sorry to part with them, they were such company.' In Greece she acquired two tortoises, called Mr and Mrs Hill after two missionaries, and a cicada whom she named Plato.

One evening she went to the Parthenon and came on some boys stoning a small object. It proved to be a young owlet, still only a ball of fluff, which had fallen from a nest in the capital of one of the great pillars. The boys were bought off, the little owl carried home and christened Athena.

Athena's disposition contradicted her appearance. She was as fierce and unmanageable as she was soft and fluffy. She flew into transports of rage, pecked savagely at everyone who came near her, and managed to destroy her cage. In despair Miss Nightingale remembered that she had once had a lesson in hypnotizing animals, when during a lunch party given by Professor Buckland, the celebrated naturalist, a little bear had become obstreperous. She followed the instructions with Athena and after a few minutes the little owl fell asleep.

Within a week Athena had become devoted to Miss Nightingale, went

everywhere in her pocket, sat on her head, and ate out of her hand. It was, however, only Miss Nightingale to whom she was devoted; she took a fiendish delight in plaguing everyone else, drank the ink on Mr Bracebridge's writing-table and scattered the sand over his papers. Plato, the cicada, she devoured.

Athena arrived in England in Miss Nightingale's pocket and settled down at Embley Park, the Nightingales' country house in Hampshire, where her iron will and her sense of humour made her a well-known character. She would hide behind the busts which stood on the library shelves and swoop down on unsuspecting visitors; she liked to sit in the best armchair and dare anyone to turn her out. She had favourites in the family and felt a special affinity for a formidable old great aunt of Miss Nightingale's, who had 'all the pent-up energies, the strong unregulated feelings, the large uncultivated powers of the brave days of old.' Athena was fond of sitting on this old lady's shoulder. It was customary for Miss Nightingale's learned friends to compliment Athena by addressing her in Greek.

Athena lived at Embley for more than three years and then, alas, met a tragic end. In 1854 the Crimean War broke out and in October of that year Miss Nightingale received and accepted the government's request to take out nurses. The expedition had to be organized in a few days. At Embley all was excitement and confusion; Miss Nightingale's family hurried to London and Athena was forgotten. Shut into an attic, she perished. When her small body was put into Miss Nightingale's hands, she, who had astonished everyone by her impassivity during the rush of the preparations, burst into tears. 'Poor little beastie,' she said, 'it was odd how much I loved you.'

Eighteen months passed and the world was ringing with Miss Nightingale's name. Her work in the hospitals of Scutari and the Crimea had brought her fame, almost worship, but she had paid a heavy price. She had caught Crimean fever and been for weeks at death's door. Now, in July, 1855, she was out of danger and recovering in the chaplain's house at Scutari, a pleasant small villa with a view over the Bosphorus —the most famous view in the world, which, she said, she had never had time to look at before. And here she received a book written by her sister Parthenope to amuse her during her convalescence. The book was called *The Life and Death of Athena, an Owlet from the Parthenon.* Parthenope had composed, lettered, and illustrated the book herself, and she was an artist of considerable talent. Miss Nightingale describes how she had it read aloud to her. In one corner of the room was an owl the troops had given her because she had told them about Athena, in another corner was a baby she was 'minding' for his mother; there was also a terrier which kept fidgeting about and trying to attract attention because, Miss Nightingale wrote, as she 'laughed and cried he knew we were reading about something we loved very much.'

A copy of Parthenope's small book is preserved in the British Museum, and by kind permission of the Trustees a condensed version is reproduced below.

THE LIFE AND DEATH OF ATHENA, AN OWLET FROM THE PARTHENON

THIS distinguished individual was born (as nearly as can be ascertained) on the fifth of June 1850. Her (future) Mistress was returning from a visit to Pittacus, the learned Conservator of the Parthenon, and his wife, the sister of the maid of Athens, when passing under the walls of the accropolis she perceived a little ball of fluff tormented by a group of children. Athena had fallen from her nest. She was rescued for the sum of 6 lepta or one farthing. On what slight accidents does fame depend!

Her mistress soon after left Athens, and not choosing to cast her loose on the stones of a troublesome world embarked her in company with a Cicada, 'Plato,' a slip from a plane tree by the Ilissus (coming home in a mustard pot), and two tortoises surnamed Mr and Mrs Hill. And now began poor Athena's griefs once more, her temper was rather defective and she fought and scratched everything that came near her. In her cage she bit, kicked, and swore vengeance for two hours, till her mistress was at her wits end. At length being tempted out with a bit of meat she mesmerized her (after a lesson learned at Oxford A.D. '47 in the inner court of Christchurch upon a little bear) and Athena's little woolly head went to sleep in her lap. She soon became quite mannerly and took her meals regularly from her mistress's hand.

And now they proceeded on their journey. Plato was dead, and Athena conveniently ate the Cicada, thereby consolidating two pets in one.

At Prague an enlightened waiter was heard holding forth to a chambermaid "Look that is the bird that all English ladies carry about with them, because it tells them when they are going to die!"

One quiet autumn evening, after an absence of ten months, her mistress mounted on foot the steep hill which led to her mountain home, came up through the garden, softly, softly, and in at the steps of the Drawing-room window. After sitting half an hour on the sofa between her mother and sister, she put her hand into her pocket and pulled out a little owlet in a bag!

Athena's head alone stuck out, she seemed however very happy and

very warm. When set at liberty she began while sitting on the table, to curtsey and bow with the greatest urbanity. And now Athena became the quiet inmate of a quiet English home. She began by making acquaintance with every cranny and corner of every room, thrust herself into every impossible place and took the greatest delight in being hunted for. She occasionally paid visits among the cottages in her mistress's pocket, tho' not in general much addicted to "doing good" (her life being one of luxurious through intellectual ease). She was of much interest to an old great aunt who with all the pent up energies, the strong unregulated feelings, the large uncultivated powers of the brave days of old, now in her 80th year kindly and patiently sat on the garden seat in the sunshine. She looked upon Athena as a great great niece, and enquired after her visitors comforts with the same dignified and hospitable care that she showed for her mistress. And Athena returned the interest by hopping on her knee or her shoulder, and settling herself comfortably there for a snooze, while the old lady never showed the smallest fear or surprise at this unaccustomed invasion of the quiet routine of her life.

She was decidedly of an aristocratic disposition, and used to fly down on the heads and pursue the heels of those whom she considered beneath her, and never made friends with any of them tho' they fed her regularly.

Her affections were rather exclusive, but how much the more did those admitted to her friendship appreciate these privileges. She would suffer her friends to stroke her quite flat, hold her by the head, pull her by the tail, blow at her, poke her, and only return for a little more play: the only thing she resented was neglect. It must however be confessed that she would bite and scratch strangers with, or without, the slightest provocation. It was very pretty to see her sitting on her mistress's finger to receive her one daily meal opening her wings wide as she swallowed each piece of meat at her hands.

The following year she took a second journey into Germany, the waters of Karlsbad having been thought good for her health. Her ideas of propriety were exceedingly strict, and one day at Bamberg she nearly barked herself into a fit at the sight of some storks sitting on a chimney top.

Her companions were long in finding out the cause of her excessive indignation till they caught a side view of the obnoxious beings. A bird, in Athena's eyes, ought to be a comfortable little round thing, with short legs and no neck at all to speak of, and here were creatures infringing on every principle that should constitute a well regulated bird, and she told them so for nearly an hour at the top of her voice, for, as she justly observed, Beauty is what I am. She returned to England to meet her mistress coming from a three months study at Kaiserswerth. From this time Athena's journeys were only to London where she spent the season, and to Lea Hurst where she spent the summer.

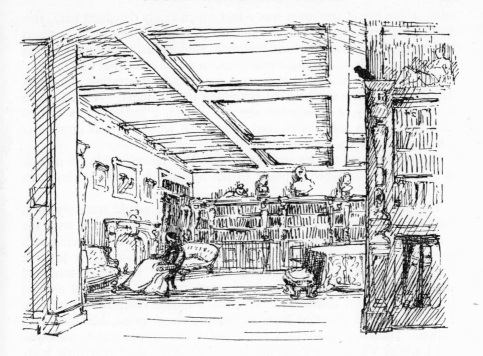

Athena's tastes were extremely literary, she read Grote with the greatest interest, sitting on her mistress's knee and growing very excited over the death of Socrates. She spent a great part of every day investigating the shelves in the library; hours indeed she used to remain at the back of the largest quartos.

Her toilette (as is supposed to be the case sometimes with literary ladies) suffered much from these excursions and by the end of the winter she generally had not a feather left in her tail. Athena had a very proper sense of her own importance, indeed a first respect for oneself is always remarked as one of the concomitant ingredients of greatness, and a perfectly necessary one of success. She objected extremely to being laughed at, and resented impertinence. If an arm chair were drawn up by the fire she always considered that it was done for her especial use and, placing herself exactly in the middle, she would comfortably shut one eye, draw up one leg and wink luxuriously and magnificently at the fire for an hour at a time.

Her favourite pastime was to fly at a nosegay, capture a dahlia and retire to sit upon it and pick it in pieces. Her conscience tho' was a very lively one, and she rarely did crimes without barking vigorously to inform the company. To knock down a jar of roses and carry off the

N

finest to the top of the room was a feat which really delighted her. Her love of high places was indeed notable. She would occasionally resort to the top of her mistress's head and crow loud and triumphantly at being in the most noble and conspicuous position which she could find.

Her conversation indeed was most varied and interesting. She had five distinct—notes may we be permitted to call them. A bark when she was naughty, a crow when she was proud, a little purr (a sort of twee twee) when she was pleased, a grumble when she was cross, and a hoot when she was melancholy.

She would go on talking sometimes the whole morning, always putting in an observation when a pause in the reading, or an enquiring tone seemed to require it.

The quickness of her eye was wonderful. She would see a fly from the farthest extremity of a large room, and descend upon it with the greatest accuracy, tho' near at hand her large nose rather interfered with her vision. She never went out for a walk above twice in her life; the little birds outside always scolded her violently, she never took the slightest notice of this, she was not popular among them and seemed rather to enjoy the distinction. One day a mouse ventured out into the Library and she pounced from her serene stand point, her high post between Theseus and Mercury at the top of the bookcase and swallowed the intruder whole! Indeed the facility of stowage in that little body was very remarkable she would in her one meal eat a thing, skin and all, a third of her size.

Her health was remarkably good, but two or three times in her life she had what her maid called "des crises," when she fell down on her side, shut her eyes, and remained insensible for an hour or more. On these occasions her friends used to wrap her in flannel by the fire, or put her in their bosoms, and after lying apparently dead, a doleful and pathetic little "twee twee" would be heard, and she would proceed to give a long and detailed account of her woes, then bursting her wraps, she would hop out and about as if nothing were the matter.

She had a warm attachment for old things and old usages, and as beforesaid a great objection to anything which she thought incorrect. One morning the biographer after a long illness came down in a cap, this Athena objected to extremely. She came and sat at the back of the chair and remonstrated warmly, and when no notice was taken of her observations, she jumped on the obnoxious cap, dragged it off the head and began to tear it.

Her courage was perfectly undaunted, she would stand at the open window on tip toe, barking at a dog or cat 50 times her size. The only time she was ever known to have been frightened, was once when a particular friend brought her a parcel, an owl with great eyes, through which shone the light of a candle. This lurid and supernatural presentiment of her own similitude was more than Athena could bear.

Her dislike to dogs and children was probably connected with early reminiscences of the woes with which she was threatened—but it became an irrational antipathy, instead of the well weighed judgment to be expected from the bird of Minerva. She did not even attend to the predilections of her mistress and was proof against the blandishments of little May H who, sitting beside her, tenderly chanted 'a ool a ool' in the most musical of voices.

The biographer cannot recall without tears her little run across the room, like the step of a partridge, her elegant manners, coming downstairs sitting on a finger quite free, but without any inclination to fly away, her talents and virtues. Indeed 'il ne lui manquait que la parole.' It will thus be seen that with the exception of a slight tendency to theft, murder, ill temper, and conceit, this remarkable person may justly lay claim to be called, as the Italians have it "una persona cómpita." Her qualities of soul, heart, and intellect was indeed first rate. We now come to the last and tragical chapter. Her mistress had been home after an exceedingly hard summer's work in London, she had been exceedingly unwell and confined to her room. Athena was her constant companion, when she could bear no one else of larger size. Athena sat on the bed and talked to her, she ran races round the room after imaginary mice. Every meal she considered to have been brought for her especial use, and she accordingly appropriated the bread and butter and pounced on the chicken; "Mademoiselle la gâte" was the warning voice, but her mistress let it be.

* * * * *

At length after a fortnight her mistress returned to town; and the day after she arrived began to consider her great expedition. As soon as her friends heard of the plan they hurried up to London, everything was in haste and confusion. Athena was put into a room by herself, the grief, the cold, and the isolation were too much for her, she fell down in a fit, there were none at hand to succour her, and when found she was lying dead on her little side. Athena's body was sent up to be embalmed, her mistress asked to see her again, and the only tear she shed through that tremendous week was when P. put the little body into her hands. "Poor little beastie, it was odd how much I loved you."

So let her lie. So wept.

In the brief but remarkable history of modern physics he has filled a unique role; his influence is such that he has been called the Socrates of atomic science.

The Wisdom of Niels Bohr

by C. P. SNOW

S a group, scientists are not given to collective modesty. They have the exuberant confidence which comes of revelling in their own success. You can see it in their self-descriptions. Rutherford used to proclaim, without undue shrinking, that this was the heroic age of physics. Sometimes he called it the Elizabethan age. As for the influence of Niels Bohr, his colleagues are fond of saying, with the same unselfconsciousness, that there has been nothing like it since Socrates.

That is the spirit, of course, in which great work gets done. The high creative ages in literature have been just the same; when men are taking part in such achievements, they shout about them, they do not travel resentfully on their hands and knees. A bit more bombast in other fields than science will be a sign of hope. The Socrates of atomic science: that was the phrase that went round the scientific world, as the twenties and thirties passed, as the science of nuclear physics was lit up with discovery after discovery, as it all came nearer to the final demonstration, the most expensive experiment ever carried out, the explosion in New Mexico in 1945.

It was an astonishing story. A scientific subject had never moved so fast. And much of that movement was brought about by nothing more sensational than talk. Talk diffuse. Talk tentative. Talk prodigiously long-winded. Talk often maddening, but probing its way with a tireless, delicate imagination. That was the part of Niels Bohr. While the enormous Wells-like machines were going up in the world's laboratories, there was talk at Copenhagen. Everyone active in atomic physics called on Bohr, in his institute in the park. There, not far from the Copenhagen lakes, some of the most momentous ideas in physics struggled to be born.

From about 1920 Bohr has occupied this unique position. For any new idea, he was the man to talk to. He was also the man to listen to, for a long time. In the short and brilliant history of modern physics, no one had ever filled such a position before. He came to it, or rather it imperceptibly grew round him, while he was still a young man.

He had emerged into fame just before the first war, during his collaboration with Rutherford at Manchester. Rutherford had recently proved, by some of the most famous of all experiments, that the mass of the atom was almost entirely concentrated in a central nucleus: so that an atom was something like the solar system, with a nucleus in the place of the sun, and electrons like planets rotating round it. But it was hard even to begin to imagine how those electrons were arranged. At that time Bohr, fresh from Copenhagen, still under thirty, arrived in England. He had some vague theoretical ideas about that electronic structure. He went to Cambridge, but got nothing out of it. He was shy, he talked too much and incomprehensibly. Sadly, he left Cambridge, and went to Manchester.

IT WAS ONE OF THE LUCKIEST OF journeys. He and Rutherford were made for one another. They were both among the most gifted men who have spent their lives in science. They were enough unlike to reinforce each other. Rutherford was the experimentalist nonpareil, Bohr the theoretician and philosopher: Rutherford was certain, Bohr hesitant. But they were like enough in their fundamental approach to be in sympathy. They were both intuitive rather than rational. There is a game of dividing scientific discoverers into two categories. The first consists of those who are, so to speak, born knowing a certain aspect of the truth and who only have to grow up in order to reveal it. This is the category of Kelvin and Dirac. The second is made up of the men who, with darts of insight, nose their way round the brute facts towards reality.

Rutherford and Bohr were both of this kind, and they understood each other at once and always.

Thus, inspired and fortified by Rutherford, Bohr produced his first paper on the quantum theory of electronic states. It was as much a landmark as Rutherford's proof of the existence of the nucleus. It paved the way for the whole of atomic theory for thirty years. It earned Bohr all the honours of a successful scientist—a chair at his own university of Copenhagen when he was thirty-one (1916), an Institute of Theoretical Physics specially built for him four years later, a Nobel prize in 1922.

He was all set for the great work of his life—which was to be, not another discovery of the magnitude of his first, but instead twenty years drawing out the half-ideas of others. It is obvious, of course, that such a task required much more than a scientist of genius. It required in addition a personality that is just as rare. The two together have only happened once. There have been several theoretical physicists of about the power of Bohr. But there has been only one Bohr.

Perhaps it helps to recall a remark which Einstein made to me the only time I talked to him. He was saying that all the major scientific discoveries had been made by happy men, free from anxiety, in tranquillity of mind. Then he stopped. There is one exception, he said. Bohr. Bohr's first great paper was conceived and carried through during a period of intense private suffering.

I do not know how well-placed Einstein was to make the observation, but there is nothing improbable about it. Bohr is a man of deep nature, magnanimous, brooding, probably predisposed to sorrow, who has known affliction. He has nothing of the opaqueness, brisk and complacent, which is one of the less likeable qualities of some eminent scientists. His is altogether a profounder personality than theirs. If it had not been so, he could not have seemed the wisest man in the scientific world.

In the first years of the 'twenties, there he was, his achievement beyond question, his personality deeper and more generous than the people round him, equipped to shed his influence on anyone who came near. And, for two reasons, many came near. The first of these reasons was a technical one. Atomic theory had reached an impasse, and everyone in the field was looking for ways round. The second reason was due to the nature and organization of the scientific profession.

The scientific profession is a small one; in a subject like fundamental physics, everyone knows everyone else. Particularly in the 'twenties, this was true the world over. Physics then was a genuinely international activity, in which any Englishman of reputation would be personally known to his German or Scandinavian or Russian colleagues. Many of these men felt linked with each other in a grand creative enterprise, and their personal relations were closer than with, say, their classical acquaintances of their own university and country. It is possible that, from 1918 until the middle 'thirties, international spirit rose higher in those circles than it had ever reached in any other professional group. This helped to lead physicists to welcome an international meeting-place. They liked travel, their lives were exceptionally leisurely, they were comfortable with each other, there was nothing more attractive than a term or two in Copenhagen.

There they talked and listened. Modern quantum mechanics; the Uncertainty Principle; nuclear structure; atomic fission; all those, which involve the subtlest concepts in modern physics, were stimulated by Bohr, questioned by Bohr, refined by Bohr, re-examined by Bohr, as the hours passed. The seminar used to collect in a lecture-room at the institute. Someone, perhaps Heisenberg or another famous foreign visitor, would give a paper; Bohr followed with comments at considerable length (for, as an admirer remarked, 'he is not succinct,' and this frailty became a standing joke); another visitor; a Dane; Bohr again; and so on. Usually in English, sometimes in German. Bohr speaks English with the utmost pertinacity and fluency, but with a monotonous Danish intonation. I once heard him lecture for two and a half hours, with Rutherford, who was easily tired, trying to stop him every quarter of an hour after the first. Despite the interest of the subject matter, it seemed a long time.

There were other gigantic talks, in Bohr's own house. The Danes have a mansion at Carlsberg, left for the purpose by the famous brewers, which is allocated for life to the most eminent Dane. It is a pleasant custom; perhaps in small countries it is easier to pay these tributes to intellect. But even in Denmark the tributes do not go quite as far as might appear. Niels Bohr is recognized by sight by a fair proportion of the citizens of Copenhagen, and in their polite fashion they touch their hats. His brother Harald is recognized by a much larger proportion. Now Harald, though a fine pure mathematician, is nothing like so eminent in his line as Niels in his. Does it mean that Danes esteem pure mathematics above physics, even physics of the highest class? It does not; it means that Harald once captained the Danish soccer team.

The talks continued, at dinner in the Carlsberg mansion, after dinner in the big drawing-room. Sometimes, on a special occasion, there would be so many present that young men were, in actual fact, sitting on the floor at Bohr's feet. At Carlsberg the talks tended to be more philosophical, less strictly scientific: on free will and the Uncertainty Principle, on the difference between physical and mathematical reality, and, as the world darkened for such men as Bohr (his politics are liberal; it was that reason, at least as much as because his mother was a Jewess, which made his friends, and the Danish police, smuggle him into Sweden in 1944), on the struggle to come.

WHY HAS HE BEEN SUCH AN influence?   Is it chiefly his personality or chiefly his mind?   That is the most difficult question to answer; and perhaps those who know him best, who have been most affected by his tentative, probing manner, would find it most difficult of all.   I have said enough, I hope, to suggest that he is a man of uncommon stature.   It is conventional among scientists to say that it does not matter who gets credit for a piece of work, so long as the truth is found.   In fact, however, the intrigues for priority are bitter ; and there are plenty of fine scientists who have not been over-careful about appropriating others' ideas.   Bohr has stood above such weaknesses.   He has given away concepts which others would have claimed.   He has been so magnanimous that posterity, judging only by the names of authors on scientific papers, may be deceived. He has been generous and sincere, strong and reflective and sorrowful, one of those figures who capture the imagination of their day.

Yet that is not all.   Perhaps it is not half of it.   His own contribution, apart from all that he has drawn out, is small in quantity, but what there is is fine.   His is not a beautiful mind, in the sense that, for example, G. H. Hardy's was beautiful; Hardy could not write an inelegant sentence, but Bohr on paper, on the rare occasions when he can force himself to write, is 'not succinct.'   Nevertheless, he is one of those men with an abnormal nose for reality.   Often such men—like Dostoevski in litera-ture—bumble and falter, have shafts of insight, encircle their object with streams of words, approach it in width as well as depth.   They can be maddening to read or listen to.   Yet, at their best, they may embrace more of the truth than more lucid persons.

There is a German saying that clarity is complementary to truth.   It sounds neater in German; it is not a saying to apply in all circumstances and at all times, but there is something in it.   It might have been invented for Bohr.   With his wonderful antennae he has felt more of physical reality than any man alive: he has led others to make sense of what he has felt: but he has not often found his own expression for it.

Yet on one occasion he was clear, curt and to the point.   It is one of the curiosities of atomic physics that experimental evidence for nuclear fission was published months before anyone came along with the right explanation.   There stood the facts; they pointed the way to atomic energy, the atom bomb; no one saw it.   At last O. R. Frisch (who is now a professor at Cambridge) grasped what must be true.   He was a refugee from Vienna who had been working with Bohr for years.   He rang Bohr up and began to account for the facts.   This could only be fission, and nothing but fission.   Surprisingly, very uncharacteristically, almost rudely, Bohr broke in: 'It is obvious.   It was staring in our faces.   We all ought to be ashamed of ourselves.'

The first Great War thrust the father, the most distinguished sailor of his day, into obscurity; the second brought the son into the picture. Mountbatten's qualities made him the only Englishman to hold supreme command of a major Allied force, the last Viceroy of an Indian Empire and the first Governor-General of an Indian Dominion, brought him an earldom and resounding fame; and that strange background of his is not irrelevant to all this.

Mountbatten of Burma

by CYRIL RAY

IT looks a very romantic affair, now, that runaway match of 1851, when the young cavalry colonel ran off with the little countess. But it is not only the sentimental mists of ninety-nine years that make it seem so, not only the tight uniform and splendid whiskers of the colonel, the curls and crinoline of the countess: they must have seemed romantic runaways even to their delighted contemporaries.

For the colonel was Prince Alexander of Hesse, still in his twenties, third son of a reigning German Grand Duke, and an officer—thanks to his sister's marriage to the Czarevitch—in the Russian Emperor's Household Cavalry. And he risked much in eloping, for all that his pretty Julie's father had been a Polish count who was also a Russian general. The young prince's father, the Grand Duke, held that he had married beneath him: the union must be regarded as morganatic, and its children, who must take their mother's name, excluded from the succession. And the Russian Emperor Nicholas had him cashiered, for marrying without formal permission. It was not until Prince Alexander of Hesse's elder brother became Grand Duke that the Countess Julie was made Princess of Battenberg, and not until his brother-in-law became Emperor of Russia, in 1855, that her husband was reinstated in the Russian Army.

Had it not been for that cashiering of 1851 the grandfather of the Earl Mountbatten of Burma would have been engaged against the British in the Crimean War, instead of commanding an Austrian division—he was a kinsman of the Empress of Austria, too—against the Italians of the Risorgimento. And had the princely honours of Battenberg not been granted to the Countess Julie Hauke the names of a British First Sea Lord and of the last Viceroy of India would have been different. Perhaps history itself might have been different.

This is not the place to list the late nineteenth-century marriages that

185

connected the newly named Battenbergs with the royal houses of England
and Greece, as well as of Russia, Austria, a couple of Balkan states, and
a German principality or so. It is enough to know that the background
and connections of Louis, second child and eldest son of the runaway
marriage, with German, Polish, and Flemish blood in his own veins and
French as his fireside language, were as cosmopolitan as an international
banker's. And it was no more remarkable that he should become an
Englishman than that he should become a Montenegrin.

What took him to England, though, was his determination to be a
professional sailor, and how that passion came to seize a Central
European schoolboy, whose only sight of the sea had been of Adriatic
waters trapped and tamed in the canals and lagoons of Venice is
something else again.

Many thousand Hessians, in the previous century, had worn British
regimentals, and there are transatlantic history books in which it is not
yet forgiven us; the first Hessian, surely, to wear the blue and the gold
lace of the Royal Navy took the oath of allegiance to Queen Victoria
in October, 1868, and a year later was Midshipman His Serene Highness
Prince Louis of Battenberg, R.N., a fifteen-year old British subject on
dinner-table terms with the Queen herself, whose grand-daughter he was
eventually to marry.

But it was not the splendour of his connections that made him a four-
ringed captain at 37, Director of Naval Intelligence at 48, a full Admiral
and First Sea Lord on the eve of the 1914 war. Any Englishman who,
in spite of the Polish destroyer-captains of the nineteen-forties, still
cherishes the sentimental fancy that what makes a sailor is English blood
and a home within seventy miles of the sea might look again at the career
of Prince Louis of Battenberg. Hard work, brains, and a passion for his
job had made a Hessian, born at Graz to an Austrian general, not only
a sailor but the most distinguished sailor of his day. Commanding a
cruiser squadron in the Fleet exercise of 1901, for instance, he was
blockaded in the Ionian Islands by the combined Channel and Mediterranean Fleets and successfully eluded them at night without even being
sighted, much less brought to action. (His son, with the same rank and
job, was given a similar task in 1949.) The admiring comment of a
rating was 'Six British Admirals outside, and one damned foreigner inside
was too clever for them all.'

It is a career indeed which, reflecting in its course no special credit
on English blood—but much on the British sailors of all ranks who had
taught the First Sea Lord his trade, and loved him for learning it so
well—reflected, in its ending, much discredit on high-placed Englishmen.
The same nineteen-fourteen hysteria—in the same men, perhaps—that
pilloried a great Secretary of State for War for once publicly admiring

the German philosophers, began a whispering campaign in the clubs against the one man who had done more than any other to make the Navy ready—whose order it was, on a *carte blanche* from Winston Churchill, First Lord of the Admiralty, that had prevented the reservists from dispersing on July 26, 1914, and kept the Fleet mobilized.

The Churchill we knew in 1940 could have saved him for further great service to the State; the Churchill of 1914, though he admired and believed in him, had not the power. In October, 1914, forty-five years to the month after his appointment as midshipman, Prince Louis resigned from the Board of Admiralty and from further service. His elder son, George, was already a lieutenant in a battle-cruiser; his younger son, Louis, a naval cadet at Osborne, was on the eve of becoming a midshipman himself.

NOW, AT THE AGE OF 49, THE OSBORNE cadet is a vice-admiral commanding a cruiser squadron, as his father, at about the same age, was before him. But there has been a seven-year period during which the career of a famous son ran far from parallel with that of a distinguished father. One great war thrust Louis of Battenberg into obscurity; a second great war swung a spotlight on to Louis Mountbatten. And in considering the qualities that made Mountbatten the only Englishman to hold supreme command of a major Allied force, that made him the last Viceroy of an Indian Empire and the first Governor-General of an Indian Dominion, that gave him an earldom and the Garter—in considering the qualities that made him one of the most glittering figures of the recent past and one of the most frequent subjects of speculation in an uneasy present—that curious background of his is not irrelevant.

For the capacity for hard work, the intelligence, and the passion for the sea that made his father First Sea Lord, though they are shared to the full by the son, might merely have made him the successful flag officer that he is today. Alone, they do not explain the years between. Is there not something of the dash of the cavalry-colonel grandfather added to the supremely good seamanship of his father? Is there not something of the charm—the wayward charm, perhaps—of the Countess Julie as well as the quiet likeability of Prince Louis? And it is certain that the English-born great-grandson of Queen Victoria, cousin of the reigning monarch, was more surely insulated against certain kinds of spite—though not against all—than the foreign-born princeling who had married Queen Victoria's grand-daughter.

Even the foreign blood seems to have its significance. The English are a mixed breed, it is true, but most Englishmen have been islanders for a long time and tend, abroad, to behave as such.

But here was an Englishman, an admiral and an aristocrat to boot, who could disarm an American with his breezy bonhomie and charm an Indian with the grave courtesy of an equal, where the one had feared high-hatting and the other was ready to resent the arrogance of a ruling race. To the easy good manners of the professional sailor Mountbatten adds an extra cosmopolitan tolerance of his own. His own breeding makes him, literally, a good European; temperament makes him a citizen of the world. The quality has expressed itself angrily at sea and gracefully ashore. I have heard him sharply rebuke the destroyer captain who sneered at an enemy that was refusing battle: 'There's nothing wrong with the Germans' guts, and you know it!' And in India he adopted India's habits: he sat on the ground with his Indian guests, greeted them with folded hands and a ceremonious bob of the head. There are few other Englishmen of his rank who could have done that without their condescension creaking like corsets.

But it is not merely that Mountbatten is accessible to people and adaptable in his manners: he is accessible to ideas and adaptable in his planning. And here he is the son of his father, who watched Blériot's cross-channel flight of 1909, eagerly went up with the first naval pilots of 1911, and filled his Admiralty memoranda with prophecies about aircraft and defence schemes against the almost as new-fangled submarines.

In Mountbatten's case the same freshness of mind manifested itself in the technical curiosity and inventiveness that made him top of his class in endless specialist courses, chief wireless instructor at the Navy's Signal School while still in his twenties, Fleet wireless officer to the Mediterranean Fleet not long after.

THESE WERE THE YEARS when Mountbatten was 'Dickie' to countless readers of the wide-ranging, tuft-hunting gossip columns of the day—the polo-playing friend of the Prince of Wales, with a rich and pretty wife and a fabulous penthouse in Park Lane. But even in those days the friends he chatted with at the much-publicized cocktail parties were as noted for their wit as for their frivolity—Mountbatten has a liking for brains, whether they are those of a playwright or of a scientist —and he was still as likely to be designing a station-keeping device for His Majesty's ships as a revolutionary new head for the polo mallet.

His own brains, indeed, are too restless to be confined to any groove. Any other man, almost, would have found it a full-time job to be as successful in his chosen profession as Mountbatten was in his twenties and early thirties: Mountbatten had to be inventing gadgets as well, creating a Royal Navy polo team out of nothing to beat a cavalry regiment for the inter-regimental cup, and leading, on leave and at week-ends, the kind of social life that has defeated many a man of infinite leisure who spends his mornings in bed.

It was this same mental restlessness, a decade later, that had one of his scientific advisers complaining that the Chief of Combined Operations never gave himself time to think, forgetting that it was his own job to do the thinking, Mountbatten's to direct and organize it, to inspire it even, and to translate it into action. And it is some similar quality— or defect—in the man that makes it difficult for him to delegate small office jobs, and that provides the foundation for the one criticism of him as a fighting sailor: that he is too impatient to get to grips, that 'there's no one better to be with in a tight spot—and no one so likely to get you into one.'

It is here, perhaps—in the handling of ships at sea—that there is as much of his grandfather's cavalry dash as of his father's seamanship. Prince Louis was probably no less brave than his son but seems, judging by his success in Fleet exercises, to have been a good deal more cautious than the Mountbatten who had so many destroyers shot from under him —*Kelly* in the North Sea, *Javelin* in the chops of the Channel, *Kelly* again off Crete. But with the hot eagerness to fight goes coolness in the fighting: he was on the bridge when the torpedo struck *Kelly* and he told me, 'I thought, as I saw it coming, that that's going to kill a hell of a lot of chaps. Curious, isn't it, one's belief in one's personal immortality?'

Later in his career, with more at stake than a destroyer flotilla, Mountbatten has shown the same impatience to get to grips with a job, the same coolness in the council chamber. He overrode the advice of Sir Reginald Dorman-Smith and his staff in treating Aung San and the Burma National Army as patriots and making them his allies; he expedited by nearly a year the end of British rule in India and the introduction of partition. He persuaded the princes, out-argued Jinnah, electrified Whitehall into drafting a Government of India Act overnight, and so charmed the Hindus that they not only accepted partition but chose him as their first Governor-General.

Statesmanship? Diplomacy? It is hard to say. For the successes have all been in the one kind of job, as head of a team with a limited objective in view. There, he has a gift for finding the right advisers and lieutenants and for kindling their imaginations, for brushing aside inessentials and for timing. Whether he has the patience for long-term diplomacy, the faculty for philosophic thought necessary in the far-ahead planning of the statesman, is doubtful.

What is certain is that after his task in India was done both mind and body needed relaxation. And Mountbatten admitted to a friend that his own immortal soul needed a rest from grandeur. Hence the sigh of relief with which the man who had partitioned an empire took over a cruiser squadron, with which the one-time Viceroy, the lover of splendour, retired to the relative obscurity of a rear-admiral's cabin.

BUT HE IS STILL SHORT OF fifty, and if there can be little ambition left —outside his own profession—for one who has been Viceroy of India in peacetime and a Supreme Allied Commander in war, the State may find duties for the admiral that the admiral does not seek. It is a widely canvassed secret that Mountbatten hopes to justify his father, as it were, by becoming First Sea Lord. The goal is well within his reach. But this government, or another, may be tempted to see if Mountbatten's legendary luck holds in some future task as big as the one he handled in India.

He is debarred from politics himself by his royal blood, but as a serving officer he may properly be employed by politicians. And of politicians he is more tolerant than are most serving sailors. His own political views, which he keeps to himself, are generally believed to be rather to the left of centre, though they are based, one imagines, more on day-to-day notions of the practical thing to do in a given set of circumstances than on any political philosophy. If he is impatient of reactionaries he is equally impatient of windy theorizers.

Himself, he is a doer, not a theorizer, an energizer rather than a temporizer, and although he is phenomenally quick-witted—'he thinks on his feet' somebody once said of him—he has no taste for thinking for its own sake. He is an empiricist and a pragmatist.

IT MAY BE, THEREFORE, that his gifts are best used in the service, that here is a brilliant First Sea Lord of the future, a first Chief of Staff to the Minister of Defence, maybe, when we get around at last to co-ordinating properly the three services. For this is the one Englishman who has not only commanded an inter-Allied force of land, sea, and air forces, but who—as Chief of Combined Operations—has controlled an inter-service organization, with high rank conferred on him in all three.

Indias, after all, are not to be partitioned every day—though there is still, come to think of it, Ireland to be federalized and brought back into the Commonwealth as India was partitioned and kept in. That is to take a freakish example, yet it is the kind of task that could bring out the best in Mountbatten—the vigour, the disinterestedness, the open-mindedness, the delight in finding a job worth doing and setting himself a D-day for it. And it would be amusing to watch whether the Irish, whose charm is counted against them, would recognize as the Indians did that in this English grandson of the Hessian colonel and the Polish countess the charm is 'a quality of the heart.'

Of the rose-red city half as old as time, fantastic beyond belief and a monument to the strangeness and variety of human civilization.

A Day In Petra

by *JULIAN HUXLEY*

The urn on the top of El Deir

W HEN I got back to Europe, a friend commented that, from my description, Petra sounded surrealist. No, said I, not surrealist, for after all it is real. But you might call it *surimaginist*, because no one could imagine such an extraordinary reality.

I had always had a hankering to visit Petra, ever since as a boy I first heard the line about the rose-red city half as old as time. (It comes from Dean Burgon's Newdigate Prize Poem.) Later, I read some account of Petra—the entrance gorge, the fabulous landscape, the city of rock-hewn tombs, the place abandoned, deserted, unknown for a thousand

191

years to the West save as a dim legend, rediscovered by Burckhardt at
the risk of his life, still visited at the traveller's peril up to a bare
half-century or so ago.

It epitomized the strangeness of the civilizations that have risen and
perished, entirely alien from our own or from any that are alive now,
and can no more be resuscitated than can a Moa or a Mammoth, however
much we today might desire it.

And now I was going there. When I found I had to visit Transjordan
on my tour of the Middle East, in preparation for the Unesco Conference
at Beirut, I wrote to ask whether a visit to Petra would be possible. In
spite of the fact that my total stay in the country was fifty-two hours,
the authorities very kindly made it possible. *Just* possible! To reach
it meant getting up at 4 a.m., travelling $2\frac{1}{2}$ hours by plane, $2\frac{1}{2}$ hours by
car, $2\frac{1}{2}$ hours on horseback, and $2\frac{1}{2}$ hours' roughish walking, apart from
meals and sightseeing; so that we were quite tired when we had to face
an official reception back at Amman at 7.30 p.m. But it was worth it.

The plane, a little five-passenger biplane, took us down to Ma'an over
the edge of the desert, stretching unbroken and interminable to the east;
to the west, a few valleys leading down to the Dead Sea, with occasional
settlements. At Ma'an we went to the Military headquarters for
breakfast; and then off by car across horrible country—level desert
strewn with black pebbles and stones. After a bit the road began to
wind down a valley in the calcareous scarp, the little fields in the valley
bottom bright with enormous red poppies. So to Ain Musa, Moses'
Spring, at the head of the Wady or dry torrent of the same name where,
at the military post in the village, we changed from car to horses—but
the most miserable specimens I have ever seen, and not even furnished
with a rein: only a halter, and a 'guide' apiece. A little way down
the stony track, I saw that one of the Arabs of our party (who with
some reason prided himself on his English) was walking, and asked
why. Affably, but with some heat, he replied, 'Because my bally horse
is no damn good. . . .'

Before us lay a great purple and brown rampart—the range of sandstone mountains from which Petra—'the Rock'—takes its name. The
outskirts of the village are the only spots of green in the huge landscape,
terraces with figs and almonds and vegetables contouring the steep slopes.
Soon we were in the desert again, but now a desert of ivory-coloured
sandstone, dissected by weathering into valleys bordered with strange
rounded domes and bosses, like human constructions which had begun
to melt and lose their sharpness of outline. Then the first rock-hewn
tombs; I wanted to explore them, but our guide hurried us on, explaining
that they are nothing in comparison with what we shall see later. And
then before us the entry of the famous Siq, the astonishing approach to

ABOVE is a medium-sized tomb carved out of the mountainside. The common tawny-brown rock has been cut away to reach the amazing parti-coloured sandstone layer, which has been deliberately used for the façade.

(Left) For over a mile the great north-east wall of the rocky amphitheatre in which Petra lies has been cut into tombs.

The double-page picture is of El Deir, the most imposing of Petra's monuments, carved out of a mountain high above the city. Only the lower storey is excavated into rooms. El Deir probably served not as a tomb but as a temple.

Colour photographs by Dr. Julian
Huxley

HORSEMEN in the Siq, the entry to Petra. The Siq is an extremely narrow water-worn canyon, with perpendicular or even overhanging sides up to 400 feet. Wild oleanders grow here and there by the dry torrent-bed.

the city. Local tradition has it that the Siq was made by Moses' rod when he struck the rock. Actually it is a gorge, or better a very narrow canyon, cut by water in the red and brown and purple sandstone which makes the inner girdle or bastion of Petra. Every traveller has been struck by it, and with reason, for it is as great a wonder in its way as the dead city itself—no, as the rest of the city, for the Siq is an essential part of Petra.

The landscape of ivory comes to an end before a barrier of low red-brown cliffs. This barrier is pierced by the torrent-bed—a narrow opening, hard to detect, even though marked by the remains of the works which the men of Petra added to the outer end of this great defensive work provided for them by nature.

Once inside and round a corner we found ourselves in an exceedingly narrow gorge with vertical sides. As the torrent-bed cuts its way through the sandstone rampart, the gorge deepens rapidly, from a mere 70 or 80 ft. at the outset to over 300 ft. near its other end, rather over a mile downstream. It curves and twists its sinuous way, never more than twelve or thirteen yards wide, and sometimes narrowing to five or even four. Here the walls curve a little away from the perpendicular, there form an overhang, according to the caprice of the floods of past ages, which have cut the canyon and polished the smooth surface of its sides. Some shrubs and little trees—mostly wild figs and oleanders—have managed to find root-hold in the cleft; and at intervals tributary torrentlets have cut back the upper lip of the gorge, revealing sunbathed sandstone ridges and peaks above the shadowed cliffs.

Today the floor is a typical torrent-bed, covered with a layer of loose stones. But there are remains of the original pavement, composed of large blocks more than $1\frac{1}{2}$ ft. square, which converted the Siq from a rough track into a real road, a noble if a strange approach to a great city.

Along the wall you can see in many places the remains of conduits, which led the water of Ain Musa into cisterns within the thirsty town. In addition to the original open conduit which the Nabataeans, the inhabitants of Petra in its heyday, cut in the solid rock, there are the remains of the more ambitious Roman system, of pipes let into the rock. Various modern travellers have described the alarming floods that nowadays sweep through the Siq after the rare but heavy rains. In Nabataean times these seem to have been largely diverted away from the road and into the city's water-supply, by means of a tunnel of which traces still remain.

It was almost impossible to visualize the traffic that passed through this astonishing place two thousand years ago: caravans of camels, spice-laden, arriving from Arabia or leaving for Damascus and Aleppo; strings of mules; horsemen; the common people, and some of the soldiers, on foot. Perhaps the King himself leaving on a campaign: two centuries later the

O

Roman Governor, messengers from Rome, Roman architects and actors, soldiers and engineers. Did they have wheeled vehicles through the Siq? I do not know.

BUT THE DIRECT PHYSICAL IMPRESSIONS were too powerful to leave our imaginations much scope. And then of a sudden a new wonder announced itself. Before this, the only sunlight had been hundreds of feet above our heads. But now, rounding a bend, we saw the two dark walls framing a vision of sunlit rose, with pilasters and architraves. Instead of shadow, sunlight; instead of nature, art.

At this point, the Siq debouches into a valley at right angles to its previous course, green with a rich growth of oleanders, and so much broader that it is flooded with sunshine. And precisely opposite the opening (doubtless deliberately, with a view to impressing visitors) the Nabataeans carved the most beautiful of all their monuments, now called by its Arab name—*Khazné Fara'oun,* the Treasury of Pharaoh.

It represents a temple façade, some 90 ft. high, carved from the rosiest-red of all the rocks of Petra, probably around the beginning of the Christian epoch. There are the remains of rich carving, both in the round and in relief; the columns across its entrance are matched by pilasters at the side. Between the two halves of the much-stylized 'broken pediment' at the top is a delicious little *tholos,* or circular temple, of extreme elegance. It is interesting that only four examples of this type of façade are known, none of them from actual buildings. Three are rock-cut monuments in Petra; and the fourth is from a wall-painting at Pompeii. The *tholos* is surmounted by an urn, which is badly damaged, since up to quite recently every Bedouin who passed would shoot at it in the hope that he could hit some secret spot which, as in a gambling machine in a modern bar, would discharge in a flood the treasure which it is firmly believed to contain. In the interior are three chambers cut in the rock, from which a strange and lovely view appears between the rosy pillars.

As we followed the valley down, the tombs became more and more numerous: indeed, at one place the right hand wall is almost a continuous cemetery. These were mostly small tombs, of the so-called pylon type, representing a single-storied small house-front, but with a slight batter and with convergence of the two sides, and pierced with a single doorway leading into the funerary chamber. The top is adorned with a battlement motif, sometimes free-standing, but usually in relief only, each battlement having three or four steps. In the later tombs of this kind, this motif is reduced to the two half-battlements at the corners, enlarged and nearly meeting in the centre, so as to give the appearance of a double staircase. (This motif seems to be confined to Nabataean tombs, here and at other sites such as Heger in the Hedjaz region of Arabia, the southernmost town of the Nabataean kingdom.) Most of the rock here is darkish brown—chocolate, or with a tinge of russet.

On the left appear the remains of the theatre, probably of the first century A.D., when Roman influence was creeping in to Arabia Petraea. It too is, of course, wholly carved out of the rock, and here and there in its back walls are square black holes, where tomb-chambers have been cut through—a surprising juxtaposition: as Professor Libbey says, 'Amusement in a cemetery! A theatre in the midst of sepulchres!'

Then the valley broadens out into a more or less level space, rather over a square mile in extent. Here, along the stream-bed, are the remains of the Roman city, built wholly or mainly after Arabia Petraea was incorporated into the Empire in A.D. 106. Little is standing now save fragments of a temple and a triumphal arch; but study has shown that there were three large markets or caravanserais, a forum and portico, a couple of gymnasia, various shops, and (as in other contemporary cities of the region like Palmyra and Jerash) a colonnade of pillars along the main road—which was here built as a continuous bridge over the torrent-bed. The archaeologists have so far found no trace of any actual buildings from the earlier purely Nabataean period; however, there must certainly have been buildings for the kings and the seat of government.

Even in the Roman period, there are no built houses or buildings which can be ascribed to the local inhabitants as opposed to their Roman rulers, and some archaeologists go so far as to suggest that the bulk of these nomads turned sedentary exploiters of caravans were content with that first approximation to a house provided by a cave. At any rate, there are hundreds of artificial caves all over the place, some of them certainly lived in; and from those shelters we may perhaps imagine them looking down with a good deal of resentment on the alien Romans who had not only conquered them but degraded Petra from its position as a metropolis (in favour of Bosra, which they proclaimed the capital of their new *Provincia Arabia*).

The city-basin appears at first sight bounded by a continuous rampart, often nearly vertical, of rock; but actually, not only does the main torrent, Wady Musa, make its entrance into and its exit from the basin, but a large number of tributary ravines run down from the heights, and these too (made accessible by staircases cut in the rock) are crowded with caves and tombs and other rock-cut monuments.

The north-eastern part of this rampart, continuing the crowded cemetery I spoke of above, is covered with tombs, including three or four huge ones of two storeys, and one monster of three storeys—so high that the top storey had to be finished in masonry, as it could not be carved from the receding lip of the cliff. These large tombs are mostly russet brown; but just beside them is a smaller one in an astonishing multi-coloured stone. Burgon's 'rose-red city' had impressed me so much that I thought all of Petra would be pink or at least russet, and I was not in the least prepared for the variety of colours to be found. Edward Lear records that his cook Giorgio, 'who is prone to culinary similes,' said 'O Master, we have come into a world where everything is made of chocolate, ham, curry-powder, and salmon.' Ivory I have already mentioned, and the various shades of red and russet (Dean Stanley speaks particularly of dull crimson, and Kammerer of raspberry); but there is also sepia, and violet, and finally these multi-coloured sands.

They have often been deliberately employed by the rock-sculptors to give a particular effect. For instance, the tomb just referred to has been cut back further than usual until its façade appears multi-coloured, but in a brown framework; and in other tombs the multi-coloured stratum has been used for the ceiling. But their effect when they appear in the natural landscape is almost as extraordinary. The celebrated sands of Alum Bay, which one can buy in striped bottlefuls, are not nearly so fine. These at Petra consist of a repeated series of coloured bands, each series usually beginning with ivory, next light bluish-grey, then indigo, and finally a flaming rust-red. The bands are wavy and of unequal width, so that the effect is of a gorgeous if somewhat barbaric piece of watered silk.

A YOUNG BRITISH OFFICER and his wife whom we had met at breakfast at Ma'an had told me that a monument called El Deir—'the Monastery' —was among the most extraordinary of Petra, and that the rough climb of under an hour needed to reach it would be well repaid. This information was very lucky. When I broached the subject of El Deir, our Lebanese friends, backed by the local guide, said it was much too far— estimates varied from 1½ to 2½ hours for the ascent, 1 to 2 hours for the descent—and said they were going to have a comfortable lunch by the Roman temple. However, we three from Unesco—two Englishmen and a Mexican—said we would try, taking the guide, a boy, and our lunch, turning back when time gave out. The guide was not at all pleased, and kept on grumbling about our going too fast for his old bones: but when we found that he could give me fifteen years, we didn't worry too much about his bones or their age.

The way led up a steep and narrow ravine, often by way of Nabataean staircases. The path at one moment led into a narrow cleft where on a shelf under an overhang there were 'baths'—cisterns of some sort—still with water in them (a rare commodity in desert Petra); higher up, in a region of scattered pines, it came out along the edge of a precipice from which an astonishing view opened into a deep and narrow canyon, with

Aaron's Grave on top of Mount Hor in the distance; and finally emerged on to a col from which the land fell, in a drop of over a vertical mile, to the Ghor beyond, that part of the Great Rift Valley which leads downhill from near the Gulf of Akaba to the Dead Sea in its deep depression. The view of this drop was stupendous, if inhospitable in the extreme—bare bones of mountains, ribs carved by subaerial denudation, a landscape all desert and all erosion, down to the rift and up to the tableland of Idumaea beyond.

This side of the col was a green sward of grass, almost level, with the mountains rising on either side. And on the north was El Deir—apparently a huge two-storey temple, with the same type of façade as the Khazné, of reddish-brown stone, but in reality just the sculptured end of the mountain which rose above and beyond it. It is much bigger than the Khazné (over 140 ft. in height), but of later date and not nearly so beautiful. French writers have compared it to the façade of St. Sulpice in Paris, and Dean Stanley (with the anti-classical eye of the Gothic revivalist) to 'a London church of the eighteenth century, massive, but in poor taste, and with a somewhat debased style of ornament.' This is a little unfair. The Deir lacks elegance, but it has a certain grandeur and in its strange setting is immensely impressive. Its solitary interior chamber is the only one in Petra to contain an altar. Although it was perhaps a royal tomb, it seems to have served mainly as a temple. In any case, public rituals were held in this high suburb, for there are remains of a theatre, or at least large-scale seating accommodation, on the flat sward. And its traditional Arab name of the Monastery may well signify that it was at one time used as a Christian place of worship—either before the Arab conquest or during the brief century when this region was in the hands of the Crusaders.

The grass by the temple where we lunched was sprinkled with white camomiles and scarlet anemones. As we ate, I heard to my surprise a great tit calling: it seemed a long way from this desert mountain to the English gardens and woodlands which the call-note automatically evoked. Libbey and Hoskins, the Americans who visited Petra in 1905, saw seven fine ibex here; we had no such luck, nor did we see the coneys (hyraxes or rock-rabbits, distant zoological relatives of the elephant) which are said to be common round Petra, where the 'stony rocks' of the 104th psalm abound for them.

After lunch we made our way up steps and rock slopes to the top of El Deir. It was a shock to come out behind the façade and to be made aware that it *was* just a façade and nothing more—a bit of the mountain converted into stupendous stage scenery, designed to adorn the perennial human drama of death.

From the top you get a greater impression of its size. The vertical drop

from the cornice made us feel giddy, and our guides looked very remote
as they busied themselves on the sward below (we discovered later that
they were engaged in picking camomiles for camomile tea!).

Everywhere on the top and the back of the Deir little water channels
had been cut. This artificial gathering of water from the tombs and
stairways seems to have been widespread. Without it, the great city (its
population is estimated to have reached 30,000) could not well have
existed in the midst of the desert.

On our return, when we told our companions of all we had seen and
that we had taken only 50 minutes up and 30 down, they were sorry
they had not come with us. But they had lost their chance, and it was
time to get on our horses again and start back (with many dismountings,
in spite of stiff and rather weary limbs, to take photographs).

Beyond the Siq, in the ivory-coloured country, a young Arab came up
with a gazelle fawn in his arms. He had just captured the exquisite little
creature, and wanted us to buy it—but that was too difficult.

In the same stretch of country we saw flocks of black and grey birds,
nearly the size of jackdaws, which I took to be some kind of chough.
But on later inquiry I found that they were Tristram's Grackles—named
after the Canon Tristram who wrote a learned work on the fauna of the
Bible. Ravens we saw too, and falcons, and handsome desert chats like
black-and-white wheatears, and grey cliff-haunting martins.

Unfortunately we had no time to visit any of the High Places to be
found on the tops of the hills and mountains. It must suffice to say that
the High Place, apparently the official centre of the city's religious life,
seems to be the best-preserved in the world, and to give a wonderful picture of the religious practices of the Edomites and their Nabataean successors (practices so violently denounced by the Hebrew prophets).
Blood-sacrifice was practised, and the two great 'obelisks' remind us that
the Gods of this and neighbouring Semitic peoples were originally supposed to inhabit sacred rocks. These were later shaped, and eventually
developed into the so-called obelisks, which combined the function of
God-rocks or God-pillars (*not* idols, for they were not representations of
anything) and of altars. Indeed there is a good deal of evidence that
Jehovah was originally a God-rock from this area. In any case, the term
rock, so often applied to Jehovah (and to other Gods) in the Old Testament, was certainly not used in any metaphorical sense, but literally, to
mean the piece of rock which was sacred as the dwelling-place of the
divinity. (Robertson-Smith, the great authority on Semitic religion,
includes such rocks under the term 'God-box.')

The main God of the Petrans was called Dusares or Dushara, which
means *Lord of Seir,* Seir being the Semitic name of the region, and roughly
equivalent to Edom. In many of the tombs and temples of Petra there are

little niches, containing squared blocks of stone which symbolize Dushara and other divinities, or their dwelling-places.

What functions did Petra's strange assemblage of rock-cut monuments serve? Though the experts still disagree, the general consensus seems to be that only a few of them were dwelling-houses, and that the great majority were either tombs or places for celebrating feasts for (or with) the dead, or both combined. Some of the larger ones were royal tombs, which may also have served as temples. And perhaps a few, such as El Deir, were only temples.

Petra is unique in two respects—in its tombs and in its fortifications. Almost all ancient cities had to be strong points against attack. They were fortified with great walls and ramparts, and were often on top of a hill or crag. Petra is unique in lying in a deep hollow, provided by nature with cliffs as ramparts and with the Siq as a defendable entry unrivalled among the defensive works of man.

In many ancient cities the necropolis or city of the dead was as important as the city of the living—sometimes even more important. So in Palmyra, in Etruscan cities, in Egypt (though there the necropolis was for kings and nobles only), at Ras Shamra, and elsewhere. Petra is unique in having used its natural ramparts as its necropolis, and also in the fact that while the city of the dead has largely survived intact, the city of the living has been crumbled by weather and earthquake to a heap of ruins, scarcely any of them still upright.

WHAT IS THE MEANING of Petra? Why is it where it is? Why and when did it grow, and when and why did it decay? Here I have no space for more than a sketch of the outlines that are beginning to emerge. Even that I give with diffidence, for our ignorance of the origins and early history of Petra is still abysmal, and can only be dissipated by the excavator's spade; and the experts disagree in their interpretation of what is known.

The essential fact is that Petra was a caravan city pure and simple. It was a key point on the caravan route from Southern Arabia—Arabia Felix, the land of the Queen of Sheba—to Syria and Egypt. The myrrh and frankincense of the Hadramaut, the ivory, apes, and black slaves (but not peacocks!) of East Africa and Abyssinia, the spices and precious woods and other luxuries (including a small fraction of the silk in transit from China) brought in coasting vessels from the Indies, the pearls of the Persian Gulf, were assembled in the Sabaean's country near Aden. They then started north on camel-back along the west of Arabia, through Mecca, up the east coast of the Gulf of Akaba, and so to Petra. From Petra one important route led westwards to Gaza and thence south again to Egypt, another continued north to Damascus and so to the Phoenician coast (or, if required, to Aleppo and Antioch). On the coast it could be put aboard ship for Greece and Italy and other Mediterranean countries.

The incense was the most valuable, or at least the most essential, element in the trade. It was available only in the semi-desert areas of Southern Arabia and Somaliland, and it was required in large quantities for the religious ceremonies of all the nations of antiquity, from Egypt to Rome (Nero is said to have consumed more than a year's supply of incense for the funeral rites of Poppaea). And of course there were other goods flowing in the reverse direction—the purple-dyed stuffs of Phoenicia are one example.

The traffic came overland because in early antiquity the land, however inhospitable, seemed less dangerous than the sea—especially the Red Sea with its rocks and reefs and its waterless coast. The caravans were a great source of profit to the communities through which they passed, for there were heavy dues and tolls to pay at each main stage: but in return the authorities had to do all in their power to guarantee safety to the caravans, which would otherwise have been pillaged and their personnel massacred by the desert nomads.

Joseph was sold by his brothers to a caravan going south through this area: this route brought Solomon his chief luxuries, and along it must have passed the Queen of Sheba on her visit. In those days the region was populated by the Edomites, although David had brought it, as well as Moab to the north, under the control of Israel ('Moab is my washpot, and over Edom will I cast out my shoe'). A Kingdom of Petra existed, under the name of Sela in the country of Seir, but it is not certain that there was an actual city at Petra, and any physical remains from that period are still buried under layers of later culture.

Somewhere about the time of the Captivity, yet another wave of desert Semites began pressing on the region, pushing the Edomites out into Idumaea, left almost empty by Nebuchadnezzar's deportations. These were the Nabataeans; and with them, Petra as we know it began to grow up. Under their rule, Petra was a compulsory stage in the caravan journey (it may have been so before, but of that we know nothing certain). The teams of men from the south handed over their goods, to be taken on by new teams to west or north; there must have been huge warehouses for the royal stores and for the bales awaiting distribution, caravanserais, stables, and all the paraphernalia of a port—though a port on the coasts of that land-sea, the desert.

The Nabataeans maintained their position as an independent kingdom, in spite of the attempts made to subjugate them, first by one and then the other of the two powerful empires of Alexander's successors, the Seleucids and the Ptolemies. Indeed they were able to exploit their intermediate position to such good effect that their wealth and power grew rapidly, until for a few decades in the early first century B.C. they actually controlled Damascus in the north as well as the north-western corner of Arabia in the south. The great majority of the rock-cut monuments date from the two centuries between 100 B.C. and A.D. 100. During this period, a Hellenistic style was adopted for an increasing number of tombs and temples, and displayed increasingly Roman tendencies as time went on.

For the power of Rome was growing, and Petra came more and more under its influence. The Jewish revolt of A.D. 67 was a stimulus, and its successful and drastic crushing by Titus in A.D. 70 an encouragement, to a policy of expansion and firmness by Rome in the area; and the result of that policy, so far as the Nabataeans were concerned, was the annexation of their kingdom in A.D. 106, and its incorporation in the *Provincia* of Arabia, with Petra degraded from its metropolitan status in favour of Bosra on the road to Damascus.

It seems probable that the Romans were able to take advantage of the Roman Peace that they brought or imposed to divert the main caravan route between Arabia and Damascus somewhat to the east, not turning aside into Petra, as the Nabataeans, much to their own profit, had previously insisted. Furthermore, the Romans only consolidated their hold on the west coast of the Red Sea during the first century, and seem then to have drained off a large part of the trade between Arabia Felix and Egypt, away from the camel caravans that passed through Petra, into their own ships. And finally from about A.D. 130 the northern and eastern caravan route via Palmyra and the Persian Gulf began to develop rapidly under Roman impulsion, presumably because more of it was under Roman control, and because their then peaceful policy towards the Parthian Empire at the eastern end of the route made it safe and practicable.

Whatever the precise causes and their relative importance, it is a fact that the fortunes of Petra went down as those of Palmyra went up; Petran merchants began to move to Bosra and perhaps even further afield; fewer and fewer monuments were carved in Petra's rock walls, until by the fourth century it was almost abandoned—save by a small Christian community who found this desert retreat to their liking. (One of the tombs was converted into a Christian Church in the year 447, under Bishop Jason, as an inscription tells us.) Of the next few centuries we know nothing. The Crusades saw Frankish fortresses in and round Petra; but after Saladin's final victory the region seems to have been abandoned to the scattered Bedouins.

All knowledge of its glorious heyday was lost; and the only traditions

that persisted then—and persist to this day—are those from the time of
Moses.   Ain Musa is the spring that Moses caused to gush forth, and
Moses is still one of the commonest names among the population of Wady
Musa; the Treasury and the Roman temple have been ascribed to Pharaoh;
and Mount Hor is crowned with the tomb of Aaron, still a goal of
pilgrimage.

SO PETRA REMAINS TODAY, provocative, unique, fantastic.   It deserves
to be a place of pilgrimage, as an outstanding witness to the prodigal
strangeness and variety of human civilization during the few thousand
years of its existence, and to the triumphs, however transient, of human
endeavour over hostile nature and grudging environment.   It should be
one of the starred exhibits in a world museum of civilization.

But for this to happen it should be properly conserved, fully studied,
and made more accessible.   Comparison of Pharaoh's Treasury today
with its condition as revealed by the careful drawings of the early visitors
to Petra shows that in less than a century it has suffered considerable
deterioration from weathering; and clearly, in spite of the desert climate,
all the rock-cut monuments will eventually, if slowly, suffer, unless
remedial action is taken.

Various of the buildings could be restored or even re-erected.   Scientific
excavation has scarcely begun, and would quite certainly bring to light
the earlier stages of Petra's history, of which we are now virtually ignorant.   A Petra museum, either in Petra itself or at Ma'an or Amman, is
needed to give the visitor the indispensable background to the site and
its ruins and monuments, as the Museum at Candia does for the ruins
of Cnossos.   And, finally, easier travel, with accommodation in or close
to Petra itself, is essential.

For this, Petra should be fitted into some general framework.   The
Middle East gives a unique picture of the growth of civilization, from
its earliest origins up to the present.   Ur and Babylon, Nineveh and
Persepolis, Isfahan and Shiraz, Baghdad and Ctesiphon, Petra and
Palmyra, Baalbek and Byblos, Damascus and Aleppo, Sidon and Tripoli,
Jerash and Dura, Ras Shamra and Qalat Seman, fortresses and castles of
all periods down to the Islamic period—what a list!   And it includes
nothing from Egypt or Turkey: if they, too, are brought in the wealth of
wonders becomes prodigious.

Why do not the countries of the Middle East club together and work
out a plan for 'cultural tourism' by which these treasures of civilization
could be made readily available for modern pilgrims?   Doubtless that
would require careful organization, and probably international help from
some body such as Unesco: but it could and should be done.

Of the magic of many far places seen during fifteen years of travel, and of the superior spell of an African town which is remote, spiritually if not geographically, from Europe's unease.

Remembering Tangier

by PHILIP JORDAN

HOSE whom the circumstances of life have caused to wander widely in this world can remember only with difficulty, I think, the occasions on which, at the immediate impact of a place seen for the first time, they have thought: 'Yes, this is it: I will live here contentedly until I die.' Such memories of my own, diffused in unending travel that lasted almost fifteen years, are as chaotic as, for the most part, their influence was ephemeral.

Many I can still recall. And I like to believe that of such I can, at will, cherish the felicity of their initial moments; physical in supreme degree, and so strong in its power to awaken whatever ability I may possess to be moved by beauty, that I can again live through a series of such revelations with both chronological and sensual exactitude. Other memories, of course, however sublime they may have seemed in those first important moments, have become pale; and the only wonder that remains is like that created in us by the dust of Pharaonic tombs, the wonder that such obsolete and shabby grains could once have constituted beauty that was neither vulgar nor depressing.

The day was warm when I first came across the Lebanon to the apricot pillars of Baalbek, rising, as they then appeared to do, far into the massive radiance of a blue sky, whose splendour was unchanged from the horizon to the zenith. The pillars were like lamps; but, despite the glow with which they dazzled eyes still accustomed to the banalities of sea-coast towns, their outlines, worn with centuries of climatic attrition and human malice, were, so it then seemed, carved with an exact accuracy normally beyond the power of men. Who, that for the first time, draws to himself from the Parthenon's majesty, lustrous and benign in the evening sun, an aureole equally serene, can never have been sure, however transiently, that here, in the shadow of this only true triumph of man's mind over earth's matter, is the place from whose immediate area he has no wish ever to depart?

Rio de Janeiro, when you come to it in an aeroplane, is like a beautiful woman, seen for the first time across a crowded room, whom you know at once it will be your destiny to pursue and your happiness finally to possess. It is true that, in the moment of vision, an almost, but not wholly unconscious imperative tells you to reject the knowledge that from her possession, disillusion, fully armed, will almost certainly spring without delay.

Yes, and there are other memories: quick minutes of abiding magic. At evening, when the sky was violent with all colour, but, because of the immensity of the Egyptian wilderness around me, nevertheless tender beyond any I have since known, I have watched a flight of geese, bowstring-taut, moving slowly south to seek comfort from a northern winter in the waters of some equatorial lake, where, perhaps, they could be as happy in their own way as, in mine, they had made my solitude for an enduring minute. Lit by vibrating fires, the thin bodies of under-nourished coppersmiths, flickering in Calcutta slums, have seemed the rarest and most precious of earth's sights; and the smell of Corfu's black soil beneath the rain gave extra beauty to that place, so that it cannot be forgotten.

All these places, whose memories, it is true, are in time and not altogether in space, have drawn that involuntary cry of 'halt' from the secret places of my heart; yet it is more by the apposite moment of their creation in my own permanent vision of the world, than by their physical structure and position that they sought to beguile, and, perhaps, who knows? to ruin me. They all have magic: all worked their differing spells so that this traveller, sufficiently weary now to desire more than a night's lodging, must disregard their individual existences, whether in time or space, and seek, in however diluted a form it may be found, a synthesis of their differing magics in one place.

But who shall say what magic is? Domrémy has it, forlorn and dirty as it is, because Saint Joan lived there: Avallon, too, because that is its name; and I know why men, approaching from the east, believe Damascus to be the fairest and most magical of cities. And a score more whose names tremble individually for a while, then fuse and fall into my memory.

Yet, if magic be not too intoxicating for daily absorption, and if we lived in a world whose currencies were minted—as they should be—from the same substance, it would not be hard for me to choose my dwelling place. My fancy would, I think, alight and come to rest in the international settlement of Tangier.

You must approach it from the sea: preferably in spring, certainly by the packet that sails from Gibraltar in the early afternoon; and, for several hours, thumps its way past the southern extremities of Spain. In these days of almost intolerably swift travel there is a nostalgic pleasure in the slow beat of antique reciprocating engines, built with loving precision to endure long into an era, the romance of whose sea-travel has been killed by the silent hum of turbines. There is, so to speak, no gongorism about that little boat: you travel in no annexe of the hotel you have just quitted, but in an honest ship that makes no pretence to be anything but what she is. She is by no means comfortable, as I remember: far from it; but in the evening light, surprisingly more tropical than it is only a few miles north, in Europe, it brings you safely across the narrows and into the harbour of this African town.

Henceforth you may take your pleasures as you will. Let it be said here that although I have visited Tangier several times, I have brought away from it little that is topographically accurate; but I have been sufficiently etched by its stylus to be sure that, however inexact I might now prove as a distant guide to its labyrinthine ways and subterranean streets, I have but to land again on the town's untidy quay to find my ways.

A green hill rises above the city, freeing itself, as it moves upwards, from its first thick integument of shining stucco, and its higher flank is only sprinkled with white villas that absorb light during the day, and, in the last minutes of a short twilight, seem generously to pour it away, like fragments of the northern lights scattered in some warmer place. As Mount Triglav in Croatia frees itself, as it soars, of clustering trees and, finally, of all vegetation, so does the hill of Tangier shake off its villas, fallen petals of a celestial magnolia, to emerge, clear, green, and smelling of thyme, in the last few yards of height, before it falls westward, on the other side, to Cape Spartel and, in spring, the peacock glory of Atlantic waters.

The climbing road into the town's centre tells the tale that, ever in fuller measure and in differing tongues, you will hear while you remain there; and the pleasure of its impact on the traveller who wishes to learn is not dissimilar to that which the reader of only one language derives from the pages of a Loeb classic: the left-hand sheet delights his mind while the right-hand, equally seductively, perhaps, albeit in differing quality, impinges on his ears, and, if the language be written in a script different from his own, his eyes as well. Here, side by side, but in no prearranged order, are the shop windows of the western world, and the open, glassless, and, to us, infinitely more mysterious bazaars of eastern peoples, common, from this place, to all towns and villages as far as the remote littorals of China. In these sheds the sacks are open, but from what strange plants come the beans and pods that crowd their neatly rolled jute necks, the newcomer can hardly say; and it is only when the tide of these intermingled lives has ebbed and flowed frequently through his being that he knows, but, by then, does not bother to admit that what lie there are precisely the same beans and pods, in differing proportions no doubt, that he buys in neat, glossy packets to consume in some hygienic form, and from which, generally speaking, processing has cleaned innocuous dirt and stolen all vitality. We are seduced by sealed packages into whose contents our fingers may not explore until we have paid for them, but those whom we like to think more primitive than we, are not to be lead astray by names or gaudy designs thought up in the air-conditioned parlours of New York or London.

Common to all, however, to bazaar-shed or glass-encased emporium, are the only real international words: Kodak, Shell, Gillette, and aspirin ; so that the traveller may wonder whether, in fact, the products of these industrial empires have brought to those who obey their laws and ordinances a happiness greater than that they slew when they first managed to create demand.

Where the road turns and gathers strength to lurch up the hillside there is an open square from whose trampled earthen floor dull Mediterranean plane trees thrust their sturdy trunks, grudgingly, to give uncomfortable shade. Here is the northern fringe of life as men and women pass it through the hot regions and over the cold mountains that lie between here and the Equator: here we are linked with that last torrid zone by an unbroken thread of immemorial custom. Throughout the day an avenue of squatting caryatids, with no visible burden on their shoulders, edges a path from the road to the entrance of the souk that lies below, their heads crowned with circular straw hats whose outer peripheries alone tremble in occasional breezes. Of their refreshing quality those who squat beneath those straw haloes seem unaware. These careless and unfinished sculptures are live Berber women from the hills, yellow as old marble, from which, until their washed-blue eyes move slowly with a maddening lack of curiosity, they might be chiselled. Ranged in small heaps before them, with a supreme and casually acquired knowledge of the power of colour, are what, from any distance, seem to be large jewels extracted from forgotten mines whose secret entries they alone have managed to remember. Here rise and tumble in their elephantine hands, whose movement is that of some sleeker and more graceful beast, the amethystine casings of the aubergine, the emerald sheen of polished pea pods, the nacreous shine of carefully peeled onions ; and washed carrots, too, spherical stones of a colour altogether rare. These good things are their wealth, and rich indeed is she among these silent women who can display and accept money for a basket of clean eggs. Yet, because their ways are not wholly debauched by our own, their poverty is no mean thing, for they are not, as they there seem, mindless creatures, content to trudge far each day to earn no more than copper pieces: they have a salty humour and much happiness which they liberally dispense when you meet them on the road.

Here, in this square, not fifty yards from where the sound of ice in cocktail shakers is knitted with that of western radios, is the blind story-teller to whose magic person an exclusively male audience seems permanently attached. And here, for those who like unclean pleasures, is the snake-charmer; and the money changer, with his metal wealth laid out, jointed serpents that will not rise and coil to the tune of peaceful pipes, in semicircular ruts cut in his polished trestle. Now indeed it is strange to know that less than fifty yards away hot water is flowing into the sunken porcelain bath-tubs of clean hotels, and that a printing press, albeit as old as the ship's reciprocating engines, is inking out the news of distant worlds that touch, without either being aware of it, the lives of these Berber caryatids, of the snake-charmer and the story-teller, and of the old crones who load themselves with a few penceworth of firewood, gathered far away.

Below the square the land falls sharply, between rows of bright shops, to the nexus of the souk, at whose entrance stand, as monuments both to the academic folly of contemporary nationalism and to men's efforts to cure it by homeopathy, the post offices of Spain and Italy. In the upper town Great Britain and France manifest the same disease. Indeed, nothing in all Tangier can more astound the British traveller than his first discovery of a British post office, complete with the prudish bronze plaques and neat white lettering we know so well, 'teleported' from, let us say, Rickmansworth or Guildford, so that when he comes outside with a five shillings book of stamps in his hand and one of Mr. McKnight Kauffer's posters in his eyes, it is, for a moment, strange to see, not English lanes in spring and hot, pig-tailed girls on bicycles, but, almost next door, comfortable Arab gentlemen in yellow slippers and djellabas, drinking mint-scented tea in the garden of a café shack, and cosily smoking from common pipes to whose flexible tubes each has fitted his own private amber mouthpiece.

Shops, mainly operated by Sephardic Jews, line the street that falls from the square to the souk's mysteries; and here their owners deal in small wares that have permanent value and can be moved easily when they once more become inclined to wander through the earth. These philatelists, these dealers in stones and precious metals, are for ever on the move, the visible crust of a hidden and scattered world pushing upwards through the generations to acceptance and positions in societies they despise but need to penetrate, because prejudice and fear have so long excluded them that they have become desirable. Their windows are crammed with trash to lure silver from the pockets of sailors, but in small back rooms, to which time alone can provide the stranger with a key, many hold much wealth in wallets and in chamois-leather bags, that their daughters may carry on the race.

Much virtue and, perhaps, more vice lie behind the doors that flank the souk's streets, paved with rectangular stones and clean as those beneath the arcades at Berne. What you choose to do is your own business, and men are compassionate of human weakness. Once, on a spring night, when I found myself there in the company of a considerable French writer, with whose name you would be familiar, his unhappy, but, by then, half-conquered craving for cocaine came on him, and for some hours, until he could no more bear the deprivation, we sought relief for him in the night cafés that do so little to attract you that you must seek them out by questioning kind strangers in the labyrinth. When dawn was near, trumpeted by that sudden cooling effluence peculiar only to places where great heat can sometimes come, he would wait no longer; and he walked up to a policeman, unmoving, I remember, beneath a street lamp, so that he was like a late 19th century theatrical poster, lithographed in lemon and blue shadings, and asked him where he might buy the drug. I need not have been fearful, as I then was, for the policeman did no more than take a small parcel from his pocket and sell it to my friend.

But if the covered streets of the Socco are lonely at night, by day they are so crowded that it is more comfortable, if you are inclined to laze, either to mount the ruined kasbah that was once the symbol of Moorish domination, and, on the walls of that fallen citadel, drink tea, or climb the hill above the town and lie in a field of thyme from which, with happiness, you can look across the bay to where the molten land above Ceuta trembles in an alien heat. You do not need to ask from what countries come those who inhabit the villas you pass on your way up, for men write their nationalities in the gardens they make and in the smells that come from the kitchens in which their food is cooked. Take my advice: climb higher to where, on warm afternoons, rich Arabs, attended by servants, will picnic without their wives and pass blissful hours at chess. Here indeed is peace.

That is, in part, the magic of this place. It is infinitely remote. The unease of Europe begins only a few miles north, but the present neuroses of our continent have failed to cross the straits. Politics! What, when you are lying in a field of thyme, are politics? A disease that consumes men in moribund societies. Here, you cannot but feel, not only is liberty unmenaced, but there do not exist men sufficiently evil to contrive its death. No doubt, this indigenous felicity is an illusion; but if magic were not an illusion it would have no meaning but fear. Perhaps, then, you think, all this will endure and you need worry about nothing more important than the need to reach the shore and swim before the sun goes down.

Alas: as you rise and stretch to go down into the city, the walls of the smashed kasbah remind you of the impermanence of all things; and you remember then those other symbols: the pillars of Baalbek, the Parthenon, and, not so far away, the salt-sewn desert that was Carthage.

It began with a small wooden keg bobbing on the water of a North Devon cove. For the next seven years the tide never turned but that Mr Duncan was there to meet it.

The Confessions of a Beachcomber

by RONALD DUNCAN

Anthony Gilbert

O move from one house to another is to do more than change one's address. We think it is merely a matter of shifting our furniture, buying new curtains, finding new tradesmen. Such tedious business accomplished, we unpack our books and assume quite confidently that our personality will soon impose itself on our new surroundings and that we shall then feel quite at home again, and everything will be as before. That is where we make a big mistake: it is not we who change a house but, more often, the house which changes us . . . Anyhow, that's been my experience.

For years, I had had my eye on an old watermill which lay in the lap of a North Devon cove. The beach was only two hundred yards from the mill. The sides of the valley were steep and uncultivated,

P

covered with giant gorse bushes, a thick mat of heather and ling giving way to a coppered wilderness of bracken. Wild sage and thyme made the cliffs smell like Harris tweed. The land had been entirely abandoned to rabbits; the small trout stream was leased by a heron, and poised buzzards overlorded all. Further up, away from the sea, both sides of the valley were wooded with scrub oak, tortured little trees, their trunks twisted like corkscrews, their branches shorn by the wind. Every tree looked as though it had been arrested in full flight with each twig pointing away from the sea.

I don't know why I had always wanted to live in this place. Perhaps I mistook its loneliness for solitude; or, what was a greater error, assumed its solitude would mean serenity. At any rate, as soon as I had heard that the mill was vacant, I went down the steep cart track to look over the place. The old miller, who had recently moved to a farm at the top of the hill, now trundled along beside me. I noticed that his legs were bandy, like two barrel staves; and that his enormous shoulders were bent as from a life spent in carrying great weights—but, as he was a miller, this did not surprise me.

The cottage looked rather like a drunken charwoman, for its thatch had slipped over its eaves; the untidy ivy hung as wisps of hair over its blowsy walls.

'It's got great character, this house has,' said the miller, trying to impress me. He was right; the cottage had character, but of what kind was another matter. At that moment I suspected that any references this old char might produce would be forged in her own untidy hand.

'And it's as old as these hills themselves,' the miller added in the vague hope that its vice might have decreased with its age.

We went inside. There were only three rooms. And, if one excluded the large open fire place from the sitting-room, then one could say there were only two.

The cottage was unfurnished, but full: full of clutter. My wife and I had to stand on each other's feet, for the floor was covered with the queerest assortment of rubbish that I had ever seen. Bits of cork, coils of rope, slabs of grease, lumps of brass, and planks of every length. In one bedroom I observed five unhung doors lying in a pile on a bed.

'I'll clear this stuff out,' the Miller offered, trying to make the deal.

'What about water?' I asked him.

'There's a well.'

'A lavatory?'

'There's a bucket.'

'You only need some nails and you could be a fakir,' my wife suggested to me.

'With inconveniences like these,' I retorted, pointing to the pump without a handle, 'none of our friends will ever visit us. This is just the place we're looking for.'

I was, at that time, trying to settle down to write a play. I was fleeing from London distractions. And, mistaking discomfort for simplicity, I bought the cottage there and then.

'What are we going to do about furniture?' my incredibly tolerant wife asked.

The miller offered to sell us a single bed, a card-table, and a rocking-chair.

'As for the rest, you'll soon pick that up,' he said with a sort of tired resignation which I didn't notice at the time.

Having removed his pile of doors from the bed, he puffed his way up the hill again.

My wife surveyed her home.

'It won't take you long to dust it,' I consoled her, 'once he's cleaned this stuff out.' Then I took my turn in our only chair as she went along to explore the cupboards.

'This is just the place to write in,' I mused. I began, absent-mindedly, to sharpen a pencil . . . And that was as near as I got to my play; for, at that moment, there was a cry of excited delight coming from the depths of the cupboard underneath the stairs . . . My wife had found an old rusty kettle, two cups, and a knife.

'If you were to stop wasting your time sharpening a pencil,' she said as she emerged, covered in cobwebs, 'and were to go and find some fire-wood, we could boil this kettle and have some tea.'

'If we had any tea,' I replied, bluntly puncturing her domestic fantasy.

'Anyhow, if you got some firewood, we could sit by the fire—or, at least, one of us could.'

I put my pencil down. It was a full four years before I picked it up again. . . .

I went outside and immediately began tugging at the gorse-roots. Either they were strong or I was weak. When we parted I was the more dishevelled. Feeling discouraged, I wandered aimlessly down the donkey path to the beach. The tide was just on the turn. A faint evening wind blew from the land, turning the backs of the waves as though they were the leaves of a book. For a few moments I stood almost mesmerized by the monotonous sound of the waves. Then, quite suddenly, I saw something interesting, something bobbing up and down about three waves out from the shore. For a moment I thought it was a seal. Then the surf seemed to roll itself up into one great wave which flung the object towards me. It was a small wooden keg.

I rolled it out of the sea, far too excited to notice that I was almost soaked to the skin. Then, with hands as clumsy as a crab, I began to claw at the lid. I could tell by its weight that it was full—but of what? In desperation, I looked for a sharp pebble and with this bashed a hole in the lid. I smelt. I stuck my finger in. I sucked. It was fresh butter. About fifty pounds of it. Like a prospector who had at last found gold by tripping over a mine, breaking his nose on a nugget, I began to giggle hysterically. Then, finding strength I did not know I possessed, I carried the keg back to the cottage.

'Butter from beach,' I announced, placing it before my wife, as though that now completed her home.

She dug her finger in. 'It's perfect!' she said. 'What a pity we haven't got any bread. . . .'

THAT'S HOW IT BEGAN; AND, FOR the next seven years, the tide never turned but that I was there to meet it. And the tide turns twice a day. The fascination of finding something for nothing completely dominated me. Often I would wake up at four o'clock in the morning, hearing the wind moaning over the cottage. For a few seconds I would lie still, wondering what might be cast up on the rocks. Perhaps another keg? This time some tea? Could I risk it and go to sleep again? But, if I did, wouldn't some neighbour find it before me? Sheer predatory greed would then fling me out of bed, and curiosity hurl me out into the cold, wet night. My flickering lanthorn would make the mist seem solid. My feet grew eyes of their own and would lift me from rock to rock with a sleepwalker's sureness; my hands, too, got to know the surface of the granite cliff with an almost indecent intimacy. I had become an addict. And the drug would drag me slithering over the wet rocks every twelve hours, whatever the season, whatever the weather.

Many mornings, there was nothing but seaweed. On such days I would return home with only firewood and sit sullen through breakfast. I would then resolve to give up this mad pursuit and get on with my work. But on the very next tide the sea would yield something to me as if unwilling to let me go. I remember the morning when I promised my wife that I would go no more to the beach if there was nothing washed up by the next tide. I knew there would be; I knew that the sea had no mercy.

The wind had been blowing from the south-west; so, instead of going towards Gull Rock, I went towards Chizel Reach. As soon as I turned the point of the cove, I saw it. The tide had only just dropped it, its sides were still flecked with foam. I raced across the rocks, terrified that the object for which I had waited and watched for so many tides might turn out to be a mirage, or, what would have been worse, be claimed by a neighbour getting his mark on it first.

For a full minute I stood still, letting my eyes caress its lovely shape, appraising its full-bodied depth, its compact, buoyant lines. I stood in awe as though before an idol. Indeed, it was my idol. I had dreamt it, wished it, willed it. This was no mere brewer's barrel which you often see being rolled into a pub's cellar, but the Emperor of all Barrels. I was reminded of a great ebony Buddha which had suddenly confronted me in an Indian jungle.

I tapped one end. It was full. If it had been empty, I would have wept with disappointment. But it was full. But of what? Oil? Treacle? Pitch? What else goes in barrels? A panic of speculation seized me. I put my nose to it but could smell nothing—only the sea. Then I began grovelling for the bung and gradually eased it out. A scarlet flow spurted into the night. It was as though I had let its blood; as if I had severed the artery of a wild boar. I put my mouth to it as one does to a fountain, and the wine gushed all over my neck. 'My God!' I cried aloud, seldom feeling so fervent, 'it's Burgundy!'

I dived frantically to replace the bung. This secure, I raced home across the rocks. As I went, I tried desperately to remember all the mathematics I had learned at school in an effort to work out how much wine was in the barrel. The nearest I could get to the formula for volume was to remember the name of the master's wife . . . No matter, the problem was not to measure, but to salve, before the tide washed the barrel out again.

I ran upstairs to my wife who was still in bed. 'What have you done?' she cried, mistaking the wine on my shirt for blood.

'Quick! Quick!' I yelled, 'give me a bottle, dozens of bottles!' And, for a start, I grabbed her hot water bottle and emptied it out of the window. Then I tore round the cottage, grabbing every jug, basin, pitcher, and pot.

All day we went to the beach, back and forth, carrying our jars of wine until even the sink and the child's bath were full. At last, we counted eighty gallons of the sea's red mercy.

After this haul, there was no stopping me. And though no more wine came in, the sea kept me faithful to her tides by casting an occasional favour.

One morning, I found the beach simply littered with airtight tins— each full of American coffee in perfect condition. And, soon after the invasion of Normandy, two American supply ships collided in a fog off our coast. Like a greedy vulture, I waited, watching for the wind to change. When it did eventually, I found a man's leg lying bootless on the beach. I knew the rest of the cargo would soon follow.

Sure enough, the next tide was profligate: cartons and crates were squandered on the shore. There must have been fifty thousand cigarettes, all perfectly dry. There were cigars too. One could pick them out of the sea and light them. And all the comforts of a bathroom culture followed, including hundreds of tubes of shaving cream, toothpaste, chewing gum, and, of course, contraceptives.

Then weeks would pass and I would find nothing but a mere slab of tallow, a dozen pit-props or a bale of raw rubber—for which the Custom and Excise would pay me £3 per bale.

And sometimes the tides would tease me pitilessly. I remember one sullen November spending all the morning watching a barrel bob up and down on the backs of the waves. It seemed as if the tide just lacked sufficient strength to land it. I could tell it was full by the way it floated. I decided to wade out and push it ashore. I stripped, the water was maliciously cold. But I kept my eye on the barrel and waded on. I began to push it ashore. Just as I had nearly succeeded in landing it, a great Atlantic roller came up behind me unawares and wrapped me helplessly round the barrel. As it turned, so did I too. And, in this ridiculous fashion, I rode the surf—with the slight difference of being underneath it. At last the great wave flung us on to the beach: I, on top of my prize. Before I could break from this compulsory embrace, the wretched thing began to roll backwards over me. I turned, chasing it as it trundled back, faster and faster down the shingle, towards the sea again. Then a small rock arrested its mad career and I caught up with it, only to watch sixty gallons of Guinness seep into the thirsty sea. . . . Few experiences have moved me as much as this did. I almost wept over the waste of it. And it is not that I like beer. I never drink it.

PERHAPS, AS A COMPENSATION FOR THIS disappointment, my next find followed within a few days.

It was a metal drum. I rolled it to shore and sniffed. Petrol!

I had, at this time, to add to my distractions, acquired an adjoining smallholding and ran an old lorry which I used for collecting bins of pig swill from a nearby R.A.F. camp and hotels. Two days previously I had run out of petrol coupons. My pigs were squealing with hunger. The hotels were all complaining that their guests were moving out because of the stench from my uncollected swill. I had failed to borrow any coupons and my present need could not have been more. And here was a full drum of petrol. But I had become so spoilt that I did not regard this as a lucky find, or even as an opportune coincidence. I took its arrival as a matter of course; as though it were quite natural that the sea should yield precisely what I needed when I needed it. Like a pampered god collecting the sacrifices laid on his altar, I casually rolled the drum to the foot of the cliff. And then emptied its contents into jerrycans which had most conveniently arrived in their dozens on a previous tide.

Like all gods, I now became criminally careless. I filled the tank of my lorry and drove up the hill to the R.A.F. camp. I noticed that the acceleration was much improved. My old crock, which lacked an exhaust pipe, whizzed round the camp like a rocket. Officers ran from messes, for the lorry was making a noise like a plane. And no wonder, for it was not petrol in my tank but octane, aviation fuel. . . .

Months later, I sat caged in a lonely cell, feeling as frustrated as a jackdaw with a cork fixed on its beak. I awaited my trial.

The charge of stealing a drum of aviation fuel during a war made my prospects look horribly bleak. I consoled myself that a period of enforced idleness would have its compensations. I began to sharpen my pencil again, almost relishing the sentence as a relief from this tyranny of the tides.

But, somehow or other, no charge of theft could be proved. For I had rolled the drum from the sea. It was, therefore, my lawyer claimed, flotsam and not jetsam. This distinction made an honest man of me. It turned out, too, that I owned manorial rights to the beach. Accordingly, I was released.

That same evening found me at my beat again. Having missed a dozen tides, there was quite a bit to pick up—including a couple of tins of corn on the cob which, of course, I washed down with Burgundy. I will not be so indiscreet as to tell all the stories of subsequent tides. But this I will admit: though the miller had cleared the mill of his clutter, I had completely filled it with my own.

My wife and I had started with only three pieces of furniture. Now, after four years, there was not space to turn. The sitting-room was stacked with deck-chairs I had salved. Lumps of tar and rope hid my books. Piles of planks and the litter of driftwood entirely engulfed us.

There were two alternatives: either to give up beachcombing or to move altogether. Only the latter was possible, for I knew that whatever one's intentions the position of the cottage entirely determined one's activities.

As we walked up the hill for the last time I noticed my shadow: the shoulders rounded from carrying great weights, but not sacks of wheat, and my legs like the staves of a barrel. As I say, it is not we who change a house of character—but it who alters us.

Now, from my home at the top of the hill, I observe my tenant in the old mill in the throes of the same tyranny: and I draw considerable satisfaction from the sight of him struggling daily under a load of driftwood as I leisurely sharpen my pencil.

Downland Spring

by DILYS POWELL

T was, I see now, with a headful of literary notions that I set off for the Plain. The shepherd on the downs, the sheep, in Matthew Arnold's phrase, crossing and recrossing the strips of moon-blanch'd green—I looked forward to heaven knows what pastoral colloquies; I had, too, at the back of my head the memory of days in Greece, the boy piping amid the intent Boeotian silence, cloaked shepherds bringing their flocks down from Parnassus towards Delphi and the Gulf.

As we drove west from Salisbury I looked about me. We were at the verge of the Plain in the valley of the Ebble, called also the Chalke Valley: the most southerly of the vales whose streams slide between the downs to join the Avon. It was the last week of March, and the fields were fawn and lemon-coloured. The road ran along a wide shallow scoop between remote hills; on the left, as we looked towards Broadchalke, water-meadows separated us from the ragged willows of the Ebble. Cottages, farm-houses, and inns were of stone or brick and flint; occasionally a wall, cream-washed, wore a gable of thatch. The landscape was wooded, enclosed, and domestic. It was far from my idea of Salisbury Plain; and there was not a sheep in sight.

A mile short of the village of Broadchalke we left the road, turned right past Stoke Farm, and took a track which presently climbed between steep naked banks. The earth was pale, and the air still smelt of winter. Mr Thomas, tenant of Stoke Farm, authority on sheep-breeding, and owner of a pedigree Clun Forest flock, had offered us the sight of his sheep, or some of them, being driven from one pasture on his thousand-acre holding to another. I imagined a romantic spectacle. But we were late. From the deserted cottage above the track two tangle-furred cats ran mewing into an outhouse; a tractor clattered, took breath, and turned in the brown field at the crest of the hill. We could find neither Mr Thomas nor his sheep.

I have often felt chilled at a first meeting with landscape admired through literature; it is as if, introduced to some famous contemporary, one were to find the idol silent, sluggish, and sallow-faced. Indeed I do not know why the stranger should expect to love at first sight. That afternoon in the Wiltshire Downs I looked at the country without seeing it; as I afterwards discovered, we had driven by Mr Thomas's noble flock of ewes with their lately born lambs and had not recognized it. Perhaps there was some excuse. I had been looking for a different picture: for the image of the shepherd immortally cherishing his sheep.

A folded flock has constant need of its shepherd. Mr Thomas's Clun

Photographs by VICTOR MITZAKIS

Recruit to a Wiltshire Flock

A track climbs from the valley of the Ebble to the chalk downs; beside it, in a pasture, this lamb was born, to thrive and to enjoy the April sunshine.

March Lambs

Like the lamb in the first picture, this ewe is of the Clun Forest breed. It is the end of March, and her twins are less than two days old; they will graze in the open, and never know a sheepfold.

218

Hampshire Downs in the Fold

On a neighbouring farm another system of sheep husbandry is practised. These Hampshire Downs, feeding on swedes and kale, belong to a folded flock.

The Modern Shepherd

The shepherd of the Hampshire Down flock, Mr Batchelor, whose sheep spend their days between hurdles, which are moved when necessary to allow a fresh section of the crop to be eaten.

On the Uplands

The assistant Shepherd, Mr Whatley, stands on ground over which the flock have eaten their way, manuring as they went. His own dog Trixie is next to him; the other dog is Mr Batchelor's Chico.

Priority for Lambs

The lamb-hurdle, or creep, allows the lambs to pass into the next fold and eat the best of the crop, while preventing the ewes from following them.

Downs and Sky

Behind the flock is the crop to be folded, and beyond lies the valley of the Ebble.

223

Bonnie at Rest

This intelligent sheepdog, Bonnie, belongs to Mr J. F. H. Thomas, owner of the Clun Forest sheep shown in the first two pictures. Bonnie is a Scotch collie—a type with a natural instinct for 'working' sheep.

Forest flock has no fold; the ewes graze in the open and lamb alone; there is no hired shepherd on Stoke Farm. The pasture to which we drove next morning lies on the south face of a little valley between the downs and the Chalke Valley; to the west a beech wood writes, in early spring, a purple V where the foothills curve into one another. The track crosses the valley between woods and pasture and rises steeply northward to the spine of the downs; on its left you can trace the rectangular terraces of Celtic fields. The path itself has an ancient name: Herepath. In this corner of earth the sheep, too, have the look of eternity.

The lambs, that bright bare March morning, were running in packs; forgetting their dams, they raced down the slope, seven or eight of them together, prancing in mock heraldic battle. The black-faced ewes cropped the turf, turned to call their children, gazed with flat amber eyes over the valley. Some, with immense flanks, would labour tomorrow or the next day; some had already at their soft thick skirts a pair of twins. None of the lambs in the field was much more than a week old; the youngest had been born within the last twenty-four hours, perhaps in the night; one tiny ropy creature, still ignorant of the laws of levitation, was attempting a vertical jump from a kneeling position. We went into the pasture, walking deliberately lest we should frighten the families. Whooiy, whooiy, whooiy, Mr Thomas called softly and reassuringly; a pace behind him his dog, the beautiful Bonny, crept and crouched and crept again . The ewes stared and moved away without haste. A lamb, tired of racing with the pack, began to cry for his mother. He run uncertainly uphill, circled, and thrust his dark muzzle against a grazing ewe; she butted him roughly away. He's not her lamb, said Mr Thomas, she won't have him.

Even with her own children a sheep's maternal feelings can be too severely tried. Victor Mitzakis wanted to photograph a ewe with twins, and Mr Thomas climbed the slope to find a good subject; he came back with a lamb dangling by its hind legs in each hand and the mother trotting behind; he baa'd as he walked to encourage her to follow. I took up one of the lambs. It lay in my arms quietly enough, but it was not the soft-coated creature it had seemed at a distance; the wool was scratchy, almost prickly. The ewe with her second twin at first cropped indifferently a few yards away. But at last her patience gave out and she began moving off; and, her owner showing an understandable anxiety, I released the animal I was holding; the mother might, Mr Thomas said, have lost interest in a child too long withheld from her.

The flock, I have said, is not folded; and the ewes of themselves, as the spring light fails, gather their lambs on the high ground away from the frosts which settle in the hollows. But the sheep need occasional help: a lamb may be orphaned; a mother may deliver herself of a lively

R

child, then wander sickly, still carrying a dead twin. Sometimes a ewe, huge with the life she carries, rolls on to her back and lies helpless; she will die if she is left for many hours. Mr Thomas, then, must be his own shepherd: early in the morning, late in the evening, he visits the flock. When, the day after our first acquaintance, we again drove with him over the chalky track, there lying on the pasture was a barrel of wool with delicate feet in the air. It did not move: could it, we asked appalled, be dead? No, no, he said, plenty of time, and sure enough as he approached the barrel gave a feeble jerk; he rolled it over, the legs found solid earth, and the ewe, with an outraged look, flounced away. You should always, said Mr Thomas, if you see a ewe on her back, turn her over.

Another sheep was pawing the turf, kneeling, panting; she was near her labour. A third had lambed early that morning. One of her twins was lying, with the mild air of the newborn, in the shade of the beeches; the other had contrived to push through the wire fence, and now waited outside complaining of thirst while his mother, still dragging the birth-membrane, pessimistically went on grazing. An older and more active lamb had escaped from the pasture and was running along the brow of the hill, up and down the length of the fence, crying to be back. Bonnie, sent to recover him, circled cautiously, lay down near him, moved gently again; but the lamb, defeating the plan to drive him through a gate, suddenly rushed at the fence and in desperation jumped it.

Half-wild, half-pacified, the flock pursued its self-contained life, while all around the extravagance of nature fought the economy of man. Partridges flew up clucking from the Herepath; on the green hillbrow west of the beech wood, above a turf-track older than the trees which grow in its furrow, a school of hares played. Farther down the secret little valley a herd of Shorthorns with a white bull stood by a pool already enamelled with ranunculus and stared at the passing car. One afternoon we drove by them over the satiny turf and took the track to the sheep-dip near the crest of the downs. The place is used a few times only during the year, and the buildings, the yard, the pen, the bath in which the sheep are dipped were desolate. But in Stoke Bushes, the ring of ivy-sleeved ash-trees higher up the slope to the north-east, there was the clamour and traffic of a rookery; and presently five ponies, white, grey, and chestnut-and-white, left their grazing and watched us. A butterfly or two, brimstone or tortoiseshell, had come out in the sunshine, and shoots were breaking the buds of the black thickets: lime-green shoots from the red scales of the briars, from the ochre of the thorns.

On Mr Thomas's farm the sheep live chiefly by natural laws. A mile away, on Major Jeans's adjoining farm, their lives are governed by the laws of the shepherd and the fold. On the afternoon when our city eyes had played us so false we had driven at last to the end of the climbing track and met at a right angle a broad chalk way running east and west along the ridge; it was, Mr Thomas told me afterwards, an old road used in the past by drovers between Salisbury and Shaftesbury. If you follow it to the west you will pass between the landmarks of Stoke Bushes to the south and, to the north a little farther on, an oval of trees named Long Folly; still further, and on your left hand, is Fox Covert, a tangle of thorns and climbing shrubs; beyond it a track turns left towards the village of Broadchalke and the valley of the Ebble. The downland in the westward angle between the track and the chalk way is broad, open, and, in spring, naked except for the early corn; but the wind with its steady hiss covers the crying of the lambs, and the curve of the ground hides the low lines of the hurdles, so that not until you are a field's-breadth away do you find the sheepfold.

Major Jeans's magnificent pedigree flock is of Hampshire Down sheep, a breed reared for the fold. On our first visit as we drove with the owner up the track from Broadchalke he talked with enthusiasm of the part played by a folded flock in the life of the soil. In this upland country, with the soil thin on the heights, it is costly, he said, to carry manure from the valleys to the tops of the hills. Yet the earth must serve; and fertility must be preserved. The flock between hurdles, feeding on its specially grown crop, manures the land and passes on; the root-crop which in these spring months is its part-diet helps to clean the soil and prepare it for a later sowing of corn. By now we were turning beside a field; presently we saw a hut with wheels and corrugated iron roof, and beside it a long low wattle fence.

We walked towards the enclosure. The air was full of the cries of lambs and the deeper plaints of the ewes, and when we came close we could see that the flock was crowded within hurdles which marked part of a hillside thickly grown with swedes and kale. Black face, black ears, black feet, and a rich cushiony fleece: for a moment I could distinguish no more than a restless huddle of bodies amidst the shoulder-high green. Then, with a surprise which betrayed my town-bred ignorance, I saw that the lambs here were already sturdy square-set creatures, not the leggy infants of Mr Thomas's beautiful Clun Forest flock. These Hampshire Down ewes, with their shepherd to tend them, had begun lambing in the pit of winter, at New Year; by March the lambs are already heavy, at six months they may weigh as much as a well-grown man.

With their shepherd, I say. As the owner appraised his flock a man, sparely but strongly built, wearing a leather jerkin, shirt-sleeves, breeches, and high boots came to meet us with the easy deliberation of the country-man; his employer, addressing him, used the honourable title of Shepherd. They're not so gay today, said Major Jeans, and explained that the lambs had lately had their tails docked: a hygienic measure against the blowfly and its maggots. Later, Mr Batchelor, the shepherd, took me into his hut and showed me the docking-iron, a shaft with a squarish blade which is heated so that it sears and seals while it cuts: seems a shame, doesn't it, he said sympathetically, to cut their tails off. The operation does not, in the eyes of the expert at any rate, affect the charm of the victim. Major Jeans, who is President of the National Sheep-Breeders' Association, pointed out to me a ram lamb with a very broad square dock: a beautiful masculine tail, he said.

With ram lambs, he went on, you must have the masculine type: otherwise you lose constitution. The growing rams are selected for breeding with this in mind: the chosen are bold-headed solid animals; or, as Mr Batchelor put it, you want dark ears, short legs, and a good topknot; the longer-legged and less fortunate are fattened for slaughter. The best ewes, too, are rectangular. Major Jeans pointed out to me one massive beauty; there, he said, that's what you want, square, straight back, low on the ground, a beautiful leg of mutton.

Mothers and sons stood together in the fold; but while the sons could move on to better food the mothers could not follow them. The system, as I gradually learned, is to divide the main enclosure into a number of folds. One is for ewes with single lambs; another for ewes which, with twins, need a better diet; a third for ewes with ram lambs; each leads into a second, a forward fold by a lamb-hurdle, a gate with wooden uprights spaced widely enough for a lamb to pass through, but not a ewe. A creep, shepherds call it; or, in the Wiltshire burr, a crape. Day and night the flock, ewes and lambs, is folded on its patch of crop, and every day the lambs jump (or creep) through to the next patch and nibble the fresh top leaves; they like it, said Mr Batchelor, because 'tis sweet. In the morning the hurdles are moved. The forward fold becomes the fold for ewes as well as their families; the ewes eat the lower leaves and stalks and with their sharp teeth gnaw at the swede-roots; and the lambs rove ahead to find the untouched fodder. The soil over which the flock has passed is stripped bare and ready for the plough; only here and there a dry bitten stump remains.

Once more we were anxious to photograph, and when we came back next day the shepherd and his assistant, Mr Whatley, were obliging enough to bring the flock out of the fold. The dogs galloped to head off the bewildered animals as they lolloped down the hillside, the men stood with outstretched guiding arms. Mr Batchelor's Chico, a model of intelligent obedience, scampered along the slope, stopped dead to look for instructions, then ran again. The dog had been named from a very good film his master had once seen; but that was a long time ago and Mr Batchelor could not say what the film was; I shall never be sure whether or no the Marx Brothers are responsible for the name of a charming sheep-dog on the Wiltshire Downs. Chico, a Blue Shag, is eleven years old, but not too old for love; a match had been arranged between him and Mr Whatley's Trixie, a pretty and gentle Border Collie with no fault except a tendency to fits, and this her owner hoped would be cured by a litter of puppies. Careless of approaching parenthood, the dogs ran to and fro at their work.

It was a fortnight later when I climbed the hill again, and this time I came alone and on foot. I had taken the bus from Salisbury to Broadchalke; the April day was gusty and the wind blew capriciously round the village church. I went inside to gaze at the carvings and corbels, the tuneful angels and the long-eared demons; in the porch a list gave the names of parishioners responsible for cleaning the brasses, and there in the south transept a woman was rubbing and polishing. I came out into a street as quiet as the church, and walked through the village where Aubrey once lived, where Maurice Hewlett wrote. The Old Malt House received me amiably and afforded me cheese, fresh bread, butter, and a pint of good bitter beer. There were other customers: an old labourer; a handsome workman with his lunch in a green tin box which, on admiration, he announced his mother had given him; a young labourer who startled me by pouring sauce over his sandwiches and offering me the bottle. The three were acquaintances and I listened, I hope without impertinence, to their talk. Snow had fallen on the hills lately; the old man felt ill but was assured that beer would do him good ('That's the stuff to put you on your feet'); the owner of the lunch-box had been mending barges (Mr Thomas, when I asked him later what on earth a barge might be, preserved his gravity with an effort; and indeed I suppose to a practical countryman it must seem ignorant not to recognize the term for part of a house-gable).

The talkers included me in their conversation. Would I like a cigarette? Quiet, wasn't it, in the downs; when I came home on long leave, said the young labourer, it seemed so quiet you could hear it singing in your ears. I said goodbye and set off, round the bend over the stream with the watercress bed, up the road towards the track. The air still shivered, but there were dog violets and sweet white violets in plenty on the banks, and the hawthorn shoots were already unclenching their small green fists; a cock pheasant squawked almost from under my feet. At the top of the hill, guided by my memory of the thickets and the young corn, I turned along the verge of a field and made my way towards Major Jeans's flock. Surely, I thought, I must be near; yet I could not remember the brown empty field. I looked again; there were the lines of hurdles and the shepherd's house, and with a start I realized that since my last visit the flock had eaten its way nearly to the brow of the hill.

Yes, said Mr Batchelor, they'll be finished with the swedes and kale soon, it'll begin to flower too, and the pollen isn't good for them. You see that patch on the hill beyond the vuzz? That's Hungry Gap; some call it purple sprouting broccoli, but the right name is Hungry Gap; they'll be on that presently. And after that? I asked. Well, there's trifolium, and winter vetch; they'll eat right across the downs. Meanwhile, I saw, the flock was tasting other fodder. For the lambs there was linseed cake and split peas in a hooded metal trough: a box trow, we call that, said Mr Batchelor, you can turn it to the weather to keep the cake dry; the trow must be big enough for all the lambs to feed at once, or some don't get their share. For the ewes Mr Whatley was taking hay from a bale and stuffing it in a long wooden cage, a hay-crib; on the stripped soil there were pale strawy patches where the cribs had stood. From time to time a ewe went to drink at the water-trough or to lick at the slab of rock-salt in the fold.

A lamb came to the hurdle, stared, and sniffed my hand. The creep, I saw, was closed; it was the start of weaning. We shut the lambs away from the yowes, Mr Batchelor said, for a little each day; that way it's gradual and they don't holler so much. But the ram lambs, so well-fed that they could not be lured into the forward fold, were still with their mothers; the little jokers beat me today, said the shepherd. As I watched the creep was opened and the segregated lambs began to jump through, crying, searching for their mothers. Presently the two men went together into a fold; yip, yip, yip, the shepherd called quietly to his sheep. With Chico's help a ewe was isolated and caught with a forked stick; and while Mr Whatley held her a foster-lamb came eagerly to drink. She won't let him suck, said Mr Batchelor.

Vigilance, devotion, hours of solitude: I thought as I went away of the shepherd's life: the six long weeks of lambing, day and night, the rearing and tending, the endless tasks in rain and wind and sun. I thought of Mr Batchelor himself, son of a shepherd, brother of a shepherd, a proud man, planning for his flock. I was to sleep in Salisbury that night, and I decided to walk back to the road and the bus by way of Stoke Farm. Hurrying a little, since the afternoon was overcast, I came to the pasture by the wood; and there, moving among the contented sheep, was the owner-shepherd.

Mr Thomas had come straight from a train journey. You've seen something, he said, of the country. Not enough, I answered; I should like to walk along the ridge from Salisbury and look across the next valley. You'll be thirsty, he said. All the same, I said, I should like to try; but out of cautious vanity, since I was not sure if I should manage it, I did not say I planned to walk over the Dorset border to Shaftesbury.

At nine o'clock next morning I left the bus at the foot of the hill out of

Salisbury and turned up a right-hand path; I struck the east-west track a minute or two later. A man and a boy were hurrying to work; but soon I left company behind me and climbed alone between hedges alive with birds, hedges white with sloe-blossom and decorated here and there by those rejects of the tinker and the tramp, the rusty tin can, the old boot and the trouser-leg. Near the race-course I met an old yellow-faced man with mittens and a stick; what time was it? he asked, would he be in time to catch the orspital? Foolishly no doubt I gave him a shilling: Gawd love you! he cried, hurrying on to hide the prize from his following family. What time was it? when were the races? asked the old woman and the girl next in the path. Last came a woman, wheedling, with a broken basket. What time was it? Would the lady like to buy a basket? That was a lovely little basket now. No, the lady had a long way to go. O you've a long ways to go! Laughing she went on.

On the Salisbury side of the Grand Stand a road leads back to the Ebble Valley, and there in a clearing in the woods was a gipsy encampment: caravans, a fire, a dog barking. In a field opposite two men were unloading a truck of hay; yes, one of them said, smiling, th'old Plain Road would take me over the hills to Shaftesbury. The Old Plain Road: this was the Plain in earnest. Just beyond the race-course, where the track is for a few hundred yards a road, I saw a shop van and a boy on a bicycle. Then I left behind the last memories of the city. I passed Hare Warren, a wood of pine, beech, ash, oak; crossed the splendid avenue of beeches leading north to Wilton, south to the Chalke Valley; observed, in the south-west angle, a flock of sheep in an ample fold; and saw ahead of me the chalk way narrowing along the silent ridge.

At the next cross-track but one a herd of cattle was hurrying towards a lorry from which a man was flinging down fodder. The lorry drove off and the herd, left to its solitude, was sufficiently curious at the sight of a stranger to come to the fence at my whistle. By now I was nearing familiar ground, and soon on my left I saw a group of Mr Thomas's heifers; we exchanged stares and I struck across the opposite field to look at the view. There at last was the valley beyond, the Nadder; contented, I walked on past Stoke Bushes, past the coppice where an ill-famed inn once stood, past Long Folly and Fox Covert until, after listening in vain for the voices of Major Jeans's flock, in the midday sun I came to Chiselbury Camp.

The track here curves along a causeway with plunging flanks. The Camp, a huge flat circle in a ring of earthworks, thrusts its savage promontory into the Nadder country; beneath it the woods and farms and fields of the valley, the car glinting on the road, the pennon of smoke from the train belong to a remote, soft, infant world. The circle itself had been sown with corn, and plovers wheeled over the furrows; on the ramparts tiny white florets crept through the turf, and the stunted cowslips trembled in the wind. I ate my sandwiches like a being watched by history.

Between Chiselbury Camp and the solitary house at the Fovant cross-road, not a soul; only the rabbits, the pheasants, the loud-winged partridges and the track now widening to a broad grassy way, now shrinking between copses of flowering thorn and naked hazel, elder, honeysuckle, and briar. Sometimes low banks separated the path from the pale rows of young corn; sometimes in the ruts the pools of rainwater still lay, fawn-coloured or milky with azure reflections. Beyond the Fovant cross-road there were two labourers in a field; three miles farther on a man was unloading roots from a truck, and two children were watching. I saw nobody else; and when, at the high point beyond Swallowcliffe Down where the track bends past the site of a prehistoric village, a hare sat looking at me, then leaped away down the western steeps of Middle Down with his stumpy shadow running beside him in the afternoon sun, I was glad of his company.

All afternoon I followed the ridge, looking now to the right where Sutton Down, with its little coronet of trees, rises from the plain, now to the left where Gallows Hill lifts its green boss on the southern flank of White Sheet Hill. The light grew softer, the shadows solider; ahead the Dorset landscape took on rich abrupt patterns. But no matter where I looked I saw an immensity of Time: time in the maiden down and the ploughed down, in Chiselbury Camp and the village church, in the great ditches, tribal frontiers perhaps, which here and there cross the Old Plain Road and hollow their way down the sudden slopes; time, too, in the tradition of the sheep and the shepherd for which I had first come looking. At last I arrived, toiling, at the crest of White Sheet Hill. A long barrow raises here its sullen mound. I climbed to the top; the wind bent the thin grass on the spine and in the ditches which edge the barrow; infinite lines of valley, down and sky ringed the monument of earth. I hesitated for a moment before I went down the hill, past the white-faced quarry, to the main road and the four-mile trudge to Shaftesbury. A grey pocked stone hedged with weeds stands at the very brow. I went to look: it was a milestone; and on hands and knees I spelt out the inscription.

XCVII
Miles from
HIDE PARK CORNER
XIV
from SALISBURY
1736

And there is time, too, in that.

*The wild flowers in this county of wild flowers bear
immortal names; and here they are woven into an
unfading garland.*

Flowers in Buckinghamshire

by *ALISON UTTLEY*

Bugle

THE windy flower-sprinkled Chiltern hills, the cherry orchards in
the villages, the great woods of beech trees, majestic and straight-
limbed, the narrow lanes alight with traveller's joy, spindleberry
and dogwood, all are beautiful as flowers themselves, and as richly
filled with colour. In early spring when the blackthorn carries
snow-white petals on its dark angular branches, so thickly covered
that the tree looks like a ghost standing in the moonlight, and in autumn
when the beech is red-gold and the cherry leaves are crimson and amber,
there is a wealth of obvious beauty, but it is down close to the earth
that the loveliest small things grow.

This is a county of wild flowers, for it has not yet been trimmed and
shaped to tidiness, and there is some individuality left in the winding
lanes and the straggling irregular fields with their mixed hedges, sometimes overgrown, sometimes layered into symmetry by a village craftsman.

Flowers grow in luxuriance even by the sides of the main traffic roads,
where wide green margins are left for the safety of the foot-traveller.

233

There in the deep grass are white pools of dog-daisies, and drifts of innocent bird's eye, the little shining speedwell which seems larger and more wide-awake here, patches of the blue pennies of wild geranium, and hot golden broom, all displayed along the broad highways where the lorries, motors, and buses stream past.

By the side of the main road to London I found little clusters of the mountain cranesbill, hiding in the verge of a steep incline. The delicate pale blue flowers were safe, for nobody had time to look at them, rising above their dark green foliage. The orange hawkweed also grows on the banks of this road. I have found it in the Lake District, where it is called Grim the Collier. The colour is rich and striking, deep copper-orange, and the flowers grow in bunches on the head of a long dusky-haired stalk. Botanists insist it is a garden escape, but it is listed as a wild flower.

Near the towns on the waste places small flowers hide the scars. Wild marjoram, silky musk-mallow, Our Lady's bedstraw, and wild thyme weave a tight net of colour which spreads round the feet of the hoardings and covers the raw slashes of road excavations, as if in protest. They will not leave their home for any navvies digging there. As long as the earth lasts they will return, for they are immortal.

Many of the narrow roads and winding lanes have green verges and ditches under the hedges. The hollows of these damp places are lined with a galaxy of flowers, with wild hyacinths, dog mercury, wood spurge, cuckoo pint and stitchwort in the spring, and myriads of white violets grow on the banks. Later on the sulphur-yellow toadflax, stiff aromatic yarrow, pink and cream and pale fawn, and the magenta-rose fringed flowers of the great knapweed spring up. 'Paintbrush' is the country name for this Rembrandt flower, which is not unlike an outspread brush soaked in purple magenta paint.

The high hedgerows bordering the lanes are grown from varied trees, maple and dogwood, ash and oak, hazel and sloe, with here a crab apple and there a whitebeam, here a spindleberry, there a wild rose. In autumn blackberries climb vigorously to hang their juicy fruit out of reach. Over the trees are festooned the delicate grey feathers of traveller's joy, the rich red berries of bitter-sweet, and long trails of black bryony like jewels in the hedge. Old red brick farms with long low cowhouses and great barns, cornfields golden with wheat and barley, all waiting for the harvest, lie beyond the fruitful flowery hedgerows.

By the lanes are clumps of marjoram, murry-coloured, purple and rose, like garden flowers in their compact neat growth, and musk-mallow with its thin silk skirts of pale pink, sweetly scented. There are the tall spires of the great mullein, a flower that always fascinates me so that I have to stop and consider its purple eye, its yellow velvet petals, and its soft flannel leaves. The main stem has many smaller mulleins springing from it, like yellow candles in the shadows of the ditch. Once I stood beside the flower, and a nightingale began to sing overhead.

I loiter along these grass-edged lanes to discover fresh beauties in the individual blossoms, for each flower is distinct and different, and each seems to contain a secret which I may discover. Here are the slender fingers of agrimony, like tiny hollyhocks, and near them the tall lovely goats'-beard; the long pointed buds, sharp as a woodcock's bill, the delicate grass-fine leaf springing in a curve from the stalk, the eight green bracts pointing from behind the yellow rays of petals of the flower-head make a most decorative picture. Most important of all, the round clock of cream and buff-coloured seeds, each with a concave pappus, like a minute saucer, is geometrically satisfying. It is a mathematical flower made out of circles and lines. I look at it as if I had never seen it before, but I discovered its beauty for myself when I was a child, straying in the forbidden mowing grass of our own fields. It is called 'John-go-to-bed-at-noon,' and off to sleep it goes, shutting its golden eye at midday, as all farm boys used to remember. It was not common on our land, but in Buckinghamshire crowds of these exquisite clocks are held up to the noonday sun.

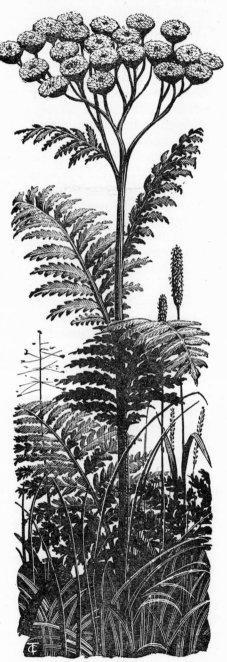

Tansy

One August Bank Holiday, when I was seeking these goats'-beard clocks to carry away, I met a procession all shining gold and yellow, so that at first I thought it was a circus coming down the lane under the arching trees. Five great wagons, newly painted canary yellow with scarlet wheels, were drawn by five splendid cart horses, bay, dappled, and black. Their waving manes were adorned with tassels and ribbons, and more ribbons were plaited in their tails. Horse-brasses jingled musically, and the carters, smiling and waving their beribboned whips, drove slowly along from an agricultural show. None of them had won a prize, but they deserved more than a first class for their beauty as they moved along that lane in the evening sunlight, with flecks of gold dust and silver light dripping from the wet trees upon the harness and polished flanks of the horses. They were radiant as the horses of the sun-god himself, and for some unknown reason they were all part of the simple beauty of the 'weeds' I sought.

One of the loveliest flowers is the bee orchis, which grows in many places in the county. I found it first at Jordans, where it grew in abundance in a field. Near Penn there was a haunt of the bee orchis, and the village children picked bunches for their mothers until a year or two ago. The field was ploughed up for corn and the flowers disappeared. I found them again on the banks of an old chalk pit, among other dwellers of chalk. The grassy slopes held large clumps of rosy sainfoin, of tall lavender scabious, and the little dark purple scabious. I thought I saw two bees on a stalk, and I stooped to blow them away. Then I found it was a bee orchis, with the dark mottled lip, the mauve petal and the brilliant green ribbon. I had been deceived by the mimicry. I then saw others, many more, half hidden in the long grass, a hive of bees.

The flowers of the chalk have a special miniature beauty. Horseshoe vetch, squinancy-wort, rampion, pyramidal orchis, and the tiny blue gentian all grow on the chalk hills, and lady's fingers creep on the chalky roadside with scarlet, gold, and tawny finger-tips. The golden yellow rock-rose holds up its flowers and slender buds to the sun, it curves its stalk like a dancer, so that I expect it to leap upward. Its roots seek the small stones, while the little blue butterflies hover over it in the heat.

The tiny flowers of the milkwort are my treasures; they have such diverse colours. One can find pink and purple, mauve and magenta, deep blue, azure, and snow-white flowers growing near one another in a tapestry of minute pattern. The field scabious, which is prolific and strong-growing, has varied shades of lavender-blue, dark purple, and amethyst in its flower heads. Every flower is different, and on the round pin-cushions flutter the six-spotted Burnet moths. Sometimes a crowd jostles on one flower, with brilliant wings swinging as the moths push for a place.

ON THE CHILTERNS I HAVE FOUND the clustered bell-flower close to the ground, and the green-winged orchis, whose reddish-purple flowers have little green wings to adorn them. Sometimes this flower is palest pink, or rose, and when I found one nearly white I made my wish over it, as all good country people must.

The early purple orchis (orchis mascula) and the marsh orchis grow in the fields, or they did until recently when there has been much building. The gypsy women, who know where everything is, gather them and fill their large baskets and offer them for sale. They sweep the fields; I think the flowers will disappear. Gypsies and ploughing are the destroyers of the orchis family. A field near my home in Buckinghamshire has lost all its gems; the purple orchis, cowslips, pinks, and white centaury, those surprising little flowers of perfect stars, all have gone, and only the coarser flowers remain. Even the willows are stripped and broken for the yellow and silver palms at Easter. It is interesting to see that the gypsies always remove the horny scales from the palm willow flowers to enhance their beauty.

Succory, or chicory, fringes the cornfields on the high lands of Penn, it straggles along the borders of the low fields of wheat in Holtspur Bottom. The starry flowers with their ragged petals, blue as the sky above, radiant as the zenith on a summer's day, grow to full height and splendour on the chalk soil. They twinkle and give out a light of their own, I sometimes think. The tough stems are hard to break and the plant is a source of trouble in the corn, but it grows chiefly on the verges of the fields, close to the footpath or by a gate. It is a 'keeper of the way,' a flower that likes company, one of those friendly plants which seem to seek human society. Many branches spring from

Bee orchis

the main stem, each with its blossoms, and the chicory is a candelabra with blue lights burning. The flower heads wither and curl, while others open out and new buds unfold. So there are full blown flowers, buds, and withered petals on the same stalk.

Soapwort grows in the south of the county, in handsome spikes of pink flowers on the margins of woods and in the hedges. It may not be truly wild, but it is not welcome in the garden. The roots run underground, spreading rapidly, sending up pale green shoots, smooth as silk, some distance away from the parent stem. I have tried for years to eradicate it from my garden, where it entered without invitation, but it still appears.

Tansy, less common here than in the north, fills the air with strong pungent odour in some of the rough pastures or by the sides of roads. The cattle leave it alone, perhaps because the taste is bitter. The flat dull gold buttons clustered tightly together on stems two or three feet high are beautiful in their own way. The feathery foliage spreads out like a group of ferns. I am prejudiced in favour of tansy, whose distinctive smell is evocative of simple people and country life, and I always carry off a piece to rub in my fingers. Tansy pudding was made in Lent, as a harsh herb accompaniment to meat. It was a flower used in the house against moth, silver fish and fleas. Many a bunch of withered green and gold hung drying from cottage ceilings.

One spring day I saw a golden flood of kingcups in a rushy meadow on the banks of the elusive little river Misbourne. The Misbourne is a river that has the habit of disappearing and then returning, and the kingcups are small or large according to the water around them. I climbed over the stone wall and walked in the boggy field to gaze at the beauty before me. The water reflected the blue sky, and the flowers were like a drift of solid gold in the vivid emerald grass. I gathered an armful, I felt greedy for this fairy gold which I had not touched for years, but my inroad made no difference. The thick hollow stalks carried high the large bright leaves, and the glittering flowers and fat buds were nearly as large as water-lilies. Such kingcups I had never seen before. They were finer, richer than the north country flowers, they were cups of yellow metal, polished to reflect every ray of sunshine. I took them home and they lasted many days in a great bowl of water.

St John's wort, harebells, and spiny pink rest-harrow all decorate the lane borders, while honeysuckle holds up its creamy crowns above the hedge tops. Bugle lies like a blue shadow in many a lane, and the rich colour of the trusses rising from the blue-green leaves always makes me stop and stare in contemplation of the massed beauty of such a simple unnoticed flower. Alkanet with its forget-me-not eye appears in villages, under the walls, and comfrey grows on the commons and by

Broom

the Thames. In the cornfields near Penn the corncockle grows, an unwelcome flower but an attractive visitor. In the steep rough lane I found a giant corncockle, nearly five feet high, with large purple-magenta flowers. In the same lane the tall shafts of the 'wild canterbury bell' grow, and the great burdock, whose prickly burrs make baskets and birds'-nests and balls.

THERE ARE RARE FLOWERS IN THE county, but I have never discovered them. The Pasque flower thrives in a secret place, in the hills. White helleborine I have not found, and even the wild daphne has eluded me. My woodman sees it each year in the woods near Stokenchurch, where he cuts the trees. An old man told me that when he was a boy he used to find hundreds of daphne in the woods, and he pulled them up and sold them for a penny each. Money was scarce, and who can blame him?

Green hellebore, a strange romantic flower, seems unreal and bewitched to me, perhaps because I associated it with fairies and strange happenings when I saw it in childhood. A green flower is a magical being to the imaginative mind.

There is a hill where it is easy to believe in witchcraft and ancient gods, and on its slopes I found two distinguished flowers which enchanted me, each in its own way. I went to Cymbeline's Mount, the ancient British earthwork, which has memories of the battle in which Cymbeline's sons were slain. It is a haunted spot, and the air is cold there, even on a hot day, and a little wind rustles the grass when everywhere is still. On the summit of the grassy mound inside the rampart grew a branching tree—but it was not a tree. It was the deadly nightshade, whose many outstretched arms carried dark berries and dull purple bells. It was sinister and beautiful in that place, in the deep silence. It was alive and waiting, and I was glad I was not alone with it. In an old herbal the list of 'Poysons' includes mandrake, nightshade, henbane, and wolfsbane, a deadly quartet.

We climbed the upper part of the hill above the Mount, picking the pyramidal orchis, delicate and sweet, walking on a narrow chalk track which winds through the ancient wood of bent box trees. The scent of this tree ravished my heart, for the burning sun brought out the full strength of its odours, and the smell of box is something a country person carries through life. Above, on the bare hillside, was a blaze of hot blue light, a broad patch of dazzling colour unlike any flowers I knew. We scrambled across the narrow valley and found the bushes of viper's bugloss, of immense size and perfect beauty. It was the day, the hour of their perfection, and they held out long trails of blue and purple bells to that scorching sky, with the wide plain of Aylesbury stretched out in all its soft greens and misty blues far below.

These are some of the flowers of the county, not the rare ones but the flowers anyone can find. I came home the other day with a bunch I picked in a lane, in a tangle of hedge and road banks. There were blue sloes, with the delicate bloom on the fruit, crab-apples from a tree which carried more crabs than leaves, crimson 'aiges' from the hawthorn, yellow mullein spires, deep purple and pale mauve scabious, marjoram, pink and deep rose, wild mignonette, and the silver seed cases of the knapweed. With these I had gathered the transparent red berries of the bitter-sweet, and orange-yellow toadflax, and pink leaves of wild cherry. Lighting up this golden bouquet of autumn were branches of late chicory, with its tender blue stars. It was an epitome of England herself, strong, beautiful, enduring flowers and fruits with immortal names.

ANIMAL

Growing Up

SIAMESE STUDIES by Dunscombe Honiball

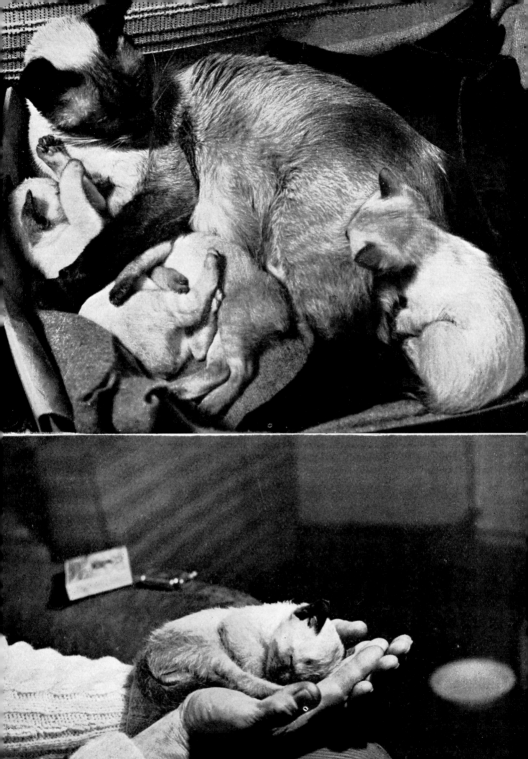

The Face on the Cover

by Lorraine Timewell

THE FACE ON THE magazine cover, from the time of the Edwardian picture postcard craze onwards, was usually somebody the public knew. Today, more often than not, it is that of a professional model, such as Gina Cameron, seen here.

Making Appointments

A MODEL'S WORK is rather like that of a theatre artist. She cannot appear and attend to business at the same time, and leaves this to her agent. Gina Cameron works through an agency run by a well-known ex-model, Rosemary Chance.

On Her Way

ALTHOUGH SHE IS on her way to be fitted for an expensive model gown, her own wardrobe is utility. Again like an actress, her well-groomed appearance and good taste in dress are part of her stock-in-trade, and Gina Cameron must contrive to look expensively simple in simple *inexpensive* clothes.

Her make-up, extra shoes, and needed 'props' are carried in a hat box.

Buying a Hat

CONTRARY TO popular belief, the models do not receive gifts of free clothing
from manufacturers, but have to buy their clothes just like any of us. Gina
buys her hats in the inexpensive department of a Bond Street milliner, and
expects later on to be able to re-trim and alter what she buys.

An Office Conference

A GOOD MODEL can model anything—even a maternity skirt—and frequently
Gina is called upon to consult with the people concerned on details of
presentation, colour and so on. Here she makes suggestions and discusses
the launching of a maternity skirt with Anna Newton and Donald Gardiner,
both on the staff of a well-known London advertising agency.

Train and Plane

GINA IS A Londoner. 'I should loathe living anywhere but London,' she
says. 'I love every inch of it—even the Albert Hall.' But she has to travel
by train or plane all over the country, and sometimes abroad as well. Most
of the models cherish ambitions to work in New York and Paris.

Sunday Afternoon

GINA IS MARRIED to John Cameron, formerly of the Metropolitan Police and the Royal Army Service Corps. They live at Barnes, overlooking the Common, and, like many other young ex-Service couples, look forward to owning their own home and running a car.

It Looks So Easy

IT LOOKS SO EASY, seeing her pose against a Coromandel screen in a gold
satin gown, or in a corner of Delanghe's Venetian salon, or against a mirror
wearing a lime-green chiffon evening dress embroidered in amethysts.
But it is a highly specialized job which requires, along with many other
qualities, relentless self-discipline.

George Bernard Shaw in the Village

by S. WINSTEN

F Shakespeare came to Ayot Saint Lawrence, he would feel perfectly at home; the old coaching inn is still there in the centre of the village and can boast of heavy beam, ingle, and log fire. The Tudor cottages beside it are externally the genuine thing and so is the manor house. If he came by stage coach, and one could almost expect all visitors to this out-of-the-way, out-of-the-past place to arrive by stage coach, he would have to follow the narrow winding lanes, old bridle tracks hardly made usable for the modern horseless contraptions. A deserted village and an amazing silence would greet him as he followed the old flint wall skirting the old churchyard with the half-demolished abbey standing picturesquely forlorn. Here a surprise would await him; round the corner, at the entrance to a park, stands what appears to be a miniature private temple, the telephone kiosk. Have these people destroyed their church and fled?

William Shakespeare indeed has every reason to come here because an aged inhabitant is at this moment calling him up from the dead; he is in fact composing a piece in which he and Shakespeare are the only characters, and they argue and fight like pugilists and compare metaphors in this flight of fancy. How dare a man who writes prose and only prose, the prose which the Elizabethan playwright had put into the mouth only of peasant and menial, how can such a man venture into the classic world?

There is no peace for Shakespeare! He stands by the kiosk wondering which way to turn, for on the right across the park there is a Greek temple, a worthy residence surely for a poet. Here there is space to think and a sky to lift the speech and transfigure the thought of the mundane world. If he had had this freedom, he contemplates, from player and public, from stress and storm, what poems he would have written instead of the hurried harangues and melancholy murders forced on him by the Burbages of the world. If he had not promised his wife to settle down and never write a word again he could have explained under what conditions he had written

T

those damnable plays for a living. These self studies would have taken the form of sonnets.

While cogitating thus, he sees coming towards him a willowy white form looking more like a ghost than a man, yet merry enough, for he is swinging a stick and striding past him, as though he, William Shakespeare, known to Queen and Knights, were not standing here. 'This is the first mortal I have seen in this place,' he thinks, 'and I venture on the opinion that he is not mortal.' Deciding to follow the lane he is soon faced with a green iron gate proudly flaunting in large letters, like an army of banners, the words: 'SHAW'S CORNER.'

'Modesty, thy name is not Shaw,' he whispers to himself, and swinging the gate wide open, walks up the path towards the porch. Here hangs a large knocker on the door, in the image of a bearded man, half smiling, half frowning, bearing the inscription: SUPERMAN.

'A tribal deity,' he mutters to himself, as he is ushered into the sitting-room. Here, to his astonishment, he sees no fewer than three further sculptures of this same figure, two of them in bronze. 'Of myself there is no graven image, but of this being I have already seen four.'

Meanwhile Bernard Shaw has posted his letter at the miniature Tudor post office and is returning, pleased with himself, because he is expecting a visitor and that will mean bringing out all the old stories and wisecracks and leading to the quip which will circle round the world and come back in dozens of Press cuttings. The toil that goes into these spontaneous utterances!

The silence of the village is harshly broken by the sound of a rattling water barrow as it trundles along the pebbly lane to supply cottagers with drinking water. Bernard Shaw decides to walk along the path of the park, towards the church with its classic columns, green rooftop, and the new graveyard. He smiles as he passes the church because he feels well disposed to it; he had sat there among the other villagers at the induction of one of the rectors, he had played the organ when alone there and had sung lustily to his playing and had heard from the lips of a young friend, when they had wandered in together, the words of the Bible which were sweetest to him: 'In the beginning was the Word, and the Word was with God, and the Word was God.' Spoken again and again while he sat at the back listening.

By this time he is rather tired and he does not swing his stick but he leans more heavily on it as he finds his way home, passing the old wooden farm from which a bevy of cats emerge and follow him to his gate.

STRANGE HOW THE MOST MODERN of people, whose utterances steal the space intended for news, should have settled in a village where the cesspool still exists and where a parish meeting is only just going to discuss the possibility of a coach once a week, so that the inhabitants might contact shops and crowds. Only four miles away as the crow flies, lucky crow, there is a modern garden city with a tremendous emporium and houses which compete for every modern device, but here in this village we have cottages without sanitation or water and the only shop sells stamps, sweets, and postcards of Bernard Shaw. The villagers are not thinking of having shops and cinemas here, but only ask for an occasional bus to take them out of themselves.

The letter which Bernard Shaw has just posted is in fact to this parish meeting and it is full of sound advice. These are the suggestions he makes:

(a) The proposed water tower to be made a thing of beauty and placed in the centre of the village, or to put it in his own words: '. . . there can be no greater mistake than to imagine that a water tower need be a disfigurement to be hidden as far as possible. On the contrary it is a golden opportunity to add to the picturesqueness of the village. A well designed water tower can be as great an ornament as a campanile, and should be in the most conspicuous position. I suggest our local sculptress should be asked to sketch a design showing what could be achieved. The middle of the park is the right place.'

(b) A straight road should be cut right through the fields because the winding lanes, however pretty, are a nuisance and a great waste of time.

(c) Certain old cottages which disfigure the landscape should be demolished and prefab dwellings placed in their stead.

Let us attend this parish meeting, the most wonderful of democratic institutions, reminiscent of old Athenian days where all could come and speak and vote. This meeting should have been held beneath the Doric columns of the classic church where orators standing on the spacious steps could utter their cry for water in measured cadence. But it is held, alas, in the very modest village hall which the inhabitants keep going with effort. These communal gatherings have already achieved many things. For example, within the last few years a notice KEEP LEFT has been erected down the lane for the guidance of motorists; the hedges, which had been allowed to overhang the narrow winding lanes for years, have now been cut down. The village green is kept tidy by voluntary effort, and most important of all, a village club has come into being with table tennis, whist drives, and talks.

Today momentous decisions are to be made. There is tension and suspense, and half the hundred souls have turned up. The village hall has never looked so small. On the wall there is a tribute to a famous citizen, an oil painting of the Earl of Cavan, Field-Marshal of His Majesty's Forces, dressed in hunting clothes and riding a regal horse.

Two important officials of the rural district council have come and have placed imposing plans on the table for all to see, plans of the proposed water tower, purely utilitarian. There is uneasiness when the suggested location is announced. Let there be water. They play ball with the ugly water tower, pitching it from one spot to another . . . so when Bernard Shaw's letter is read, it is brushed aside with loud laughter, the tension is relaxed. Who are we to question the experts?

And then, beauty or no beauty, just when all think that water is soon to be within reach of everybody, it is announced that the meeting was only called because Whitehall wanted the plans in at the earliest moment. As to being put into operation, why, it may take years . . . 'We might get water from the Sahara through atomic energy by then and the water tower prove superfluous,' the artist declares.

But Bernard Shaw would not be defeated. He was back in the old Vestry days when he fought single-handed in St Pancras for sanitation. He himself designed a water tower in coloured paper which would certainly have made this place break with its past Elizabethan tradition. There he sat, on his couch by the window, panama on head to protect him from the sun, for his room is a regular sun trap, cutting his strips of paper and sticking them into shape on a brown piece of cardboard, enjoying it like a child.

WITHOUT GEORGE BERNARD SHAW, this village would not have attracted so many visitors. Wells and Webb, T. E. Lawrence and Granville-Barker, Gene Tunney and Lord Montgomery, Lady Gregory and Frank Harris, Sybil Thorndike and Vivien Leigh, Haldane and Saroyan have found their way here among others. The story goes that Ellen Terry herself ventured this way and even reached as far as the village post office but here lost courage, purchased a postcard of G.B.S., and fled. One by one he has seen his friends come and go, and now most of them have gone for ever. Often I wonder what G.B.S. thinks about as he walks along the lonely lanes, so full of memories. He will tell you that he inherited the gift of solitude from his mother, but solitude is only a recent acquisition and does not become the actor. You can see him gazing for the hundredth time at the roof of a cottage because this reminds him of an Irish homestead, you can see him taking the fiftieth snap of a very familiar scene because the familiar yields new secrets. He will point out the gravestone which convinced both his wife and himself that this village was the place for them and for all who wished to live to a good old age.

BORN MARCH 5 1825
DIED FEBRUARY 13 1895
Her Time Was Short

'One day,' he once said to me, 'life will be so miraculous that three hundred years will seem too short.'

What else is there to show in the village? He prefers now to go for a walk round his own garden. The lamb in bronze by Troubetzkoy frisks just outside his window and a path leads to his recent acquisition, a life-size bronze of Saint Joan looking over the fields with her eyes shaded, fist clenched and a live 'perfectly modelled body that makes the bronze live, the only one I would let into my garden to live with.' He so hates the thought of London now, though he has a flat in the heart of it, that if he had to go there he would feel like his Saint Joan faced with imprisonment.

'To shut me from the light of the sky and the sight of the fields and the clouds . . . without these things I cannot live.' I shall never forget the look of delight on his face when, ready to go to London, he discovered that he need not go after all. He was like a schoolboy told on a sunny day that there was a holiday.

Often he says that he could do without people, but he is always happy to meet our visitors at our place. Scientist and artist, politician and philosopher, clergyman and doctor, author and actor, Indian, Chinese, villager . . . he is always ready to advise them on the subjects in which they have made world reputations. Thus he gets more from them by this challenging method than if he remained quiescent. Yet I have seen him with my son, a mathematician, listening eagerly to his exposition of an abstruse problem; they were seventy years apart but he who was older was still eager to learn. Later I found G.B.S. with mathematical books round him indulging this intellectual passion.

He is always complaining that he cannot give as much as he desires to the subjects that interest him and prays for complete release from postman and Press. I wonder what would happen, however, if as with many a cottage here the postman passed his house and the Press forgot his presence, if his world of interest contracted into this small village lying asleep at his gate. Impossible. His perspicacity prevents his becoming a mere country gentleman, a mere cypher. Is there another writer in this country who employs his own 'remembrancer' lest we forget?

The beauty of this rural scene rarely enters his work. There is no danger of his becoming a Hertfordshire writer as did a fellow Irishman J. M. Synge in the Aran Islands, Wordsworth in the Lake District and Hardy in Wessex. Yeats said to Synge: '. . . . Go to the Aran Islands, live there as if you were one of the people themselves.' Shaw's last play is pitched in Belgrave Square and the Panama. Yet, when he is not mischievously inclined he will tell you in ecstatic terms that he owes everything to the beauty of Ireland and that the happiest moment of his life was when, as a boy, he heard from his mother that he was leaving the Dublin streets for the Dalkey countryside. 'I am a product of Dalkey's outlook.'

But when Ireland suggested that he spend the last years in the country of his inspiration, he would not hear of it. He preferred the village in which he now lives, his 'adopted native place,' which cannot boast of mountain, sea or distant grandeur. . . .

HE IS ESSENTIALLY A DAYLIGHT person and his best writing has been done between breakfast and lunch. This, he explains, is what makes his work so different in quality to the nocturnal brooders. The difficulty is that as he mostly writes plays, and these are performed at night, people come to them with the wrong kind of mentality, wanting the triangle and the vicious circle for their relaxation. In the ideal state of affairs the mornings would be given over to leisure pursuits and the afternoons, which A. E. Housman called the 'dead part of the day,' could be given over to socially necessary routine jobs. Once, in teasing mood, I suggested that the B.B.C. might give over a whole day for the broadcast of his *Back to Methuselah,* a national holiday declared so that all could listen-in. In this way the whole world could pay tribute to a great writer. He took this suggestion seriously and thought it inevitable.

What would the night be like without the wireless concert, the play, and the talk? Years ago the playing of a Beethoven symphony was an event, but now one only has to switch on to get a good concert. Here in his dining-room he is seated in his wing chair conducting, remonstrating, bursting into song, his clear strong voice often drowning the wireless. And he has his audience, for on the mantelpiece are ranged Lenin and Stalin, Yeats and Granville-Barker, Chekov and another Russian gentleman with the saddest face I have ever seen. Of course, there are portraits of himself: the John and the De Smet.

Often with the wind coming in my direction I can hear his wireless, and from the programme can guess that he must be dozing. All the noise of hell would fail to wake him, but when I come into the room and lay the gentlest hand on his he wakes at once to lively activity. He wakes from a world of dream, where he is with his old cronies again, enjoying his prime, his travels and living the great moments all over again. He complains that the things which happened yesterday have slipped his memory but the things that happened years back are now strangely illumined. In old age one pieces together the jigsaw puzzle of memory. What otherwise might appear as a chaos of ideas and images forms into a co-ordinate whole.

I AM GLAD WHEN THE DAYS BEGIN to lengthen and G.B.S. can have an hour or two, after his shut-eye, in the afternoon sunlight. It makes all the difference to his long day. Spring came early this year and I have seen him in the first days of February sitting on his verandah enjoying the sunlight while writing his postcards and letters. Quick to shed all winter trappings at the first suggestion of spring, he is most unwilling to put on extra wrappings against the wintry blast of summer. 'Trees shed their clothing in winter and I am like that. I like the cold.' He feels this affinity with trees because, like them, he is rooted here. Often, when he comes to see us, he admires the weeping willows in our garden: two old luxurious trees that form a wonderful canopy and seem to be laughing rather than weeping, like his plays, in fact. He felt a strong desire to have two such willows in his own garden and therefore asked us to plant a couple that would in the course of time develop like ours. On a cold and rainy day of the following year my wife and I planted them while he held the helpless delicate branches in position. 'In ten years' time,' he said, 'they'll look quite handsome. How quickly ten years pass.'

This is his plaint always. The years pass like a day and it takes him five years to do what it formerly took him five months. He sees the pines and chestnuts, bounding his grounds and giving him the privacy which he enjoys, and is amazed at their height and splendour, because it seems only yesterday that his wife planted them when they bought the house forty years back. She planted these and she planted a grove for the genius to walk in and to meditate. Yet I think that the greatest thoughts come to him when he sits down in the simple little hut tucked under an oak, down in the meadow, among the wild grass. Away from the house he becomes workmanlike and conscientiously does his few hours as Gandhi did his spinning.

A copper beech and a cedar at the entrance knew this house first as a rectory and have watched only adults walking in and about the grounds. The laughter of children has never been heard there. Only the yapping of a small aggressive cairn belonging to the late house-keeper. Trees, however, do not need the laughter of children to tell them that there is real happiness here, the singing heart of Bernard Shaw. Though he proclaims that he has never sought happiness and has known it rarely, he is within himself immensely happy and radiates it.

He modestly insists that his retention of good sight, hearing, and memory is due solely to inheritance, for both his parents lived to a good age. The G.B.S. he dangles before the public is entirely his own creation and would be unrecognizable by his parents. He was born adult, wise, forthright, and obviously older than his parents. He has created a personification of deep conviction and buoyant imagination, a person 'full of sound and fury signifying' everything. His success amuses him above everything, and even he sometimes fails to distinguish between creator and created.

England
Expects—

by OGDEN NASH

with a reply by Virginia Graham

LET us pause to consider the English,

Who when they pause to consider themselves they get all reticently

thrilled and tinglish,

Because every Englishman is convinced of one thing, viz.:

That to be an Englishman is to belong to the most exclusive club

there is;

A club to which benighted bounders of Frenchmen and Germans and

Italians et cetera cannot even aspire to belong,

Because they don't even speak English, and the Americans are worst

    of all because they speak it wrong.

Englishmen are distinguished by their traditions and ceremonials,

And also by their affection for their Colonies and their contempt for

    their Colonials.

When foreigners ponder world affairs, why sometimes by doubt they

    are smitten,

But Englishmen know instinctively that what the world needs most is

    whatever is best for Great Britain.

They have a splendid Navy and they conscientiously admire it,

And every English schoolboy knows that John Paul Jones was only

    an unfair American pirate.

English people disclaim sparkle and verve,

But speak without reservations of their Anglo-Saxon reserve.

After listening to little groups of English ladies and gentlemen at

    cocktail parties and in hotels and Pullmans, of defining Anglo-

    Saxon reserve I despair

But I think it consists of assuming that nobody else is there,

And I shudder to think where Anglo-Saxon reserve ends when I

    consider where it begins,

Which is in a few high-pitched statements of what one's income is and

just what foods give one a rash and whether one and one's

husband or wife sleep in a double bed or twins.

All good young Englishmen go to Oxford or Cambridge and they all

write and publish books before their graduation,

And I often wondered how they did it until I realized that they have

to do it because their genteel accents are so developed that they

can no longer understand each other's spoken words, so the

written word is their only means of intercommunication.

England is the last home of the aristocracy, and the art of protecting

the aristocracy from the encroachments of commerce has been

raised to quite an art,

Because in America a rich butter-and-egg man is only a rich butter-and-

egg man or at most an honorary LL.D. of some hungry university,

but in England why before he knows it he is Sir Benjamin Buttery,

Bart.

Anyhow, I think the English people are sweet,

And we might as well get used to them because when they slip and fall

they always land on their own or somebody else's feet.

A Reply

by *VIRGINIA GRAHAM*

LET us also pause,

(Which we have lots of time to do because

As everybody knows the English do no work, preferring, in fact being

　　　ever so partial

To lying on sofas gorging chocolates given them by General Marshall)

Let us pause, therefore, and consider the American,

Which we can do much better than either a wop or a jerry can

On account of the language which, through the good offices of

　　　Mr Goldwyn and Mr Mayer

We have, from childhood, studied with some cayer.

Americans are distinguished by the fact they have wives,

And these not only regulate, command, and absorb their husbands' lives,

But they also belong to Country Clubs and play Bridge

In the intervals of getting things out of the fridge.

Americans live in palatial homes run by delightful coloured servants or

    electrically inspired knobs, but it is undeniably odd

That though their country, so they say, belongs to God

He omitted to give them the grace whereby they might one day

Build a cathedral one could be taken to look at after luncheon on

    Sunday.

Indeed, every American who has a leaning towards culture

Has to come flying across the Atlantic like a predatory vulture,

For in America there has never been anybody who could make a nice

    bit of buhl

Which looked right, somehow, at the edge of a swimming puhl

All good Americans go to Harvard or Yale

Where they take degrees in anything they fancy, however fanciful, and

    where every able-bodied male

Votes for the female who is the cutest and has the nicest bust

On the campus, into which (the bust we mean) it is his aim and object

    to thrust

A pin.

When at last somebody or other, probably the best pitcher in the baseball

    team has got it in,

They leave to become lawyers or to go into businesses owned by their

    fathers who are owned by their mothers who are owned by dear

    white-haired old grannies

In pince-nez; but wherever they park their fannies,

And whether they be Republicans or sinners,

They see to it they have a nice glass of rye with their dinners.

For though they are confident that the world loves them and that with-

    out them the world would get into a fearful botch,

Their faith is remarkably fortified by imported Scotch

As is it also by the sound of their own voices

Which run on uninterrupted from the day they are born to the day they

    are carried to their Cemeteries Beautiful in motor hoices.

As they do not listen much to others it is more than somewhat natural

    they consider the English to be somewhat more than an enigma,

But the English, on the whole, do not count this as a stigma.

Anyhow we think the Americans are sweet,

And we might as well get used to them because when we slip and fall

    they are invariably under our feet.

A Short Trot with a Cultured Mind

by PATRICK CAMPBELL

BOUT Christmas time, many years ago, when I was a pale boy of twenty-four, writing zoological notes for a provincial newspaper, I was suddenly promoted, without warning, to the post of literary editor, on the grounds that the book page required the supervision of a cultured mind.

I was taken aback by the honour. At that time I had read, and enjoyed, only one book from cover to cover—*The Postman Always Rings Twice,* by James M. Cain.

I conducted some research work around the office. For a while I thought I might have been made literary editor by mistake, or even *in spite of* the fact that the book page required the supervision of a cultured mind; but then I discovered that the manager believed I'd been to Oxford, and had taken honours in Modern Greats.

He was not entirely correct. In point of fact I'd had two motor accidents my first term, been gated during the second, and had then resigned, rather than face the rigours of a third.

But the most important thing in newspaper work is to snap at your chances as they arise. I snapped at mine.

The following Saturday morning saw me installed in the literary editor's room. Tyrell, my predecessor—he'd gone to Manchester to write about football—had left it clean and sweet save for a box of digestive tablets and a pair of black socks in the middle drawer of the desk.

The book parcels had already arrived. I unwrapped them, and made out a careful list of publications received. Then I sat back to see what would happen next. I had an open mind.

It seems to me now to be a curious thing that I should have assumed this responsibility so lightly. I cannot recall having asked anyone what I was supposed to do, or, indeed, any preliminary discussion about the job whatever. I was just shoved into it, and left free to edit. On the whole, this was probably just as well, since I might have been chopped for an answer if I'd been asked, at the editorial conference, what I thought about Balzac's influence on the modern novel—or anything like that. I might even have gone on being Zoological Correspondent, at 35s. a week, with lunch money, for ever.

As it was, seated at my own desk, surrounded by heaps of new books, I felt fine. I didn't know what was going to happen next, but I felt fine.

When it did happen, it happened rather quickly. The reviewers arrived.

I knew most of them by sight. In the main, they were casual labourers in the literary field, being either scholarly incompetents, or else in possession of some other job, like the Civil Service, which gave them the time and the necessary financial backing to write.

They greeted me politely, and offered their congratulations. I noticed that nearly all of them were carrying attaché cases, or small canvas bags.

'Well,' I said, making it sound brisk but friendly, 'until I find my feet perhaps you'd all like to take anything that catches your fancy. Just let me have your copy by Thursday afternoon, and, of course, write on one side of the paper——'

I was surprised to see the reviewers fall upon the books. There was quite a struggle. It was all I could do to make out a list of titles for each man as he stuffed them into his bag. By the time they left I was close to exhaustion.

I looked round my office. There was a lot of torn paper and string, two paper-backed things about missionary work in Nyasaland, and *The Care and Training of Airedale Dogs*. Everything else had been swept away.

It seemed to me that the first morning's work had gone well. It looked, indeed, as though we were going to have a comfortable amount of over-matter for the next issue. Then Shakey Dodds put his eye, and the peak of his cap, round the edge of the door.

This curious old man was some sort of part-time freelance. He was believed by many to live in the basement of the office, retiring at night to a nest of back numbers somewhere behind the machines. Certainly, during the daytime, he was invariably on view, either writing at the 'Advertisements Received' counter in the front hall, or padding about upstairs, peering round the edges of doors, tipping his cap, and sorting out his endless sheets of dog-eared, yellow notes.

'Good morning, Mr. Dodds,' I said, 'what can I do for you?'

The old man hopped in. 'Um, ha,' he said, pushing out his moustache, 'yes—the Westerns—did you keep any Westerns for me? Um, ha, Mr Tyrell always used to keep me the Westerns . . .' All the time he was darting nervous glances at the debris.

'Westerns?' I said. 'I'm awfully sorry. I think they've all gone. I didn't know you were coming. I'm new to this job, you see, and——'

'Um, ha,' said Mr Dodds, and suddenly pounced upon the remnants of one of the parcels. He rooted with his stick in the heap of brown paper, and brought out a large volume entitled, *Some Aspects of Norman Architecture*. 'Two guineas!' exclaimed Mr Dodds, and stuffed it into his pocket. He was half-way out of the door when I called him back.

'Excuse me,' I said, 'I hope you don't mind my asking, but—do you *know* anything about Norman architecture?'

The trouble with Shakey was that no one was ever able to read his copy. I didn't want to lose a good book for the sake of a few squiggles on cheap notepaper.

The old man looked puzzled. 'No,' he said. 'Um—why do you ask?'

'Well,' I said, 'if you're going to review it——'

'I'm *not* going to review it,' snapped the old man, 'I'm going to sell it. Tyrell always gave me ten shillings' worth of Westerns. If you can't keep the Westerns for me I'll have to have something else.' His eye lit upon *The Care and Training of Airedale Dogs*. He pouched it before I could stop him. He paused briefly at the door, holding up the Norman architecture. 'At least,' he said, angrily, 'I could *read* Zane Grey,' and was gone.

I sat at the desk for a while, lost in thought. Then Mossie, the tea-boy, came in with a bun and a cup.

'Mossie,' I said, 'what's this about selling review books? Is it all right?'

Mossie looked at me calmly. 'God love you,' he said, 'haven't you heard about that?'

'Look here, Mossie,' I told him, 'I'm an editor now. You can leave out that sort of talk.'

Mossie bowed. 'I beg your pudden,' he said. He was a frightful boy, really—miles above his station.

'Come on, Mossie,' I said. 'What's it all about?'

He lit the stump of a cigarette. 'The reviewers,' he said, 'don't get paid for reviewin'. Consequently, the poor perishers has to whip as many bewks as they can, and trade 'em in to Humphreys round the corner. Toity-tree an' a toid poi cent,' said Mossie, with one of his charming lapses into dialect, 'is de reglar rake-off. And now, if you don't mind, I'll get on with me work. The editor wants to see me about the leadin' article.'

He put his head round the door a moment later. 'Here's a drop of gravy for you,' he said, 'you can spread it on your bib.' He threw a large parcel into the room.

I opened it. The complete works of Sir Walter Scott, in five volumes. I opened the first one. It was priced at three guineas. And so were all the others!

I couldn't believe it. I'd never actually read Sir Walter Scott, as I'd always thought that he wrote for children. But here he was turning up at three guineas a slice!

I don't quite know how it happened. Suddenly, I found myself parcelling Sir Walter up again. My heart was beating quickly. It was the first time in my life that I had ever engaged in anything that wasn't —entirely on the level.

I was half-way down the stairs when I thought of something. I rushed up to my room again, shoved a sheet of paper into my typewriter, and hurriedly wrote:

OMNIBUS EDITION OF SIR WALTER SCOTT

This splendidly turned out omnibus edition of Sir Walter Scott should prove a real treasure to all lovers of good books. The type is clean, and the illustrations clever. The style and quality of the writing, of course, need no commendation.

I put the notice in my tray, and shot out by the back door. Ten minutes later I came out of Humphreys' bookshop with five guineas in my pocket. It had been incredibly easy. Humphreys had even thanked me!

At six o'clock that night the phone rang. It was Miss Kelly, the editor's secretary. As soon as I heard it was Miss Kelly, the editor's secretary, I dropped the receiver. I snatched it up again, to hear Miss Kelly saying that she'd been trying to get hold of me all afternoon.

'I'm sorry,' I said, 'I was playing golf.'

'That's all right,' said Miss Kelly, 'it's just that the editor was looking——'

'For the omnibus edition of Sir Walter Scott,' I said to myself.

'For the omnibus edition of Sir Walter Scott,' said Miss Kelly. 'He's promised it to Professor Nutley. We're going to run a two-column feature on page three.'

'The omnibus edition of what?' I asked.

'Sir Walter Scott,' said Miss Kelly. 'It should have arrived today.'

'That's queer,' I told her. 'It certainly hasn't reached me.'

'Right oh,' said Miss Kelly, a jolly girl. 'It should be in by Monday. If you let me have it first thing I'll pass it on.'

I was unable to say good-bye. Two minutes later I was pedalling, bowed low over the handlebars, down to the office.

We had no Sunday edition. The front door was closed. It took me some time to rouse the caretaker. I galloped upstairs. My review was still lying in the tray. I tore it to pieces. That much, at least, had been attended to.

I passed that evening, and the whole of Sunday, partly in coma, and partly in prayer. I was leaning against the door of Humphreys' bookshop when it opened at 9.30 on Monday morning.

'Mr Humphreys,' I said, without preamble, 'can I buy the umnibas

U

addation—the omnibus edition—of Sir Walter Scott? I find there's been a mistake.'

'The Scott?' said Mr Humphreys. He thought for a moment. 'Sold it Saturday morning,' he said, with some satisfaction.

'Who,' I said, 'who bought it? Quick!'

'Mr Abbalabba.'

'Stop playing the fool!' I cried. 'Who bought those books?'

'Mr Abbalabba,' said Humphreys, in an injured voice. 'Student chap, at the university. . . .'

I ran Mr. Abbalabba to ground in his rooms. He was about 9 ft. high, and blue-black. He had a cup of tea in one hand and a piece of toast in the other. Behind him, on the table, was the omnibus edition of Sir Walter Scott.

'Mr Abbalabba,' I said, 'I want those books.'

Mr Abbalabba's face opened in an enormous smile.

'How you find me?' he said. 'Good morning.'

'It doesn't matter how I found you,' I told him. 'How much do you want for those books?'

Mr Abbalabba took a large mouthful of toast.

'Twanty pown,' he said. 'Vairy good boooks—Irvinghoo, Bob Roy . . .'

'Twenty pounds!' I exclaimed. 'You couldn't possibly have paid more than ten.'

'Twanty-tooo pown,' said Mr Abbalabba, his face hardening a little.

'Look here,' I said, 'I know quite well what you paid——'

'Twanty-treee pown,' said Mr Abbalabba.

In the end he consented to accept a cheque for £11 10s.

'I trost you,' he said, examining my signature, 'a leetle beet.' Then he tried to sell me a rug. I snatched up Sir Walter Scott and retired.

Professor Nutley did a splendid job on the omnibus edition. I was amazed, to tell the truth, at the amount that he was able to write about it. It looked fine, with a couple of illustrations.

A few days later I was walking past Humphreys' bookshop—on the other side of the road—when I was surprised to see Professor Nutley, with a parcel, slipping in by the side entrance.

A moment afterwards I was even more surprised to see Mr Abbalabba coming out. Under Mr Abbalabba's arm was Professor Nutley's parcel.

'Hallo, you sir!' cried Mr Abbalabba, spotting me at once. 'You buy Walltare Scott! Vairy nice! Irvinghoo, Bob Roy, Goo Mannering. Twanty pown . . .' He came rushing across the street.

I stood my ground. 'I'm very sorry,' I said, 'I am no longer in the business.'

It had the merit of being entirely true.

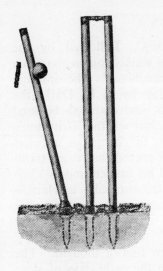

Cricket
Gadgets

by

JOHN ARLOTT

"EUREKA" STUMP.

ADVANTAGES.—(1) They are the same in action as the ordinary stump, and with the use of Dibble given with each set are fixed in a few minutes. (2) They are always of an uniform height and width. (3) Driving being unnecessary, the tops do not get damaged, consequently the bails keep their position. (4) As they revolve the grooves are easily brought parallel for replacing bails. (5) The wicket-keeper can with safety keep close to the stumps, as they do not fly out of the ground. (6) Can be attached to any existing stumps. (7) They do not loosen or break the ground. (8) The time saved by the use of the Eureka stumps cannot be overrated.

THE social historian of the future may find the key to our attitude to cricket in that, while other games have rules, cricket is governed by THE LAWS. Thus the reformer in football seeks merely to change a rule, but his cricketing counterpart seeks an amendment of the Laws.

Cricket, for all the evidence which may be adduced to the contrary, is usually regarded as a conservative game, and cricketers as conservative people. The legendary reactionary cricketer is that sporting Victorian, the Hon. Robert Grimston, of whom his biographer, Frederick Gale, said, simply and without qualification, 'he was averse to all change.'

Grimston progressed, single-mindedly and naturally, from school at Harrow to a position of power at Lord's. One morning in the eighteen-forties, paying his daily call at Lord's ground earlier than usual, he approached a group of workmen who were digging some ground where the Grand Stand is today. 'Would any of you fellows like to earn a

275

guinea?' he asked—'then bring your pickaxes.' Followed by the labourers, each with pickaxe over shoulder, he walked on to the pitch and, pointing, said, 'Destroy that infernal machine.' The infernal machine was a lawnmower, borrowed that day by J. H. Dark, the proprietor of Lord's ground, from Bob Thoms, and about to be used on the Lord's pitch for the first time. It is not clear whether Grimston's objection was based upon his normal aversion to change or a belief in the greater efficiency of the sheep which had grazed that twice transplanted and historic turf ever since Lord opened his first ground in 1787.

Yet this same Robert Grimston introduced the catapulta to Harrow School for coaching batting. Was Grimston in fact so conservative? We find that he experimented with electricity in its earliest days. Are cricketers, after all, really averse to change?

We may find, by way of the catapulta, a new line of thought. The invention of the catapulta obviously dates from the early days of siege warfare, but the elaborate adaptation of the old siege engine to cricketing use must be credited to the Kent cricketer Nicholas Wanostrocht, who played under the name of 'N. Felix.' Felix was a schoolmaster, and since

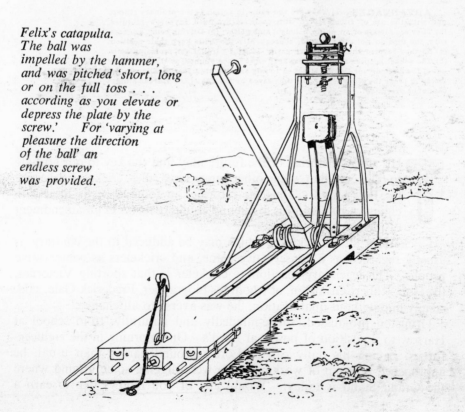

Felix's catapulta.
The ball was
impelled by the hammer,
and was pitched 'short, long
or on the full toss . . .
according as you elevate or
depress the plate by the
screw.' For 'varying at
pleasure the direction
of the ball' an
endless screw
was provided.

JOHN HOLROYD & CO. LTD., HULME, MANCHESTER. 125

MACHINE FOR BATTING PRACTICE.

THIS machine is so constructed as to combine the various styles of bowling practised by professional cricketers, viz.:—slow, medium, and fast, with a "break" from the on or off side as desired.

With the help of a boy to operate the machine, gentlemen possessing a suitable room or plot of land, may obtain excellent practice, and become expert batters without the expense of a professional bowler.

he taught Latin we may assume that he came upon the idea of the catapulta in his classical reading. Felix's remarkable batting against fast bowling was certainly due in part to his practice with the machine.

But now statistical vindication of the catapulta has been produced by Mr G. B. Buckley in the record of a match between the Gentlemen of South Hants and the Players of all Hampshire. The professionals were

The automatic ball brushing machine, for 'brushing six to eight balls at the same time, cleaning them thoroughly in less than a minute.' The price was 21s.

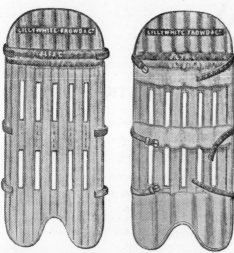

Lillywhite Frowd's 'Acme' ventilating leg guard was 'confidently recommended as the best Leg Guard ever brought out. With thoroughly good resistance, it is at once the coolest and by far the lightest Guard ever made.' From 9s. 6d. a pair (1896).

immeasurably the stronger side and, to redress the balance, the Gentlemen were allowed the use of the catapulta as a bowler —and the machine took six wickets in the first innings.

Felix included a drawing and a description of the catapulta in his book *Felix on the Bat*, the first elaborately produced book on cricket; it was illustrated by two of his former pupils, G. F. Watts and Sir John Gilbert.

In 1845 Felix's catapulta was to be had of Mr Dark at Lord's Cricket Ground, Marylebone, for eleven guineas, 'complete with the latest improvements.' Advertisements for catapultae are to be found in the cricketing periodicals for many years, all, apparently, variations on Felix's machine. In 1898, however, one of the first firms of machine-tool makers, Holroyds, whose factory was then at Hulme, Manchester, included in their catalogue a 'Machine for Batting Practice' based on a completely different principle. Whereas the original catapulta controlled the pace, length and direction of the ball, this new machine could also spin the ball —'from the on or off side as desired.' The *History of Warwickshire Cricket* (1911) carried an advertisement for a 'Patent Bowling Machine' which, although even lighter than the Holroyd machine, could *vary the amount of break transmitted.* But now, almost forty years have passed with no substantially new bowling machine to expose, with mechanical accuracy and pitilessness, the shortcomings of batsmen.

Felix also claimed to have introduced batting gloves, and Wenman, the wicket-keeper, Felix's contemporary in the great Kent side of the eighteen-forties, wore one of the first known leg-guards. An actual pad worn by Wenman has come into the possession of the M.C.C.: it is half the length of the pad we know today and was probably worn *under* the trouser. The first attempt to protect the legs of a batsman was made much earlier. In the 1790s Robert Robinson of Hambledon batted in 'pads' made from two thin boards set at an angle. The ball came off them with immense noise, and Robinson was laughed out of his 'invention.'

I am much exercised as to whether 'Shock' White of Reigate ought to be included among cricketer-inventors. In 1776 he used a bat of the same width as the wicket—with it, John Nyren recalls, 'he effectually defended his wicket from the bowler.' If White's bat was not strictly an invention, it caused the introduction of the bat-gauge and the law restricting the width of the bat.

In October, 1855, the bearers of two great cricket names, John Wisden and Frederick Lillywhite, went into partnership in a 'cricketing and cigar depôt' in New Coventry Street, Leicester Square. Their partnership lasted only three years, but from almanacks, companions, guides, catalogues, annuals and, often, the factories of Wisden and Lillywhite, their relatives, descendants and partners come the records of subsequent cricket inventions. Often their lists of the eighteen-seventies contain four or five hundred different items of cricket gear. Why, I wonder, do we never see now the leg-guard, advertised in 1896, which fastened with a single strap? And why does not everyone use the 'ventilating' leg-guard, which, affording quite as much protection as a modern pad, would be so much cooler. It was the firm of Frowd and Surridge that in 1887 advertised in James Lillywhite's *Cricketers' Annual* the 'Eureka' stump, which, when

hit by the ball, heeled over, on a bearing, at ground level—while its point remained firmly where it was first pitched.

Victorian cricket installations are to be seen on our grounds all up and down England. Many a village batsman straps on his pads in a metal pavilion, thirty feet by twelve, with a wooden floor, 'two dressing-rooms and lobby,' which, verandah, roof-ridge decoration and all, cost his club fifty-two pounds fully sixty years ago, and is still waterproof. In the early years of this century the counties began to install the new automatic scoring-boards in place of the old 'telegraph.' They were the cricket novelty of their day, but their claim to be 'Easily worked by a lad of 16: cannot get out of order' was, as any county secretary will confirm, argued from mechanical rather than human premises. Proud indeed, however, was the club which could present to the cricket world, when W. G. came to play on *their* ground, one of the new automatic score-boards and a gaily be-flagged and painted pavilion (with verandah, *extra*).

The period between the wars saw leather and vellum covering used to prevent practice bats from splitting. Perhaps the best of the new cricket machines and the one which is most widely used is the ingeniously simple slip-catching machine: a ball thrown into it is slung out at unpredictable height, pace and angle to reproduce slip-catches.

I am convinced that time and change have done little to alter the character of cricket as it is played in England, but the oblique impact of progress on the game is to be gleaned from many corners of its history.

The minutes of the Teignbridge Cricket Club in 1860 'noted that several members of the club travelled by railway to Newton and back.' Twelve years before that, along the growing railways, Clarke's All England Eleven had spread its gospel of the length ball, and the straight bat all through England and Scotland. The eleven played eight three-day matches—at Bradford, Ripon, Sunderland, Darlington, Leeds, Leamington, Chelmsford, and Southampton—in twenty-four playing days of September, 1848. In 1891, when Surrey won the Championship with Lockwood and Lohmann, Abel and Read, their spectators could travel to the Oval by the new electric railway. On August 11, 1944, players at Lord's dropped flat on the ground as a flying-bomb passed over the ground, fell just outside and blew debris on to the pitch. In 1948 the English and South African teams finished a Test Match in Johannesburg on Thursday, flew twelve hundred miles to Cape Town on Friday morning, and practised there the same afternoon for the Test Match which they began on Saturday morning.

Progress, progress—but at the moment a certain number eleven batsman, a friend of mine, is making inquiries at the Patent Office with a view to tracing a batting machine, however old.

STAMPS tell the STORY

by Douglas Armstrong

THE HISTORY of our own times is written in stamps: many aspects of the post-war world are reflected in the postage stamps of the nations depicted here, with Victory and Peace furnishing the theme of the 3d. British issue (top right).

The design of the shilling issue (bottom, centre), is the work of the distinguished artist, Edmund Dulac. Flanking it (left), is an Australian stamp commemorating the Pan-Pacific Scout Jamboree of 1948–49. On the right, the re-birth of Italy is the inspiration of a one lira stamp showing a hand planting a sapling.

Ceylon celebrates her new-found constitution; and a representation of the famous Asoka Pillar symbolizes India's transition from Empire to Dominion.

THE ARTS

PHILATELY pays frequent tribute to the achievements of art, music, literature and the drama. On the occasion of the centenary of his death, music-lovers will welcome the miniature portrait of Chopin that adorns one of a long series of stamps portraying Polish 'intellectuals.' 'The Knight of the Doleful Countenance' is seen on a Spanish stamp which marked the fourth centenary of the birth of Miguel de Cervantes Saavedra, creator of the immortal Don Quixote. It was issued in 1947 on a special 'Stamp Collectors' Day.' Another cultural issue from Spain commemorated, in 1946, the second centenary of the painter Goya. It consisted of three stamps, each being a reproduction in miniature of the well-known self-portrait of the 'Artist in a Temper.' France recalled Chateaubriand's influence upon European literature by the symbolic design of a

special 18 francs stamp commemorating his death in 1848.

A galaxy of great writers is celebrated on a striking set of literary stamps put forth by the Hungarian post office in 1948. Taken from it are the two stamps illustrated at the bottom of the opposite page—Poe and Byron.

The Strindberg centenary was celebrated in many countries, and Sweden honoured the memory of the author of 'The Father' with a special trio of stamps showing his likeness by the artist Richard Bergh. Sarah Bernhardt was born in 1844 and at her centenary France did her homage by reproducing this striking portrait.

Finland marked the 80th birthday of her great musician Jean Sibelius with a particular stamp of 5 marka. The theatre was not overlooked by the Polish authorities in the long series of stamps dedicated to the arts. Modrzejewska appears on the 5 zloty value between Boguslawski and Jaracz.

THE Czechoslovakian tragedy is epitomized in these two stamps. One is a 'mourning' stamp for the late President Benes; on the other appears the Communist President Gottwald, haranguing the mob.

INDIA mourns Mahatma Gandhi.

ONE of the first permanent postage stamps of the new State of Israel.

HOISTING the green banner of Egypt over the Citadel of Cairo, after British evacuation.

WORLD AFFAIRS

EGYPT's ill-starred incursion into Palestine is perpetuated by this commemorative stamp showing a column of troops winding its way to Gaza.

COLD war in the Antarctic: Britain, the Argentine and Chile support their claims with miniature maps.

PORTRAITS of the two Princesses on one of the special stamps issued by Southern Rhodesia to honour the Royal visit in April, 1947.

AUSTRALIA celebrates the wedding day of Princess Elizabeth.

ROYAL OCCASIONS

COMMEMORATIVE stamps (above), issued by South Africa and the native territory of Basutoland in honour of the Royal tour in 1947. Below them are two of the 250 stamps originating from countries of the British Commonwealth on the occasion of the silver wedding of their Majesties. Left, Great Britain. Right, South Africa.

THE late King George II of the Hellenes.

AFTER a reign of 50 years Queen Wilhelmina abdicated in favour of her daughter, the Princess Juliana, whose first stamp portrait as Queen appears here.

What it Felt Like to be a Gentleman

by C. WILLETT CUNNINGTON

NOBODY nowadays dreams of proclaiming himself a gentleman unless he isn't one. The title has become a thing to be shunned; it has ceased to be respected and may presently cease to be respectable. It is true that in the plural the word may still be applied, without offence, to political meetings and public lavatories. But in the singular it is now almost as suspect as was the word 'aristocrat' in the French Revolution.

Yet in former times it was quite good manners to describe yourself as a gentleman even if you were one; no doubt there have always been false claimants to this distinction who—in the words of a writer of six centuries ago—'yelpeth of their gentility for they ween they are of gentle blood.' However, we are concerned only with the genuine article.

Even before the Conquest he had a status distinct from the nobility, a status based primarily on birth with ancestors who had always been free men. He stood between the noble and the serf. The consciousness of possessing this precious inheritance, freedom, has coloured the mental outlook of the English gentleman; even more important was the awareness of duties owed by him, not to a master or to a State, but to a peculiar concept of behaviour. He had to preserve a social standard.

He might or might not possess wealth or property; his singularity was that he might accept or refuse, if he chose, the duties and privileges of gentility. He could, if he liked, cease to be a gentleman. It is to be noted that only his social group possessed that sort of option, and it gave him a peculiar sense of freedom. His necessary accomplishments were set out, in 1622, by Henry Peacham, M.A., in his *The Compleat Gentleman, fashioning him absolut, in the most necessary and Commendable Qualities concerning Minde or Body*. In it stress is laid on intellectual and physical 'qualities,' not—be it observed—on moral. In the same century the eminent divine and mathematician, Dr Barrow of Trinity, used these significant words: 'For what is a gentleman, what properties hath he, what qualities are peculiar to him whereby he is distinguished from others? Are they not especially two, courage and courtesie?'

One observes that such qualities are not wholly inborn but are capable of being instilled by training; already, by that date, the original meaning of 'gentleman' was expanding beyond the accident of birth by the acquired characteristic of 'courtesie.'

All through the seventeenth and eighteenth centuries there was nothing as yet in the status of the English gentleman to provoke hostility towards him in the masses outside his charmed circle. For though his position depended in large measure on his birth, the demarcation was not absolute; in this country there was none of the unbridgeable aloofness which distinguished the French 'aristocrat.' In fact, the English gentleman was not necessarily an aristocrat, nor was the English aristocrat always a gentleman. Younger sons of gentlefolk might even earn their living in the professions without losing caste. Consequently, the English gentleman did not excite the hatred which ultimately brought the French aristocrat to the guillotine.

There was also this curious fact, that some members of a family might be obviously gentlemen and others obviously not, though all had been brought up in the same environment. Evidently there was some inborn element necessary which was not always transmitted. And occasionally a sort of 'sport' would crop up in strange soils, producing what was called 'one of Nature's gentlemen.'

THEN WITH THE RISE TO SOCIAL POWER OF THE prosperous middle class in the last century, the meaning of the word 'gentleman' began to undergo a fundamental change, destined eventually to destroy his status. The term became endowed with a *moral* significance. Hitherto he had claimed no moral superiority; courtesy was not more creditable to him than manual dexterity was to the artisan. But as soon as he began to claim a moral superiority the very foundations of his existence were changed. He was asserting a claim unjustified by facts, to his own ultimate undoing.

There is, of course, abundance of evidence of such a claim by the early Victorian gentleman. How significant is that passage in Cardinal Newman's *Idea of a University* in which a gentleman is defined: 'It is almost a definition of a gentleman to say that he is one who never inflicts pain'; and in elaborating this new moral concept Newman adds: 'He is never mean or little in his disputes, never takes an unfair advantage; he is patient, forbearing, and resigned.' A singular description to come from the sharpest pen in Europe. A little later Emerson defined the gentleman as 'a man of truth, lord of his own actions, and expressing that lordship in his behaviour.'

To ensure that the sons of gentlefolk should be trained to possess that refined moral outlook, exclusive schools, called by unconscious irony 'Public,' instilled it into them so effectively that a permanent mark was printed on their characters. Dr. Arnold's moral impulses and inhibitions established a tradition. He was wont to contrast what he called 'the *good*

Poor' with 'the Trades Unions, a fearful engine of mischief, ready to riot or assassinate.' Obviously it was the moral duty of the high-minded gentleman to check, as far as possible, the depraved impulses so prevalent —alas!—in the Lower Orders. Unfortunately it was an attitude of mind which in time caused him to be disliked by those less gifted. They had not minded so much his superior accomplishments; they grew to detest his superior morals, or, rather, the assumption of them.

At any rate, the Victorian gentleman, viewing humanity from the top of his pedestal, found it helpful to establish a code of behaviour to sustain such a position, postulating that all would obey the code who possessed his moral outlook; those who did not, or could not, were beyond the pale.

It became a convenient symbol of gentility. A newspaper article of just a hundred years ago, evidently written by one who was himself no gentleman—probably just a journalist—gives us a detached view of the picture: 'The gentleman may kill a man in a duel but he mustn't eat peas with a knife. He may thrash a coalheaver but he mustn't ask twice for soup. He must never forget what he owes to himself as a gentleman; but he need not mind what he owes, as a gentleman, to his tailor. He may do anything—or anybody—within the range of a gentleman but he must never on any account carry a brown paper parcel or appear in the streets without a pair of gloves.'

An unsympathetic judgment, perhaps, but it implied a growing dislike towards that figure.

Even his restrictions were irritating; no gentleman would smoke in St James's Street—it faces a royal palace, and one might not smoke in the presence of royalty. No gentleman might smoke a pipe in the streets because it was a symbol of the artisan.

This conspicuous insistence on his select status would have been tolerated no doubt, just as differences of rank in the Services were tolerated, if there had not been that fatal assumption of moral superiority, reiterated in every novel and play. The masses grew tired of this moral Aristides.

Then his pedestal crashed in the first Great War. The creature survived nevertheless, and, I suppose, survives still in sheltered nooks, though in diminishing numbers.

No longer claiming moral superiority—at least publicly—and no longer allowed to possess wealth, all that is left for him to cultivate without interference is a sense of the irony of his position.

He knows his day is over. Perhaps the purpose for which the English gentleman came into being is fulfilled; he no longer has duties or responsibilities. In fact, he is—free. Freer than any other section of the community, just as he was a thousand years ago. All that is left him is to face the ultimate with the very qualities he possessed three centuries back. 'Are they not especially two, courage and courtesie?'

To